2016 SQA Past Papers With Answers

Higher
ENGLISH

2014 Specimen Question Paper,
2015 & 2016 Exams

HODDER
GIBSON
AN HACHETTE UK COMPANY

This book contains the official SQA 2014 Specimen Question Paper and 2015 and 2016 Exams for Higher English, with associated SQA-approved answers modified from the official marking instructions that accompany the paper.

In addition the book contains study skills advice. This advice has been specially commissioned by Hodder Gibson, and has been written by experienced senior teachers and examiners in line with the new CfE Higher syllabus and assessment outlines. This is not SQA material but has been devised to provide further guidance for Higher examinations.

Hodder Gibson is grateful to the copyright holders, as credited on the final page of the Answer Section, for permission to use their material.
Every effort has been made to trace the copyright holders and to obtain their permission for the use of copyright material. Hodder Gibson will be happy to receive information allowing us to rectify any error or omission in future editions.

Hachette UK's policy is to use papers that are natural, renewable and recyclable products and made from wood grown in sustainable forests. The logging and manufacturing processes are expected to conform to the environmental regulations of the country of origin.

Orders: please contact Bookpoint Ltd, 130 Park Drive, Milton Park, Abingdon, Oxon OX14 4SE. Telephone: (44) 01235 827720. Fax: (44) 01235 400454. Lines are open 9.00–5.00, Monday to Saturday, with a 24-hour message answering service. Visit our website at www.hoddereducation.co.uk. Hodder Gibson can be contacted direct on: Tel: 0141 333 4650; Fax: 0141 404 8188; email: hoddergibson@hodder.co.uk

This collection first published in 2016 by
Hodder Gibson, an imprint of Hodder Education,
An Hachette UK Company
211 St Vincent Street
Glasgow G2 5QY

Typeset by Aptara, Inc.

Printed in the UK

A catalogue record for this title is available from the British Library

ISBN: 978-1-4718-9087-1

3 2 1

2017 2016

Introduction

Study Skills – what you need to know to pass exams!

Pause for thought

Many students might skip quickly through a page like this. After all, we all know how to revise. Do you really though?

Think about this:

"IF YOU ALWAYS DO WHAT YOU ALWAYS DO, YOU WILL ALWAYS GET WHAT YOU HAVE ALWAYS GOT."

Do you like the grades you get? Do you want to do better? If you get full marks in your assessment, then that's great! Change nothing! This section is just to help you get that little bit better than you already are.

There are two main parts to the advice on offer here. The first part highlights fairly obvious things but which are also very important. The second part makes suggestions about revision that you might not have thought about but which WILL help you.

Part 1

DOH! It's so obvious but …

Start revising in good time

Don't leave it until the last minute – this will make you panic.

Make a revision timetable that sets out work time AND play time.

Sleep and eat!

Obvious really, and very helpful. Avoid arguments or stressful things too – even games that wind you up. You need to be fit, awake and focused!

Know your place!

Make sure you know exactly **WHEN and WHERE** your exams are.

Know your enemy!

Make sure you know what to expect in the exam.

How is the paper structured?

How much time is there for each question?

What types of question are involved?

Which topics seem to come up time and time again?

Which topics are your strongest and which are your weakest?

Are all topics compulsory or are there choices?

Learn by DOING!

There is no substitute for past papers and practice papers – they are simply essential! Tackling this collection of papers and answers is exactly the right thing to be doing as your exams approach.

Part 2

People learn in different ways. Some like low light, some bright. Some like early morning, some like evening / night. Some prefer warm, some prefer cold. But everyone uses their BRAIN and the brain works when it is active. Passive learning – sitting gazing at notes – is the most INEFFICIENT way to learn anything. Below you will find tips and ideas for making your revision more effective and maybe even more enjoyable. What follows gets your brain active, and active learning works!

Activity 1 – Stop and review

Step 1

When you have done no more than 5 minutes of revision reading STOP!

Step 2

Write a heading in your own words which sums up the topic you have been revising.

Step 3

Write a summary of what you have revised in no more than two sentences. Don't fool yourself by saying, "I know it, but I cannot put it into words". That just means you don't know it well enough. If you cannot write your summary, revise that section again, knowing that you must write a summary at the end of it. Many of you will have notebooks full of blue/black ink writing. Many of the pages will not be especially attractive or memorable so try to liven them up a bit with colour as you are reviewing and rewriting. **This is a great memory aid, and memory is the most important thing.**

Activity 2 – Use technology!

Why should everything be written down? Have you thought about "mental" maps, diagrams, cartoons and colour to help you learn? And rather than write down notes, why not record your revision material?

What about having a text message revision session with friends? Keep in touch with them to find out how and what they are revising and share ideas and questions.

Why not make a video diary where you tell the camera what you are doing, what you think you have learned and what you still have to do? No one has to see or hear it, but the process of having to organise your thoughts in a formal way to explain something is a very important learning practice.

Be sure to make use of electronic files. You could begin to summarise your class notes. Your typing might be slow, but it will get faster and the typed notes will be easier to read than the scribbles in your class notes. Try to add different fonts and colours to make your work stand out. You can easily Google relevant pictures, cartoons and diagrams which you can copy and paste to make your work more attractive and **MEMORABLE**.

Activity 3 – This is it. Do this and you will know lots!

Step 1

In this task you must be very honest with yourself! Find the SQA syllabus for your subject (www.sqa.org.uk). Look at how it is broken down into main topics called MANDATORY knowledge. That means stuff you MUST know.

Step 2

BEFORE you do ANY revision on this topic, write a list of everything that you already know about the subject. It might be quite a long list but you only need to write it once. It shows you all the information that is already in your long-term memory so you know what parts you do not need to revise!

Step 3

Pick a chapter or section from your book or revision notes. Choose a fairly large section or a whole chapter to get the most out of this activity.

With a buddy, use Skype, Facetime, Twitter or any other communication you have, to play the game "If this is the answer, what is the question?". For example, if you are revising Geography and the answer you provide is "meander", your buddy would have to make up a question like "What is the word that describes a feature of a river where it flows slowly and bends often from side to side?".

Make up 10 "answers" based on the content of the chapter or section you are using. Give this to your buddy to solve while you solve theirs.

Step 4

Construct a wordsearch of at least 10 × 10 squares. You can make it as big as you like but keep it realistic. Work together with a group of friends. Many apps allow you to make wordsearch puzzles online. The words and phrases can go in any direction and phrases can be split. Your puzzle must only contain facts linked to the topic you are revising. Your task is to find 10 bits of information to hide in your puzzle, but you must not repeat information that you used in Step 3. DO NOT show where the words are. Fill up empty squares with random letters. Remember to keep a note of where your answers are hidden but do not show your friends. When you have a complete puzzle, exchange it with a friend to solve each other's puzzle.

Step 5

Now make up 10 questions (not "answers" this time) based on the same chapter used in the previous two tasks. Again, you must find NEW information that you have not yet used. Now it's getting hard to find that new information! Again, give your questions to a friend to answer.

Step 6

As you have been doing the puzzles, your brain has been actively searching for new information. Now write a NEW LIST that contains only the new information you have discovered when doing the puzzles. Your new list is the one to look at repeatedly for short bursts over the next few days. Try to remember more and more of it without looking at it. After a few days, you should be able to add words from your second list to your first list as you increase the information in your long-term memory.

FINALLY! Be inspired...

Make a list of different revision ideas and beside each one write **THINGS I HAVE** tried, **THINGS I WILL** try and **THINGS I MIGHT** try. Don't be scared of trying something new.

And remember – "FAIL TO PREPARE AND PREPARE TO FAIL!"

Higher English

The course

The Higher English course aims to enable you to develop the ability to:

- listen, talk, read and write, as appropriate to purpose, audience and context
- understand, analyse and evaluate texts, including Scottish texts, as appropriate to purpose and audience in the contexts of literature, language and media
- create and produce texts, as appropriate to purpose, audience and context
- apply knowledge and understanding of language.

The basics

The grade you finally get for Higher English depends on three things:

- The two internal Unit Assessments you do in school or college: "Analysis and Evaluation" and "Creation and Production"; these don't count towards the final grade, but you must have passed them before you can get a final grade.
- Your Portfolio of Writing – this is submitted in April for marking by SQA and counts for 30% of your final grade.
- The two exams you sit in May – that's what this book is all about.

The exams

Reading for Understanding, Analysis and Evaluation

- exam time: 1 hour 30 minutes
- total marks: 30
- weighting in final grade: 30%
- what you have to do: read two passages and answer questions about the ideas and use of language in one of them (25 marks), and then compare the ideas in both passages (5 marks)

Critical Reading

- exam time: 1 hour 30 minutes
- total marks: 40 (20 marks for each Section)
- weighting in final grade: 40%
- what you have to do: Section 1: read an extract from one of the Scottish Texts which are set for Higher and answer questions about it; Section 2: write an essay about a work of literature you have studied during your course.

1 Reading for Understanding, Analysis and Evaluation

Questions which ask for understanding (e.g. questions which say "Identify … " or "Explain what … " etc.)

- Keep your answers fairly short and pay attention to the number of marks available.
- Use your own words as far as possible. This means you mustn't just copy chunks from the passage – you have to show that you understand what it means by rephrasing it in your own words.

Questions about language features (e.g. questions which say "Analyse how … ")

- This type of question will ask you to comment on features such as Word Choice, Imagery, Sentence Structure and Tone.
- You should pick out a relevant language feature and make a valid comment about its impact. Try to make your comments as specific as possible and avoid vague comments (such as "It is a good word to use because it gives me a clear picture of what the writer is saying"). Remember that you will get no marks just for picking out a word, image or feature of a sentence structure – it's the comment that counts.
- Some hints:
  - **Word choice:** Always try to pick a single word and then give its connotations, i.e. what it suggests.
  - **Sentence structure:** Don't just name the feature – try to explain what effect it achieves in that particular sentence.
  - **Imagery:** Try to explain what the image means literally and then go on to explain what the writer is trying to say by using that image.
  - **Tone** This is always difficult – a good tip is to imagine the sentence or paragraph being read out loud and try to spot how the words or the structure give it a particular tone.

The last question

- Make sure you follow the instruction about whether you're looking for agreement or disagreement (or possibly both).
- When you start on Passage 2, you will have already answered several questions on Passage 1, so you should know its key ideas quite well; as you read Passage 2, try to spot important ideas in it which are similar or different (depending on the question).
- Stick to **key ideas** and don't include trivial ones; **three** relevant key ideas will usually be enough – your task is to decide what the most significant ones are.

2 Critical Reading

Section 1 – Scottish Text

The most important thing to remember here is that there are two very different types of question to be answered:

- Three or four questions (for a total of 10 marks) which focus entirely on the extract.
- One question (for 10 marks) which requires knowledge of the whole text (or of another poem or short story by the same writer).

The first type of question will often ask you to use the same type of close textual analysis skills you used in the Reading part of your Analysis and Evaluation Unit. The golden rules are to read each question very carefully and do exactly as instructed, and to remember that (just like the "Anlaysis" questions in the Reading for Understanding, Analysis and Evaluation paper) there are no marks just for picking out a word or a feature – it's the comment that matters.

The second type of question requires you to discuss common features (of theme and/or technique) in the extract and elsewhere in the writer's work. You can answer this question with a series of bullet points or by writing a mini-essay, so choose the approach you feel most comfortable with.

Finally, a bit of advice for the Scottish Text question: when you see the extract in the exam paper, don't get too confident just because you recognise it (you certainly should recognise it if you've studied properly!). And even if you've answered questions on it before, remember that the questions in the exam are likely to be different, so stay alert.

Section 2 – Critical Essay

A common mistake is to rely too heavily on ideas and whole paragraphs you have used in practice essays and try to use them for the question you have chosen in the exam. The trick is to come to the exam with lots of ideas and thoughts about at least one of the texts you have studied and use these to tackle the question you choose from the exam paper. You mustn't use the exam question as an excuse to trot out an answer you've prepared in advance.

Structure

Every good essay has a structure, but there is no "correct" structure, no magic formula that the examiners are looking for. It's **your** essay, so structure it the way **you** want. As long as you're answering the question all the way through, then you'll be fine.

Relevance

Be relevant to the question **all of the time** – not just in the first and last paragraphs.

Central concerns

Try to make sure your essay shows that you have thought about and understood the central concerns of the text, i.e. what it's "about" – the ideas and themes the writer is exploring in the text.

Quotation

In poetry and drama essays, you're expected to quote from the text, but never fall into the trap of learning a handful of quotations and forcing them all into the essay regardless of the question you're answering. In prose essays, quotation is much less important, and you can show your knowledge more effectively by referring in detail to what happens in key sections of the novel or the short story.

Techniques

You are expected to show understanding of how various literary techniques work within a text, but simply naming them will not get you marks, and structuring your essay around techniques rather than around relevant ideas in the text is not a good idea.

Good luck!

Remember that the rewards for passing Higher English are well worth it! Your pass will help you get the future you want for yourself. In the exam, be confident in your own ability. If you're not sure how to answer a question, trust your instincts and just give it a go anyway – keep calm and don't panic! GOOD LUCK!

National
Qualifications
SPECIMEN ONLY

SQ14/H/01

English
Reading for Understanding,
Analysis and Evaluation

Date — Not applicable

Duration — 1 hour 30 minutes

Total marks — 30

Attempt ALL questions.

Write your answers clearly in the answer booklet provided. In the answer booklet you must clearly identify the question number you are attempting.

Use **blue** or **black** ink.

Before leaving the examination room you must give your answer booklet to the Invigilator; if you do not, you may lose all the marks for this paper.

The following two passages focus on the importance of trees.

Passage 1

In the first passage Janice Turner, writing in The Times newspaper, considers the value of trees.

Read the passage below and attempt the questions which follow.

Watching the tree surgeon from the window, I felt I was witnessing a crime. One I'd authorised, like a Mafia hit. The holm oak — a dense, virulent, evergreen ball — loomed over the garden like a storm cloud. It had to be cut back. But as the chainsaw whined and branches tumbled, I wondered if I really had the right.

5   I'm a resolute city-dweller, but trees seem ever more precious these days, a rebuke to built-in obsolescence, a steady point in a churning world. My pear and apple trees are remnants from when South London orchards ran all the way down to meet the sea. The walnut reaches out a mammoth limb from my neighbour's garden to mine like God's arm on the ceiling of the Sistine Chapel in Rome.

10   They are our living past, clocking up the years, ring by ring. Trees are calming like cathedrals, reassuring us that they will endure even though we will not. No wonder the ancients believed they were gods; there are worse things to worship than a tree.

And this week, reading how some protesters had been arrested trying to prevent ancient woodland being destroyed to make way for a three-mile link road to Hastings, I thought: yes, I'd
15   go to prison for a tree. Indeed, the protesters who are digging tunnels in the mud and standing before the diggers are not "eco-warriors" or "hippies". Among them are young families, retired folk and ordinary dog-walkers. "Local grandmothers", it was reported, came to swing in giant hammocks strung between the 400-year-old oaks.

But this is their last stand. They can only slow the developers. By March the trees will be
20   felled. Local people have fought for 20 years to save them, but they are on the wrong side of what the government is determined to market as progress, however short-term and dubious the economic benefits. The Chancellor of the Exchequer gave £56.8 million of government money for this very road, which will fill up with extra traffic, as new roads do, and lead in time to a spanking new industrial estate, although Hastings town already has plenty of boarded-up
25   premises from which to trade.

Development versus the trees. The government tells us that those who want to protect open countryside and woodland from being turned into endless Lego-brick estates are not conservationists, they are selfish, privileged people who, sitting comfortably in their own cheaply bought piles, have no care for struggling young couples who can't afford a family home.
30   Anyway, what's a bunch of trees?

But people with no respect for trees show a special kind of arrogance: they think they're bigger than history. I'd argue that cutting down an ancient oak is worse than killing most types of animal. Certainly the more numerous species such as dogs, cows, monkeys or cats. A chainsaw slicing into a 300-year-old trunk is more brutal and grotesque than hunting 100 foxes. Chopping
35   down a fine old tree is more like shooting an elephant or harpooning a whale: the aching poignancy of an enormous creature whose size and strength nonetheless cannot save it. Except even the mightiest mammal can be bred to maturity in a few years. Not so a tree.

Yet it is astonishing, given how much people love them — planting them to mark special moments or honour dead loved ones, measuring their lives by their seasonal changes — that
40   officialdom loathes trees. Insurance companies fretting about subsidence would rather you took them all down just in case. Councils detest them, employing municipal butchers to hack away at whole groves. Embarrassed stumps with a couple of twigs are all that remain.

45 It's a wonder any tree survives a health and safety audit. One City Council tried to remove a whole row of horsechestnuts because conkers fell on cars and children might slip on leaves. Our local primary school cut down a fine tree beneath which generations of children had played, because the new head deemed its twigs and leaves too messy. A posh gardener once suggested we cut down most of our trees and start again with fresh, more groovy varieties. This misunderstood the very point: trees are the antithesis of fickle fashion. But some crass homeowners can't bear the fluff-balls from plane trees messing up their hall carpet or the lime

50 sap puking down on their shiny car bonnets. Neater to reach for the axe. Maybe garden centres should start selling plastic ones: say goodbye to autumnal hell.

Visiting Burma, I learnt that its teak forests were flogged off to China by the generals, who were desperate for quick cash, like a beautiful girl being forced to sell her hair. Iceland is barren because Vikings cut them all down in a year and Peru is logging away its resources.

55 Our country's trees will tumble to make way for the machines of progress. But for how much economic growth is it worth mowing down a wood? Trees are beyond priceless: they are our history inscribed in the natural world. Which rich men, planting beautiful orchards to their own glorious memory, have always known.

Adapted from an article in The Times newspaper, January 2013.

MARKS

Questions

1. Re-read lines 1–12

    (a) From the first paragraph, identify two feelings the writer had as she watched the tree in her garden being cut back. **2**

    (b) Analyse how the writer's use of language in lines 5-12 emphasises the importance of trees. You should refer in your answer to such features as sentence structure, word choice, imagery, contrast, tone . . . **4**

2. Re-read Lines 13–25

    According to the writer in lines 13–18, in what ways are the protestors different from how we might expect them to be? **2**

3. **By referring to at least two features of language in lines 19–25** analyse how the writer conveys her feelings of unhappiness about the Hastings development. You should refer in your answer to such features as sentence structure, word choice, contrast, tone . . . **3**

4. Re-read lines 26–37

    (a) From lines 26–30 identify two claims the government makes about the protestors. **2**

    (b) **By referring to at least two features of language in lines 31–37**, analyse how the writer conveys the strength of her belief in tree conservation. **4**

5. Re-read lines 38–54

    (a) Identify any **four** reasons given in these lines for cutting down trees. You should use your own words as far as possible. **4**

    (b) By referring to at least one example, analyse how the writer's use of imagery emphasises her opposition to cutting down trees. **2**

6. Evaluate the final paragraph's effectiveness as a conclusion to the passage as a whole. **2**

Passage 2

In the second passage below, the science writer Colin Tudge gives his own views on trees.

Read the passage and attempt the question which follows. While reading, you may wish to make notes on the main ideas and/or highlight key points in the passage.

In New Zealand a few years ago I experienced more powerfully than ever the sheer gravitas of trees: in the presence of the world's largest kauri. Kauris are conifers, the biggest of their family. The great trunk of the kauri rises like a lighthouse out of the gloom: fifteen metres in circumference — it would touch all four walls in an average living room — and straight up,
5 leafless, for twenty metres or so. And then on its great horizontal boughs rests a virtual park, a floating island with an entire ecosystem of ferns and flowers. Kauris are about 2000 years old. For the first 1400 years of the kauri's life, moas strutted their stuff around its base. Moas included the world's tallest-ever birds, like giant emus, which were preyed upon by commensurately huge but short-winged eagles. The moas and their attendant eagles are now
10 long gone. The kauri lives on.

The remaining kauri forest has been horribly reduced these past two hundred years, but the way modern New Zealanders look after the trees that are left to them is a model for all the world. Rare trees are no longer felled but existing planks are prized and meticulously re-cycled. Meanwhile, you can follow slatted wooden paths among the vast conifers. That's conservation;
15 that's intelligent ecotourism.

Similarly, if new farming economies are to come about, then trees must be at the centre of them. Yet, tree-based farming systems have to fight for survival against the massed ranks of the powers-that-be. How ludicrous. The world's most powerful governments have made themselves answerable to the big companies — and they take pride in this. They call it "realism".

20 So although the things that need doing seem obvious, governments — and the big corporations whose interests they serve — have a quite different agenda. If we want life to be agreeable or indeed to continue at all we just have to ignore the pressures from our ostensible leaders, and do things the way they should be done: building new ways of life, whatever the pressures from on high. Again, trees show the way.

25 Outstanding among the world's many popular initiatives is the Greenbelt Movement, a campaign among Kenyan women to re-plant trees in places they used to grow. Now they have planted 30 million. They have transformed landscapes and changed entire economies and the whole tenor of life. This kind of thing, very simple, and achieved in the teeth of the modern economy (for who makes money out of it?), contributes far more to human wellbeing than, say, cheap white
30 goods from China, on which the economy of the modern world, egged on by our world leaders, is being built.

The broadest issue of all is the western conceit that we can "conquer" nature, or indeed control it. This idea truly took off in the 19th century, and yet is taken still as a mark of modernity. In 1879 the poet Gerard Manley Hopkins lamented the felling of poplars: "O if we but knew what we
35 do/When we delve or hew — Hack and rack the growing green!" We still don't know what we are doing but the hacking and racking continue more vigorously than ever. The only halfway sane approach if we want this world to remain habitable, is to approach it humbly. Trees teach humility. We need to take the world far more seriously. It would be a good idea to begin with trees.

Adapted from an article published on Colin Tudge's website in 2005.

Question

7. Both writers express their views about the importance of trees. Identify key areas on which they agree. In your answer, you should refer in detail to both passages.   5

You may answer this question in continuous prose or in a series of developed bullet points.

[END OF SPECIMEN QUESTION PAPER]

[BLANK PAGE]

SQ14/H/02

English
Critical Reading

Date — Not applicable

Duration — 1 hour 30 minutes

Total marks — 40

SECTION 1 — Scottish Text — 20 marks

Read an extract from a Scottish text you have previously studied and attempt the questions.

Choose ONE text from either

Part A — Drama	Pages 2—9
or	
Part B — Prose	Pages 10—19
or	
Part C — Poetry	Pages 20—31

Attempt ALL the questions for your chosen text.

SECTION 2 — Critical Essay — 20 marks

Attempt ONE question from the following genres — Drama, Prose, Poetry, Film and Television Drama, or Language.

Your answer must be on a different genre from that chosen in Section 1.

You should spend approximately 45 minutes on each Section.

Write your answers clearly in the answer booklet provided. In the answer booklet you must clearly identify the question number you are attempting.

Use **blue** or **black** ink.

Before leaving the examination room you must give your answer booklet to the Invigilator; if you do not, you may lose all the marks for this paper.

SECTION 1 — SCOTTISH TEXT — 20 marks

Choose ONE text from Drama, Prose or Poetry.

Read the text extract carefully and then attempt ALL the questions for your chosen text.

You should spend about 45 minutes on this Section.

PART A — SCOTTISH TEXT — DRAMA

Text 1 — Drama

If you choose this text you may not attempt a question on Drama in Section 2.

Read the extract below and then attempt the following questions.

***The Slab Boys* by John Byrne**

In this extract, which is taken from Act 1 of the play, the discovery of Phil's folio causes conflict in the Slab Room.

(*Alan turns over the folio . . . idly looks inside.*)

Alan:	(*Taking out drawings*) Hey, these aren't yours, are they?
Spanky:	No, they must be Phil's . . . ho, put them back. If he catches you going through his stuff he'll break your jaw.
5 Alan:	I'm not touching them. Hey some of these are not bad . . . look at this one . . .
Spanky:	I'm telling you Alec . . . (*Crosses to have a look.*) God they are good, aren't they? There's one of Elvis...'s dead like him, isn't it? Right . . . shut the folder or I'll get the blame. I get the blame for everything around here . . .
Alan:	Hey . . . how about that red chalk drawing?
10 Spanky:	That's his old man . . .I recognise his ears . . . like Dumbo. And there's one of his maw. Christ, you can tell, can't you?
Alan:	Tell what?
Spanky:	Nothing . . . tell it's his mother. Shut that folder, I said.
Alan: 15	Look at the way he's done those hands. Whenever I have a bash at hands they turn out looking like fankled pipecleaners . . .
Spanky:	Which is exactly how your features are going to look if Phil comes back. Get that shut . . . I'm not telling you again.
Alan:	I wonder how he got that effect?
Spanky:	What effect?
20 Alan:	There . . . The way he's got the nose coming forward from the head . . .
Spanky:	Mines comes forward . . .
Alan:	Some of these are quite accomplished . . .
Spanky:	Aw . . . 'quite accomplished', are they? And what d'you know about it?
Alan: 25	Not a great deal but anyone can see they're rather good. He's wasting his time in here . . .

Spanky: Yeh, you have a word with him kiddo . . . I'm sure he'll appreciate it. Now for the last time, are you going to shut that folder or . . .

(*Enter Curry*)

Curry: I've just been having a natter with your dad, Alan . . .

30   Alan: Oh . . .? (*Tries to gather up drawings*)

Curry: On the phone. You never let on Bob Downie was your father . . . eh?

Godstruth, see you young fellows . . . Chief Designer at Templars . . .? I'd have been as proud as punch . . . Hullo, what's this? Some of your artwork? Let's have a butcher's . . .

35   Alan: No, these aren't . . .

Curry: Tch, tch, tch, tch . . . a chip off the old block, eh?

Alan: I'm afraid they aren't . . .

Curry: A right talented pair of buggers . . . I remember when Bob Downie used to work here he was always . . .

40   Alan: These aren't mine, Mr Curry.

Curry: What?

Spanky: Yeh, they're not his.

Alan: I was just . . .

Curry: Who belongs to them then? They aren't yours, Farrell, that's for sure. You've
45   got trouble trying to draw water from that tap over there . . .

Alan: They were just lying around . . .

Curry: And they can't be Hector's. Too bold for him . . .

Alan: I think they must be . . .

Curry: (*Interrupting him*) You're not going to tell me they're McCann's. What's this . . .
50   (*Turns drawing over*) That's the Art School stamp isn't it? Jimmy Robertson and I used to go up to Saturday morning classes together . . . [*Reads*] 'Glasgow School of Art . . . First Year Entrance Exam . . . Nineteen Fifty Sev . . .' What??

Spanky   Eh?

55   Curry: Whose are these?? Come on . . .

Spanky: How should I know?

Curry: (*Finding label on front of folder*) "P. J. McCann, 19 Darkwood Crescent, Ferguslie Park . . ." So that's what the loafer's been up to. A flyman, eh?

Well we'll soon see about this . . . Farrell!

60   Spanky: What?

Curry: Away down to the ablutions and fetch that crony of yours up here.

Spanky: I'll need to wash my hands first.

Curry: Get a move on! Tell him to drag that miserable carcase of his up those flaming stairs. You and McKenzie can take an arm and a leg each if he can't manage.

65   Spanky: And just leave the rest of his body down there?

Page three

MARKS

70 Curry: Get those mitts washed! Bloody corner boy. Now, Alan, where were we? Ah, yes . . . now, I'm going to rough in a few roses here. I dare say your dad's covered some of this ground with you . . . still, no harm in seeing it again, eh? I showed Bob Downie a few tricks while he was with us. Expect he told you, eh? Now, what's the first . . . Farrell, will you gee yourself up a bit! You'd think it was a damned bath you were having! Right Alan . . . what's the first thing we do when we're starting a charcoal sketch.

Questions

1. By referring closely to two examples of dialogue from lines 3–17, explain what Spanky's comments suggest about Phil.　　2

2. Throughout the play, Curry often reminisces about various incidents in his life. By referring to two examples of dialogue in this extract, explain what these memories suggest about him.　　2

3. Describe the contrasting attitudes shown by Curry to the Slab Boys and to Alan. Explain how this is shown by referring closely to the extract.　　4

4. Choose any example of humour in this extract and explain how it is used to engage the audience's sympathy for Spanky.　　2

5. By referring to this extract and elsewhere in the play, discuss how the theme of frustrated ambition is developed in the text.　　10

OR

Text 2 — Drama

If you choose this text you may not attempt a question on Drama in Section 2.

Read the extract below and then attempt the following questions.

The Cheviot, the Stag and the Black, Black Oil by John McGrath

Fiddle plays:	"The Lord is my Shepherd". *The Company hum quietly as one of the actors is dressed as* The MINISTER *and the* OLD MAN *places his pulpit in position.*

MINISTER:

5

10

15

20

Dearly beloved Brethren, we are gathered here today in the sight of the Lord and in the house of the Lord, to worship the Lord and sing His praises, for He is indeed, the Lord and Shepherd of our souls. Oh you are sheep, sheep who have gone astray, who have wandered from the paths of righteousness and into the tents of iniquity. Oh guilty sinners, turn from your evil ways. How many times and on how many Sabbaths have I warned you from this very pulpit of your wickedness and of the wrath of the Almighty. For I will repay, saith the Lord. The troubles that are visiting you are a judgement from God, and a warning of the final judgement that is to come. Some of you here today are so far from the fold, have so far neglected the dignity of your womanhood, that you have risen up to curse your masters, and violate the laws of the land. I refer of course to the burning of the writs. And everybody here gathered knows to which persons I am referring. There will be no more of this foolishness. Be warned. Unless you repent, you are in great danger of the fire, where there will be much wailing and gnashing of teeth. On that fearful day when God divides the sheep from the goats, every one of us, and particularly those whom I have spoken of today, will have to answer for their flagrant transgression of authority.

He goes off.

OLD MAN:

And it worked . . .

25   SECOND GIRL:

Everywhere, except in Knockan, Elphin and Coigeach.

FIRST GIRL *comes on stage and says, to mounting cheers from the others.*

FIRST GIRL:

30

Here the people made a stout resistance, the women disarming about twenty policemen and sheriff-officers, burning the summonses in a heap, and ducking the representatives of the law in a neighbouring pool. (*Big cheer.*) The men formed a second line of defence — (*Groan*) — in case the women should receive any ill-treatment. (*More groans.*) They, however, never put a finger on the officers of the law — all of whom returned home without serving a single summons or evicting a single crofter!

35   *A big hooch from the Company, the fiddle strikes up and they leap onto the stage to dance to celebrate this victory, the women leading off.*

At the end, all go off except the actor playing the OLD MAN, *who comes to the mike and talks to the audience as himself.*

MARKS

OLD MAN.   What was really going on? There is no doubt that a change had to come
40   to the Highlands: the population was growing too fast for the old,
                inefficient methods of agriculture to keep everyone fed. Even before
                the Clearances, emigration had been the only way out for some. But this
                coincided with something else: English — and Scottish — capital was
                growing powerful and needed to expand. Huge profits were being made
45   already as a result of the Industrial Revolution, and improved methods of
                agriculture. This accumulated wealth had to be used, to make more
                profit — because this is the law of capitalism. It expanded all over the
                globe. And just as it saw in Africa, the West Indies, Canada, the Middle
                East and China, ways of increasing itself, so in the Highlands of Scotland
50   it saw the same opportunity. The technological innovation was there:
                the Cheviot, a breed of sheep that would survive the Highland winter
                and produce fine wool. The money was there. Unfortunately, the
                people were there too. But the law of capitalism had to be obeyed.

Questions

6. Explain how the minister's speech reveals that he regards himself as a force of
    authority and control.   **3**

7. By referring closely to an example of stage directions or dialogue, analyse how
    humour is used in lines 26–34.   **2**

8. Music is evident on two occasions in this short extract. In each case, explain what
    the music contributes to the scene.   **2**

9. In lines 39–54, the Old Man presents a series of financial details. By referring to at
    least two examples, explain how these details are relevant to the themes of the
    play.   **3**

10. The role of women is a significant issue in this play. By referring to this extract and
    elsewhere in the play, discuss how this theme is developed.   **10**

OR

Text 3 — Drama

If you choose this text you may not attempt a question on Drama in Section 2.

Read the extract below and then attempt the following questions.

Men Should Weep by Ena Lamont Stewart

Isa comes out of the bedroom. She has a tawdry lacy, low-cut slip on, and over it a dirty film starish négligée

	ISA:	Whit's a the row?
5	MAGGIE:	(*emptying the contents of her purse on the table*) Alec's shiverin; he can hardly staun on his feet. Rin doon quick and get's a gill o whisky.
	ISA:	A *gill*? There's no much in a gill.
	MAGGIE:	An get a packet o Woodbine tae. An here! You've tae leave aff tormentin him!
	ISA:	Me? Tormentin him? I'm no tormentin him!
10	MAGGIE:	Aye are ye! Threatenin tae leave him when ye ken he's that daft aboot ye. Goad kens why, for ye're a worthless slut if ever there wis yin.
	ISA:	You keep yer insultin names tae yersel, ye dirty aul bitch!
	MAGGIE:	I'll learn ye tae ca me a bitch! (*She slaps Isa's face.*)

At this moment John comes in

15	JOHN:	Here! Whit's a this?
	ISA:	She hit me! She's that rotten tae me!
	JOHN:	Maggie! Whit dae ye think ye're daein?
	MAGGIE:	Naethin she didnae deserve. She ca'd me a bitch.
	JOHN:	Well, ye're certainly actin like yin.
20	MAGGIE:	John!
	JOHN:	Ma Goad! Whit a hell o a hoose tae come hame tae!
	MAGGIE:	It's no ma fault! I've din a hale copper-fu o washin an scrubbed three floors an the hale lot o yous had naethin tae dae but lie in yer beds! Ye couldna even wash up a dish for me. It's me that aye has tae dae twa jobs when you get the sack.
25		
	JOHN:	Aw, shut up harpin on that string. It's no ma fault. I've been oot lookin for work.
	MAGGIE:	Aye, I've seen yous men lookin for work. Haudin up the street corners, ca'in doon the Government . . . tellin the world whit you'd dae if you wis rinnin the country . . .
30		
	JOHN:	Shut yer mouth or I'll shut it for ye!
	MAGGIE:	(*shocked*) John! (*Pause*) Whit I meant wis . . . ye could have tidied the place up afore ye went oot.
35	JOHN:	Tae Hell wi this Jessie business every time I'm oot o a job! I'm no turnin masel intae a bloomin skivvy! I'm a man!

Page seven

ISA: (*softly*) Quite right. A woman disnae respect a man that's nae a man. (*To Maggie*) Well, whit aboot this whisky?

JOHN: Whit's this? Whisky? There's nae drink comin intae this hoose!

ISA: It's for Alec. He's nae weel, she says.

40 MAGGIE: He's lyin doon.

JOHN: If he's nae weel it's mair likely because his system's poisoned wi the stuff a'ready. Alec! Get oot o that bed an show yer face!

MAGGIE: I tell't ye he's nae weel, John.

John goes across to the bed and drags Alec out.

45 JOHN: Get outside and breathe some fresh air, at least whit passes for fresh air roon here. Ye're getting nae whisky. D'ye understan?

MAGGIE: (*turning on him fiercely*) Who earned that money? You or me?

John, as if he had been shot, drops Alec and turns away, slumps down in a chair and puts his head in his hands.

50 *Alec craftily sneaks some of Maggie's cash and slinks out.*

Maggie, resentful, eyes first Isa and then the demoralised John.

ISA: That's the stuff! He's needin somebody tae tak him in haun. He's beyond me. (*She cries, not very convincingly*). I canne dae naethin wi him.

MAGGIE: Oh, wull ye listen tae her! See they crocodile tears? It's a wunner ye can
55 squeeze oot a drap frae they wee marble eyes!

JOHN: Don't cry, Isa; he's nae worth it.

MAGGIE: It's her that's the worthless yin! If she'd leave him alane … …

JOHN: Maggie! That's no fair! She's upset.

MAGGIE: (*bitterly hurt at John's perfidy*) Oh, yous men! Big saft idiots the lot o ye.

60 JOHN: It's your fault. You spoiled him frae the day he wis born. He's still your wee pet lamb no matter whit he gets up tae.

ISA: Aye, he's jist a great big baby. If he disnae get whit he wants, he greets; tears rinnin doon his cheeks. It fair scunners me. I like a man tae be a man. Staun up for hissel.

65 MAGGIE: (*to John*) And I like a man . . . (*Her voice breaking*) . . . tae stand up for his wife.

She seizes her coat and hauls it on, jams on her terrible old hat (this should be black or dark brown) and goes to the table to pick up her money: when she sees how little Alec has left her, she can't help making a small sound.

Questions

11. By referring closely to the dialogue between Maggie and Isa in lines 3—13, explain what is revealed about the difference between Maggie's attitudes to Isa and to Alec.

2

12. Much of the dialogue in lines 20—66 is about how a man is expected to behave. With close reference to the text, discuss Maggie, Isa and John's differing attitudes to this issue.

3

13. Analyse how the stage directions in lines 48—49 add to our understanding of John's character.

3

14. Maggie is disappointed by John's behaviour in this scene. By referring closely to this scene, explain two examples of his behaviour which she finds disappointing.

2

15. Discuss this scene's importance to the development of Maggie's character. You should refer to this extract and in more detail to the play as a whole.

10

SECTION 1 — SCOTTISH TEXT — 20 marks

Choose ONE text from Drama, Prose or Poetry.

Read the text extract carefully and then attempt ALL the questions for your chosen text.

You should spend about 45 minutes on this Section.

PART B — SCOTTISH TEXT — PROSE

Text 1 — Prose

If you choose this text you may not attempt a question on Prose in Section 2.

Read the extract below and then attempt the following questions.

In Church by Iain Crichton Smith

He was grateful now for the silence and for the wood which had a certain semblance of order after the scarred ground worked over and over, continuously revised by shells, so that it looked like carbon paper scribbled over endlessly by a typewriter that never stopped.

5 He looked up again and as he did so he saw two birds attacking another one. They seemed to synchronise their movements and they were low enough for him to see their beaks quite clearly. The third tried to fly above them but they attacked, probing upwards from below. He could no longer see the plane, just the birds. The third bird was weakening. He couldn't make out whether it was a buzzard or a crow. The other two
10 birds were zeroing in at it all the time, pecking and jabbing, going for the head.

He couldn't stand watching the fight any more and turned away into the wood, and it was then that he saw it — the church. It was completely intact though quite small and with gravestones beside it. It was strange to see it, like a mirage surrounded by trees whose brown leaves stirred faintly in the slight breeze. From the sky above, the birds had
15 departed: perhaps the two had killed the third one or perhaps it had escaped. It reminded him of a dogfight he had seen between a German triplane and a British Sopwith Camel. After a long duel, the German triplane had destroyed the British plane but was in turn shot down by another British fighter. The triplane made a perfect landing. The British troops rushed up to find the pilot seated at the controls, upright, disciplined,
20 aristocratic, eyes staring straight ahead, and perfectly dead. Later they found the bullet which had penetrated his back and come out at the chest.

He pushed open the door of the church and stood staring around him. He had never been in a church like this before with the large effigy of the Virgin Mary all in gold looking down at him, hands crossed. The stained glass windows had pictures of Christ in green
25 carrying a staff and driving rather shapeless yellow sheep in front of him. In one of the panes there was another picture of him holding out his hands in either a helpless or a welcoming gesture. There were no Bibles or hymn books on the seats as if no one had been there for some time. At the side there was a curtained alcove which he thought might be a confessional. He pulled the curtains aside but there was no one there.

30 He sat down and gazed for a long time at the huge golden cross which dominated the front of the church. The silence was oppressive. It was not at all like the churches at home. There was more ornament, it was less bare, more decorated. The churches at home had little colour and less atmosphere than this. He could feel in his bones the presence of past generations of worshippers, and then he heard the footsteps.

MARKS

35 He turned round to see a man in a black gown walking towards him. There was a belt of rope round his gown and his hands could not be seen as they seemed to be folded inside his gown. The face was pale and ill looking.

"What do you want, my son?" said the voice in English.

Questions

16. Analyse how Iain Crichton Smith uses both word choice and sentence structure in the first two paragraphs (lines 1—10) to emphasise:

    (i) war's futility

    (ii) cruelty   4

    You should comment on both word choice and sentence structure in each part of your answer.

17. Explain how the anecdote about the dogfight in paragraph 3 develops the theme of the futility of war.   2

18. Analyse how Iain Crichton Smith conveys the narrator's unfamiliarity with his surroundings. (lines 22—38)   4

19. In his stories set in wartime, Iain Crichton Smith develops the theme of the destructive nature of war. By referring to this and at least one other story by Crichton Smith, discuss how he develops this theme.   10

OR

Text 2 — Prose

If you choose this text you may not attempt a question on Prose in Section 2.

Read the extract below and then attempt the following questions.

A Time to Keep by George Mackay Brown

I dug out a new field at the side of the house — because no-one on God's earth could plough such a wilderness — and all the while I was tearing up stones and clumps of heather I thought to myself, "What a fool! Sure as hell the laird will raise your rent for this day's work." And my spade rang against stones or sank with a squelch into a sudden
5 bit of bog.

I looked up once and saw a dozen women trooping across the fields to the school.

It was Good Friday.

I looked up another time and saw a horseman riding between the hills. It was the laird. He turned his horse towards the school also. The Easter service was being held
10 there.

Two of my lambs had been born dead that morning. They lay, red bits of rag, under the wall. I would bury them afterwards.

There was one stone in the new field that just showed a gray curve through the heather. I took the biggest hammer in the barn and was an hour breaking it up and
15 tearing the sharp bits out of the ground.

That was enough labour for one day. The sun was going down. I turned for home.

Ingi was not in. The house was dead. The pot sat black upon a black fire. My shoulders ached with the misery and foolishness of increasing my own rent. I was very hungry too.

20 Ingi was at the service with the laird and the other women, listening to the story of the lash and the whins and the nails and the last words. All the women were there sitting before the missionary with open mouths, listening to that fairy tale. I and a few others in the island knew better. Mr Simpson, B.Sc., from Glasgow had not been our schoolmaster four winters for nothing.

25 I spent the rest of that day in the ale-house with half a dozen other ploughmen.

And how I got home to the croft again I do not know. I woke up in the morning on the rack of my own bed, with all my clothes on.

There was a jam jar with new daffodils in it in the window.

Ingi heard my awakening, a groan and a creak.

30 She rose up quickly from the chair where she was peeling potatoes and put her cold hand on my forehead. "You'll be fine now," she said. "Bella had two lambs in the night, such bonny peedie things! Your throat must be dry. I'll get you some water."

Bella was the old ewe. None of her lambs, so I had been told when I bought her, ever died.

35 "You listen to me," I said to Ingi. "You spend too much money every Wednesday at that grocery van. Don't you buy any more jars of jam, and sponge-cakes from the bake-house in Hamnavoe. We're poor people. Remember that."

The daffodils in the window were like a dozen old women shawled in brightness.

The fire burned high in the hearth and the kettle sang.

40 I closed my eyes.

MARKS

Questions

20. By referring closely to lines 1—15 analyse how George Mackay Brown conveys:

   (i) the poverty of the land

   (ii) the narrator's inadequacy as a farmer.   4

21. By referring to at least two examples, analyse how George Mackay Brown uses sentence structure to develop the narrator's worsening mood in the extract.   4

22. By referring closely to one example of Ingi's actions or speech, explain how she influences or tries to influence his mood.   2

23. In his short stories, George Mackay Brown creates characters who are flawed but nonetheless engage the reader's sympathy. By referring to this story and at least one other by George Mackay Brown, discuss how he achieves this.   10

OR

Text 3 — Prose

If you choose this text you may not attempt a question on Prose in Section 2.

Read the extract below and then attempt the following questions.

***The Trick is to Keep Breathing* by Janice Galloway**

In this extract, Joy attends her first appointment with a psychiatrist, having been referred by her GP, Dr Stead.

I knew right away this was going to be a disappointment.

Lesson 1: Psychiatrists aren't as smart as you'd think.

I knew three things right away:

1. I hate facile questions (So-why-do-you-think-you're-here is so easy to subvert);

5 2. You have to try: it's the whole purpose of being here; and

3. You have to be on your guard. There is no defence against the arbitrariness of things. You have to be suspicious of everything.

All three things whispered in my ears like Angels and Devils in a TV cartoon which made it very difficult to think straight. Dr One didn't know that. All he knew was I wasn't 10 answering.

So, he said. Why do you think you've been sent to us?

He thought I wasn't trying.

Lesson 2: Psychiatrists are not mind-readers. They just try to look as though they are.

He tried another tack.

15   Tell me from the beginning what you think is making you feel bad, he said. Take your time and tell it in your own words.

For some reason, I hadn't expected this. I'd done that story so many times I knew it like a nursery rhyme but now my throat was contracting. I couldn't think about even the first line without feeling I was about to short-circuit. On top of everything else I was ashamed 20 of how stupid I'd been. I hadn't thought it through. It was perfectly logical he should start like this yet I hadn't seen it coming. The devils whispered What did you expect? A course of shock therapy the minute you walked in the door? The angels whispered Try. Dr Stead went to a lot of trouble to get you this appointment. You have to try. There was only one way out of this. My mouth knew more than the rest of me put together. I had to 25 trust my mouth. I closed my eyes and the mouth said

My mother walked into the sea.

I remember the voice: chiselled as crystal. Cold as a razor. I hadn't known it would start like this but then I was redundant. The voice didn't need me. It didn't even like me. I let the story come out in this disembodied glass voice and listened, out of harm's way in 30 the corner of the room.

She didn't die right away. At the funeral, the man I lived with shook my hand. I left him. I had an affair with a married man. He left his wife to come and stay with me. Things were difficult. My house started caving in and we had to move somewhere else. Then we went away and he drowned

35 The end of the story seemed to come up too soon. I heard the last bit twisting out of kilter then stopping without warning. The room felt suddenly eerie: like the Bates Motel in Psycho. If you listened hard you could probably hear the liver-coloured furniture breathing, little creaks and rustles where people had been before. I had to think hard to remember where I was.

40   He drowned.

Something was happening to my stomach. As though I'd stamped my foot down hard at the end of a staircase and the floor wasn't where I thought it was. The side of the pool, the circle of men, blue eyes and the sky. I suddenly remembered what I was saying wasn't a story. It wasn't the furniture breathing, it was me. What I was saying was true.

45   Lesson 3: Psychiatrists give you a lot of rope knowingly.

Questions

24. By referring closely to lines 1—13, explain how Galloway makes the reader aware of Joy's attitude towards the psychiatrist.   2

25. "Tell me from the beginning . . . in your own words." (lines 15—16)

    Referring closely to at least two examples in lines 15—30, analyse how the writer conveys Joy's state of mind at this point.   4

26. Referring closely to at least two examples from lines 31—45, analyse how the writer highlights the significance of Michael's death.   4

27. By referring to this extract and elsewhere in the novel, discuss how Galloway develops the theme of loss.   10

OR

Text 4 — Prose

If you choose this text you may not attempt a question on Prose in Section 2.

Read the extract below and then attempt the following questions.

Sunset Song by Lewis Grassic Gibbon

In this extract, which is from Part I I (Drilling), Peesie's Knapp is on fire.

And faith, quick though they were, it was father that saved Chae Strachan's folk. He was
first down at the blazing Knapp, John Guthrie; and he ran round the biggings and saw the
flames lapping and lowing at the kitchen end of the house, not a soul about or trying to
stop them though the noise was fair awful, the crackling and burning, and the winter air
5 bright with flying sticks and straw. He banged at the door and cried *Damn't to hell do
you want to be roasted?* and when he got no answer he smashed in the window, they
heard him then and the bairns scraiched, there was never such a lot for sleep, folk said,
Chae'd have slept himself out of this world and into hell in his own firewood if John
Guthrie hadn't roused him then. But out he came stumbling at last, he'd only his breeks
10 on; and he took a keek at John Guthrie and another at the fire and cried out *Kirsty, we're
all to hell*! and off he tore to the byre.

But half-way across the close as he ran the barn swithered and roared and fell, right in
front of him, and he'd to run back, there was no way then of getting at the byre. By then
Long Rob of the Mill came in about, he'd run over the fields, louping dykes like a hare,
15 and his lungs were panting like bellows, he was clean winded. He it was that helped Mrs
Strachan with the bairns and such clothes as they could drag out to the road while Chae
and John Guthrie tried to get at the byre from another angle: but that was no good, the
place was already roaring alight. For a while there was only the snarling of the fire
eating in to the wooden couplings, the rattle of falling slates through the old charred
20 beams, and then, the first sound that Will and Chris heard as they came panting down the
road, a scream that was awful, a scream that made them think one of the Strachans was
trapped down there. And at that sound Chae covered his ears and cried *Oh God, that's
old Clytie*, Clytie was his little horse, his sholtie, and she screamed and screamed,
terrible and terrible, Chris ran back to the house trying not to hear and to help poor
25 Kirsty Strachan, snivelling and weeping, and the bairns laughing and dancing about as
though they were at a picnic, and Long Rob of the Mill smoking his pipe as cool as you
please, there was surely enough smell and smoke without that? But pipe and all he dived
in and out of the house and saved chairs and dishes and baskets of eggs; and Mistress
Strachan cried *Oh, my sampler!* and in Rob tore and rived that off a blazing wall, a
30 meikle worsted thing in a cracked glass case that Mistress Strachan had made as a bairn
at school.

MARKS

Questions

28. By close reference to the text, explain how two aspects of John Guthrie's and Long Rob's character are revealed in this extract.   **4**

29. By referring to at least two examples from **paragraph one** analyse how the writer conveys a sense of urgency.   **2**

30. By referring to at least two examples from **paragraph two** analyse how the writer conveys the ferocity of the fire.   **4**

31. The community is presented positively in this extract. By referring to this extract, and elsewhere in the novel, discuss how Grassic Gibbon conveys positive aspects of the community.   **10**

OR

Text 5 — Prose

If you choose this text you may not attempt a question on Prose in Section 2.

Read the extract below and then attempt the following questions.

The Cone-Gatherers by Robin Jenkins

In this extract, Mr Tulloch arrives to speak with the brothers after their expulsion from the beach hut by Lady Runcie-Campbell.

When he caught sight of Neil ahead of him, he halted and watched from behind a slender spruce long ago wind-blown, with its roots in the air. From that distance, judged only by his gait, Neil appeared like an old man. He was gathering beech seed, which he had been instructed to do whenever bad weather kept him from climbing. He would cautiously go
5   down on his haunches, wait, apparently to gather strength and endurance against the pain of that posture, and then would begin to pick up the seed-cases or mast, squeeze each one with his fingers to find if it were fertile, and drop it if it were not. The watching forester knew most of them would not be, unless this luckily was the tree's year of fertility: otherwise as many as ninety out of a hundred would be barren. To fingers
10   crippled with rheumatism it would not be easy to examine them with the necessary patience. When that area had been searched, Neil hobbled on his haunches to another. Thus he would go on until break-time. Such fidelity to so simple but indispensable a task was to the forester as noble and beautiful a sight as was to be seen in that wood so rich in magnificent trees. To praise it would be to belittle it, so inadequate were words; but to
15   fail to appreciate it or to refuse to defend it, would be to admit the inadequacy of life itself.

He stepped out from behind the hanging roots, and without hurry approached the intent seed-gatherer.

Neil looked up, saw him, stared a moment, and then went on with his inspection of the
20   beech nut. That one was fertile. He held it out to his employer.

"That's the first good one in the last half hour, Mr Tulloch," he said.

"Well, it's a slow business, Neil," replied the forester, smiling, "but look at the result." Walking forward he touched the huge grey trunk.

Behind him Neil began to sob. He did not turn to look, but kept stroking the tree.

25   "Don't fret over it, Neil," he said.

"It's not for me," sobbed Neil. "It's for Calum." And he began to pour out an account of the expulsion from the beach hut, all mixed up with the story of the insult in the hotel bar. The forester had heard about that episode from one of his workers, but he had been given to believe that the soldier had apologised, and that afterwards the sympathy of
30   nearly everybody in the pub had been with the brothers.

"I'm responsible for him, Mr Tulloch," said Neil. "If you were to ask me to whom I'm to give account for the way I've looked after him, I couldn't tell you; but I'm responsible just the same."

"No man on earth has ever looked after his brother so well," replied Tulloch. "We all
35   know that. You can give a good account, no matter to whom."

He turned round and saw, with a shock he did not show, how stooped and contorted Neil was then, by rheumatism and despair: it was as if, in some terrible penance, he was striving to become in shape like his brother.

Page eighteen

"Why is it, Mr Tulloch," he asked, "that the innocent have always to be sacrificed?"

40   "Is that really true, Neil?"

"Aye, it's true.   In this war, they tell me, babies are being burnt to death in their cradles."

The forester was silent; his own brother had been killed at the time of Dunkirk.

"I suppose it's so that other babies will be able to grow up and live like free men," he
45   said.   "But I see what you mean; in a way, aye, the innocent have to be sacrificed."

"We were driven out like slaves, Mr Tulloch.   Her dog was to be saved from the storm, but not my brother."

"I think maybe she was taken by surprise, Neil.   She didn't expect to find you there. After all, you did get in by the window.   Maybe she got a bit of a shock."

50   "Did she think we were monkeys that would bite her?"

"I think she was in the wrong, Neil, but I would like to be fair to her.   She's a good woman really; but she's got a code to live by."

Neil shook his head dourly.

"My brother's the shape God made him,' he said. 'What right has she, great lady though
55   she is, to despise him?"

"No right at all, Neil.   But don't think about it anymore.   I'm seeing her this afternoon, and I'm going to tell her I'm taking you back to Ardmore."

Questions

32.   By referring closely to lines 1–38, analyse how Jenkins evokes both sympathy and admiration for Neil.   4

33.   By referring closely to lines 39–55, explain the reasons for Neil's attitude to Lady Runcie-Campbell.   4

34.   Explain the reasons for Mr. Tulloch's attitude to Lady Runcie-Campbell and the 'code' by which she makes decisions, referring to lines 39–57 in your answer.   2

35.   Neil's words "Why is it...that the innocent have always to be sacrificed?" clarify one of the central concerns of the text.

With reference to such features as setting, characterisation and narrative in this extract and elsewhere in the novel, discuss how Jenkins develops our understanding of this central concern.   10

SECTION 1 — SCOTTISH TEXT — 20 marks

Choose ONE text from Drama, Prose or Poetry.

Read the text extract carefully and then attempt ALL the questions for your chosen text.

You should spend about 45 minutes on this Section

PART C — SCOTTISH TEXT — POETRY

Text 1 — Poetry

If you choose this text you may not attempt a question on Poetry in Section 2.

Read the extract below and then attempt the following questions.

Holy Willie's Prayer by Robert Burns

This extract begins at stanza five of the poem.

Yet I am here a chosen sample,

To show thy grace is great and ample;

I'm here, a pillar o' Thy temple,

    Strong as a rock,

5 A guide, a buckler, and example,

    To a' Thy flock.

O Lord, Thou kens what zeal I bear,

When drinkers drink, an swearers swear,

An' singin' there, an' dancin' here,

10   Wi' great an' sma';

For I am keepet by Thy fear,

    Free frae them a'.

But yet, O Lord! confess I must ___

At times I'm fash'd wi' fleshly lust:

15 And sometimes too, in wardly trust,

    Vile self gets in:

But Thou remembers we are dust,

    Defil'd wi' sin.

O Lord! yestreen, Thou kens, wi' Meg —

20 Thy pardon I sincerely beg !

O! may't ne'er be a livin' plague

    To my dishonour !

An' I'll ne'er lift a lawless leg

    Again upon her.

MARKS

25 Besides, I farther maun allow,

Wi' Leezie's lass, three times I trow;

But Lord, that Friday I was fou,

When I came near her;

Or else, Thou kens, Thy servant true

30   Wad never steer her.

Maybe Thou lets this fleshly thorn

Buffet Thy servant e'en and morn,

Lest he o'er proud and high should turn,

That he's sae gifted;

35 If sae, Thy han' maun e'en be borne,

Until Thou lift it.

Lord, bless Thy chosen in this place,

For here Thou hast a chosen race:

But God confound their stubborn face,

40   And blast their name,

Wha bring Thy elders to disgrace

An' open shame.

Questions

36.   Explain what Holy Willie means when he calls himself "a chosen sample".   **2**

37.   Holy Willie's words and feelings/actions contradict one another.

With reference to two examples from lines 1—30 from this extract, analyse how Burns conveys this contradiction.   **4**

38.   The tone changes in lines 31—42. With reference to two examples from lines 31—42, identify the change of tone used by Holy Willie.   **4**

39.   Burns creates a variety of characters in his poetry. From your reading of this poem and at least one other by Burns, discuss the contrast between Holy Willie and at least one other character.   **10**

OR

Text 2 — Poetry

If you choose this text you may not attempt a question on Poetry in Section 2.

Read the poem below and then attempt the following questions.

Originally by Carol Ann Duffy

We came from our own country in a red room
which fell through the fields, our mother singing
our father's name to the turn of the wheels.
My brothers cried, one of them bawling, *Home*,
5   Home, as the miles rushed back to the city,
the street, the house, the vacant rooms
where we didn't live any more. I stared
at the eyes of a blind toy, holding its paw.

All childhood is an emigration. Some are slow,
10 leaving you standing, resigned, up an avenue
where no one you know stays. Others are sudden.
Your accent wrong. Corners, which seem familiar,
leading to unimagined pebble-dashed estates, big boys
eating worms and shouting words you don't understand.
15 My parents' anxieties stirred like a loose tooth
in my head. *I want our own country*, I said.

But then you forget, or don't recall, or change,
and, seeing your brother swallow a slug, feel only
a skelf of shame. I remember my tongue
20 shedding its skin like a snake, my voice
in the classroom sounding just like the rest. Do I only think
I lost a river, culture, speech, sense of first space
and the right place? Now, *Where do you come from*?
strangers ask. *Originally*? And I hesitate.

MARKS

Questions

40. By referring closely to **stanza 1** analyse the use of poetic technique to emphasise the dramatic impact moving to another country had on the family.   **2**

41. Look at **stanza 2**.

    "All childhood is an emigration"

    Explain fully what the poet means by this.   **2**

42. In lines 12–16 analyse the use of poetic technique to convey the distress of the family members caused by their "sudden" emigration to a new environment.   **3**

43. Evaluate the effectiveness of **stanza 3** as a conclusion to the poem. Your answer should deal with ideas and/or language.   **3**

44. Discuss how Carol Ann Duffy uses contrast in this poem and at least one other to highlight the poems' main concerns.   **10**

OR

Text 3 — Poetry

If you choose this text you may not attempt a question on Poetry in Section 2.

Read the poem below and then attempt the following questions.

***For My Grandmother Knitting* by Liz Lochhead**

There is no need they say
but the needles still move
their rhythms in the working of your hands
as easily
5 as if your hands
were once again those sure and skilful hands
of the fisher-girl.

You are old now
and your grasp of things is not so good
10 but master of your movements then
deft and swift
you slit the still-tickling quick silver fish.
Hard work it was too
of necessity.

15 But now they say there is no need
as the needles move
in the working of your hands
once the hands of the bride
with the hand-span waist
20 once the hands of the miner's wife
who scrubbed his back
in a tin bath by the coal fire
once the hands of the mother
of six who made do and mended
25 scraped and slaved slapped sometimes
when necessary.

But now they say there is no need
the kids they say grandma
have too much already
30 more than they can wear
too many scarves and cardigans —

gran you do too much

there's no necessity...

At your window you wave

35   them goodbye Sunday.

With your painful hands

big on shrunken wrists.

Swollen-jointed. Red. Arthritic. Old.

But the needles still move

40   their rhythms in the working of your hands

easily

as if your hands remembered

of their own accord the pattern

as if your hands had forgotten

45   how to stop.

Questions

45. By referring to **two** examples from lines 1—14, analyse the use of poetic technique in clarifying the main ideas of the poem.   **2**

46. In lines 15—26 the poet expands upon the life of the grandmother when she was younger.

    Choose two poetic techniques and analyse how they help convey the grandmother's life as a younger woman.   **3**

47. By referring closely to lines 27—33 identify the attitude of the grandchildren to their grandmother and explain how this is conveyed.   **2**

48. Evaluate how effective you find lines 34—45 as a conclusion to the poem.

    Your answer should deal with ideas and/or language.   **3**

49. By referring to this poem and at least one other by Lochhead, discuss the importance of the theme of memory in her work.   **10**

OR

Text 4 — Poetry

If you choose this text you may not attempt a question on Poetry in Section 2.

Read the poem below and then attempt the following questions.

***Sounds of the Day* by Norman MacCaig**

When a clatter came,
it was horses crossing the ford.
When the air creaked, it was
a lapwing seeing us off the premises
5 of its private marsh. A snuffling puff
Ten yards from the boat was the tide blocking and
unblocking a hole in a rock.
When the black drums rolled, it was water
falling sixty feet into itself.

10 When the door
scraped shut, it was the end
of all the sounds there are.

You left me
beside the quietest fire in the world.

15 I thought I was hurt in my pride only,
forgetting that,
when you plunge your hand in freezing water,
you feel
a bangle of ice around your wrist
20 before the whole hand goes numb.

MARKS

Questions

50. By referring closely to lines 1–9, analyse MacCaig's use of poetic technique to create a vivid sense of place.

4

51. By referring closely to lines 10–12, analyse MacCaig's use of poetic technique to convey the abrupt change in the persona's circumstance.

2

52. By referring closely to the lines 13–20, analyse how MacCaig highlights the impact which the parting has on the persona.

4

53. By referring to this poem and at least one other by Norman MacCaig, discuss his use of contrast to explore theme in his work.

10

OR

Text 5 — Poetry

If you choose this text you may not attempt a question on Poetry in Section 2.

Read the poem below and then attempt the following questions.

Heroes **by Sorley MacLean**

I did not see Lannes at Ratisbon
nor MacLennan at Auldearn
nor Gillies MacBain at Culloden,
but I saw an Englishman in Egypt.

5   A poor little chap with chubby cheeks
and knees grinding each other,
pimply unattractive face —
garment of the bravest spirit.

He was not a hit "in the pub
10   in the time of the fists being closed,"
but a lion against the breast of battle,
in the morose wounding showers.

His hour came with the shells,
with the notched iron splinters,
15   in the smoke and flame,
in the shaking and terror of the battlefield.

Word came to him in the bullet shower
that he should be a hero briskly,
and he was that while he lasted
20   but it wasn't much time he got.

He kept his guns to the tanks,
bucking with tearing crashing screech,
until he himself got, about the stomach,
that biff that put him to the ground,
25   mouth down in sand and gravel,
without a chirp from his ugly high-pitched voice.

No cross or medal was put to his

chest or to his name or to his family;

there were not many of his troop alive,

30 and if there were their word would not be strong.

And at any rate, if a battle post stands,

many are knocked down because of him,

not expecting fame, not wanting a medal

or any froth from the mouth of the field of slaughter.

35 I saw a great warrior of England,

a poor manikin on whom no eye would rest;

no Alasdair of Glen Garry;

and he took a little weeping to my eyes.

Questions

54. By referring closely to the first stanza, evaluate its effectiveness as an opening to the poem.　2

55. By referring closely to lines 5—11 **and** lines 35—38, discuss the speaker's attitude towards the English soldier.　4

56. By referring to at least **two** examples from lines 12—26, analyse the use of poetic technique to convey the horror of war.　4

57. MacLean often chooses to write about people or places. Referring closely to this poem and to another poem or poems by MacLean, discuss how the poet develops a theme or themes through his observation of people or places.　10

OR

Text 6 — Poetry

If you choose this text you may not attempt a question on Poetry in Section 2.

Read the poem below and then attempt the following questions.

***The Ferryman's Arms* by Don Paterson**

About to sit down with my half-pint of Guinness
I was magnetized by a remote phosphorescence
and drawn, like a moth, to the darkened back room
where a pool-table hummed to itself in the corner.
5   With ten minutes to kill and the whole place deserted
I took myself on for the hell of it. Slotting
a coin in the tongue, I looked round for a cue —
while I stood with my back turned, the balls were deposited
with an abrupt intestinal rumble; a striplight
10   batted awake in its dusty green cowl.
When I set down the cue-ball inside the parched D
it clacked on the slate; the nap was so threadbare
I could screw back the globe, given somewhere to stand.
As physics itself becomes something negotiable
15   a rash of small miracles covers the shortfall.
I went on to make an immaculate clearance.
A low punch with a wee dab of side, and the black
did the vanishing trick while the white stopped
before gently rolling back as if nothing had happened,
20   shouldering its way through the unpotted colours.

The boat chugged up to the little stone jetty
without breaking the skin of the water, stretching,
as black as my stout, from somewhere unspeakable,
to here, where the foaming lip mussitates endlessly,
25   trying, with a nutter's persistence, to read
and re-read the shoreline. I got aboard early,
remembering the ferry would leave on the hour
even for only my losing opponent;
but I left him there, stuck in his tent of light, sullenly
30   knocking the balls in, for practice, for next time.

MARKS

Questions

58. The main themes of the poem are introduced in the title and first six lines

    Identify **one** main theme and show how poetic technique is used to introduce this theme.   3

59. By referring closely to lines 6–20, analyse the use of poetic technique to achieve a change of mood from alienation and uncertainty to one of confidence.   4

60. Evaluate the effectiveness of the second stanza as a conclusion to the poem.   3

61. In this poem, Paterson uses an apparently ordinary experience to explore a deeper truth about humanity.

    By referring to this and another poem or poems by Don Paterson you have studied discuss how he uses poetry to explore the deeper truths behind ordinary experience.   10

[END OF SECTION 1]

SECTION 2 — CRITICAL ESSAY — 20 marks

Attempt ONE question from the following genres — Drama, Prose, Poetry, Film and Television Drama, or Language.

You may use a Scottish text but **NOT** the one used in Section 1.

Your answer must be on a different genre from that chosen in Section 1.

You should spend approximately 45 minutes on this Section.

DRAMA

> Answers to questions on **drama** should refer to the text and to such relevant features as characterisation, key scene(s), structure, climax, theme, plot, conflict, setting . . .

1. Choose a play in which a central character struggles to cope with social convention **or** financial difficulties **or** family duties.

    Briefly explain the reasons for the character's struggle and discuss how the dramatist's presentation of this struggle enhances your understanding of character and/or theme in the play as a whole.

2. Choose a play in which the concluding scene provides effective clarification of the central concerns.

    By referring in detail to the concluding scene, discuss in what ways it is important for your understanding of the play as a whole.

3. Choose a play in which the conflict between two characters is an important feature.

    Briefly explain the nature of this conflict and discuss how the dramatist's presentation of this feature enhances your understanding of the play as a whole.

PROSE — FICTION

Answers to questions on **prose fiction** should refer to the text and to such relevant features as characterisation, setting, language, key incident(s), climax, turning point, plot, structure, narrative technique, theme, ideas, description . . .

4. Choose a novel or short story in which there is a disturbing or violent incident.

    Explain briefly what happens during this incident and discuss to what extent the disturbing or violent nature of the incident is important to your understanding of the text as a whole.

5. Choose a novel or short story in which a specific location or setting is crucial to the plot.

    Discuss how the writer makes you aware of the setting's importance and how this feature is used to enhance your appreciation of the text as a whole.

6. Choose a novel or short story in which a central character is presented as a menacing or threatening presence.

    Discuss how the writer's presentation of this character adds to your understanding of the text as a whole.

PROSE — NON-FICTION

Answers to questions on **prose non fiction** should refer to the text and to such relevant features as ideas, use of evidence, stance, style, selection of material, narrative voice . . .

7. Choose a piece of **travel writing** in which the writer's use of language engages your interest in his/her portrayal of a country or culture.

    Discuss how the writer uses language to successfully engage your interest in this portrayal.

8. Choose a work of **biography** or **autobiography** in which the writer's description of an emotional experience creates a powerful impression.

    Briefly explain the emotional experience and then discuss how the writer's description of this experience creates this powerful impression.

9. Choose a piece of **journalism** in which the writer persuades his or her reader to a point of view by effective use of language.

    Briefly explain the writer's point of view, and then discuss how the writer's use of language is effective in persuading the reader.

POETRY

> Answers to questions on **poetry** should refer to the text and to such relevant features as word choice, tone, imagery, structure, content, rhythm, rhyme, theme, sound, ideas . . .

10. Choose a poem in which the poet explores one of the following emotions: grief, happiness, love, alienation.

    Discuss how the poet's exploration of the emotion has deepened your understanding of it.

11. Choose two poems which deal with the same theme.

    Discuss how the theme is explored in each poem and explain which poem you believe offers a more memorable exploration of the theme.

12. Choose a poem which features a relationship.

    Discuss how the poet's presentation of this relationship adds to your understanding of the central concern(s) of the poem.

FILM AND TELEVISION DRAMA

> Answers to questions on **film and television drama*** should refer to the text and to such relevant features as use of camera, key sequence, characterisation, mise-en-scène, editing, setting, music/sound, special effects, plot, dialogue, . . .

13. Choose a film or television drama in which a central character is in difficulty.

    Briefly explain what the difficulty is, and then discuss how the film or programme makers' presentation of the character's difficulties enhances your understanding of a central concern of the text.

14. Choose a film or television drama which contains a particularly memorable or thrilling chase sequence.

    Explain how the memorable or thrilling aspect of this chase was achieved by the film or programme makers and then discuss the significance of this sequence in your appreciation of the text as a whole.

15. Choose a film or television drama which presents an epic voyage or a difficult quest.

    Explain how the film or programme makers evoke the epic nature of the voyage or the difficulty of the quest and discuss how this evocation enhances your appreciation of the text as a whole.

* "television drama" includes a single play, a series or a serial.

LANGUAGE

> Answers to questions on **language** should refer to the text and to such relevant features as register, accent, dialect, slang, jargon, vocabulary, tone, abbreviation . . .

16. Choose a particular area of journalism such as sports reporting, investigative journalism, motoring journalism, science reporting.

    Identify the key features of the language used in this particular journalistic area and discuss that area's contribution to effective reporting.

17. Choose a form or forms of electronic communication such as e-mail, social networking, text messaging, online forums.

    Identify some of the distinctive features of the language used and discuss to what extent these features contribute to effective communication.

18. Choose a political speech which makes use of persuasive language.

    By referring to specific features of language in this speech, discuss to what extent you feel the speech is successful in achieving its purpose of persuasion.

[END OF SECTION 2]

[END OF SPECIMEN QUESTION PAPER]

[BLANK PAGE]

National Qualifications 2015

X724/76/11

FRIDAY, 15 MAY

9:00 AM – 10:30 AM

English
Reading for Understanding, Analysis and Evaluation — Text

Total marks — 30

Read the passages carefully and then attempt ALL questions, which are printed on a separate sheet.

The following two passages consider the negative impact of intensive farming.

Passage 1

Read the passage below and then attempt questions 1 to 8.

In the first passage, Isabel Oakeshott gives a disturbing account of her visit to Central Valley, California, an area where intensive farming is big business.

On a cold, bright November day I stood among a million almond trees and breathed in the sweet air. I was in Central Valley, California, in an orchard stretching over 700,000 acres. Before me was a vision of how the British countryside may look one day. Beyond the almond orchards were fields of pomegranates, pistachios, grapes and apricots. Somewhere in the distance were almost
5 two million dairy cows, producing six billion dollars' worth of milk a year.

It may sound like the Garden of Eden but it is a deeply disturbing place. Among the perfectly aligned rows of trees and cultivated crops are no birds, no butterflies, no beetles or shrubs. There is not a single blade of grass or a hedgerow, and the only bees arrive by lorry, transported across the United States. The bees are hired by the day to fertilise the blossom, part of a
10 multibillion-dollar industry that has sprung up to do a job that nature once did for free.

As for the cows, they last only two or three years, ten-to-fifteen years less than their natural life span. Crammed into barren pens on tiny patches of land, they stand around listlessly waiting to be fed, milked or injected with antibiotics. Through a combination of selective breeding, artificial diets and growth hormones designed to maximise milk production, they are pushed so
15 grotesquely beyond their natural limit that they are soon worn out. In their short lives they never see grass.

Could the British countryside ever look like this? If current trends continue, the answer is yes. Farming in Britain is at a crossroads, threatened by a wave of intensification from America. The first mega-dairies and mega-piggeries are already here. Bees are disappearing, with serious
20 implications for harvests. Hedgerows, vital habitats for wildlife, have halved since the Second World War. The countryside is too sterile to support many native birds. In the past forty years the population of tree sparrows has fallen by 97%.

With an eye to the future, Owen Paterson, the UK environment secretary, has been urging families to buy British food. Choosing to buy fewer imports would reduce the relentless pressure
25 British farmers are under to churn out more for less. Paterson's vision is of a more eco-friendly way of eating, based on locally-produced, seasonal fruit and vegetables and, crucially, British meat.

But, as I discovered when I began looking into the way food is produced, increasingly powerful forces are pulling us in the opposite direction. We have become addicted to cheap meat, fish
30 and dairy products from supply lines that stretch across the globe. On the plus side, it means that supermarkets can sell whole chickens for as little as £3. Things that were once delicacies, such as smoked salmon, are now as cheap as chips. On the downside, cheap chicken and farmed fish are fatty and flaccid. Industrially reared farm animals — 50 billion of them a year worldwide — are kept permanently indoors, treated like machines and pumped with drugs.

35 My journey to expose the truth, to investigate the dirty secret about the way cheap food is produced, took me from the first mega-dairies and piggeries in Britain to factory farms in France, China, Mexico, and North and South America. I talked to people on the front line of the global food industry: treadmill farmers trying to produce more with less. I also talked to their neighbours — people experiencing the side effects of industrial farms. Many had stories about
40 their homes plummeting in value, the desecration of lovely countryside, the disappearance of wildlife and serious health problems linked to pollution.

I wanted to challenge the widespread assumption that factory farming is the only way to produce food that everyone can afford. My investigation started in Central Valley, California, because it demonstrates the worst-case scenario — a nightmarish vision of the future for parts of
45 Britain if current practices continue unchecked. It is a five-hour drive south of San Francisco and I knew I was getting close when I saw a strange yellowish-grey smog on the horizon. It looks like the sort of pollution that hangs over big cities, but it comes from the dairies. California's bovine population produces as much sewage as 90 million people, with terrible effects on air quality. The human population is sparse, but the air can be worse than in Los Angeles on a
50 smoggy day.

Exploring the area by car, it was not long before I saw my first mega-dairy, an array of towering, open-sided shelters over muddy pens. The stench of manure was overwhelming — not the faintly sweet, earthy smell of cowpats familiar from the British countryside, but a nauseating reek bearing no relation to digested grass. I saw farms every couple of miles, all with several
55 thousand cows surrounded by mud, corrugated iron and concrete.

It may seem hard to imagine such a scene in Britain but it is not far-fetched. Proposals for an 8,000 cow mega-dairy in Lincolnshire, based on the American model, were thrown out after a public outcry. On local radio the man behind the scheme claimed that "cows do not belong in fields". It will be the first of many similar fights, because dairies are expanding and moving
60 indoors. The creep of industrial agriculture in Britain has taken place largely unnoticed, perhaps because so much of it happens behind closed doors. The British government calls it "sustainable intensification". Without fuss or fanfare, farm animals have slowly disappeared from fields and moved into hangars and barns.

Adapted from an article in The Sunday Times newspaper.

Passage 2

Read the passage below and attempt question 9. While reading, you may wish to make notes on the main ideas and/or highlight key points in the passage.

In the second passage, Audrey Eyton considers the reasons for the introduction of intensive farming and explains why it could be viewed as a mistake.

The founding fathers of intensive farming can claim, "It seemed a good idea at the time!" Indeed it did, in Britain, half a century ago. The post-war government swung into action with zeal, allocating unprecedented funds to agricultural research. The outcome was that the mixed farm, where animals grazed in the fields, was replaced by the huge factories we see today.

5 The aim in confining animals indoors was to cut costs. It succeeded. Indoors, one or two workers can "look after" hundreds of penned or tethered pigs, or a hundred thousand chickens. Great economies were made and thousands of farm workers lost their jobs. This new policy of cheap meat, eggs and cheese for everyone was completely in tune with the national mood, as Britain ripped up its ration books. It was also in tune with nutritional thinking, as nutritionists at
10 that time thought greater consumption of animal protein would remedy all dietary problems.

So factory farming marched on. And became more and more intensive. Where first there were one or two laying hens in a cage, eventually there became five in the same small space. The broiler chicken sheds expanded to cram in vast acres of birds. Many beef cattle were confined in buildings and yards. Until mad cow disease emerged, such animals were fed all kinds of
15 organic matter as cheap food. In the UK dairy cows still spend their summers in the fields, but many of their offspring are reared in the cruelty of intensive veal crate systems.

The aim of those early advocates of intensive farming was "fast food" — fast from birth to table. Again, they succeeded. Chicken, once an occasional treat, now the most popular meat in Britain, owes its low price largely to the short life of the bird. Today's broiler chicken has
20 become the fastest growing creature on earth: from egg to take-away in seven weeks. Most farm animals now have less than half of their pre-war lifespan. Either they are worn out from overproduction of eggs or milk, or have been bred and fed to reach edible size in a few short weeks or months.

But meat, eggs and dairy products have indeed become cheap, affordable even to the poor. All
25 of which made nutritionists exceedingly happy — until they discovered that their mid-century predecessors had made a mighty blunder. Before intensive farming brought cheap meat and dairy products to our tables, man obtained most of his calories from cereal crops and vegetables. The meat with which he supplemented this diet had a much lower fat content than intensively produced products. Now, however, degenerative diseases like coronary heart disease
30 and several types of cancer have been linked to our increased consumption of fatty foods. War-time Britons, on their measly ration of meat and one ounce of cheese a week, were much healthier.

With this knowledge, the only possible moral justification for intensive farming of animals collapses. The cheap animal production policy doesn't help the poor. It kills them. In addition,
35 the chronic suffering endured by animals in many intensive systems is not just a sentimental concern of the soft-hearted. It is a scientifically proven fact. Cracks are beginning to show in our long-practised animal apartheid system, in which we have convinced ourselves, against all evidence, that the animals we eat are less intelligent, less in need of space and exercise than are those we pat, ride or watch.

40 It is also a scientifically proven fact that intensive farming has caused the loss of hedgerows and wildlife sustained by that habitat, has polluted waterways, decimated rural employment and caused the loss of traditional small farms. We need to act in the interests of human health. We need to show humane concern for animals. We need to preserve what remains of the countryside by condemning the practice of intensive farming. We need to return the animals to
45 the fields, and re-adopt the environmentally friendly, humane and healthy system we had and lost: the small mixed farm.

Adapted from an article in The Observer newspaper.

[END OF TEXT]

National
Qualifications
2015

X724/76/21

**English
Reading for Understanding, Analysis
and Evaluation — Questions**

FRIDAY, 15 MAY

9:00 AM – 10:30 AM

Total marks — 30

Attempt ALL questions.

Write your answers clearly in the answer booklet provided. In the answer booklet you must clearly identify the question number you are attempting.

Use **blue** or **black** ink.

Before leaving the examination room you must give your answer booklet to the Invigilator; if you do not, you may lose all the marks for this paper.

MARKS

Attempt ALL questions
Total marks — 30

1. Read lines 1—5.

   Identify any **two** positive aspects of Central Valley, California, which are conveyed in these lines. Use your own words in your answer.   2

2. Read lines 6—10.

   By referring to at least **two** examples, analyse how the writer's use of language creates a negative impression of Central Valley.   4

3. Read lines 11—16.

   By referring to both word choice **and** sentence structure, analyse how the writer makes clear her disapproval of dairy farming methods used in Central Valley.   4

4. Read lines 17—19.

   Explain the function of these lines in the development of the writer's argument. You should make close reference to the passage in your answer.   2

5. Read lines 23—34.

   In your own words, summarise the differences between UK Government food policy and consumer wishes.   4

6. Read lines 35—41.

   Analyse how both imagery **and** sentence structure are used in these lines to convey the writer's criticism of industrial farming.   4

7. Read lines 42—55.

   Explain how the writer continues the idea that the Central Valley dairy farming is "nightmarish". Use your own words in your answer. You should make **three** key points.   3

8. Read lines 56—63.

   Evaluate the effectiveness of the final paragraph as a conclusion to the writer's criticism of industrial farming.   2

Question on both passages

9. Look at both passages.

   Both writers express their views about intensive farming.

   Identify **three** key areas on which they agree. You should support the points you make by referring to important ideas in both passages.

   You may answer this question in continuous prose or in a series of developed bullet points.   5

[END OF QUESTION PAPER]

**National
Qualifications
2015**

X724/76/12

**English
Critical Reading**

FRIDAY, 15 MAY

10:50 AM – 12:20 PM

Total marks — 40

SECTION 1 — Scottish Text — 20 marks

Read an extract from a Scottish text you have previously studied and attempt the questions.

Choose ONE text from either

Part A — Drama	Pages 2–11
or	
Part B — Prose	Pages 12–21
or	
Part C — Poetry	Pages 22–33

Attempt ALL the questions for your chosen text.

SECTION 2 — Critical Essay — 20 marks

Attempt ONE question from the following genres — Drama, Prose Fiction, Prose Non-fiction, Poetry, Film and Television Drama, or Language.

Your answer must be on a different genre from that chosen in Section 1.

You should spend approximately 45 minutes on each Section.

Write your answers clearly in the answer booklet provided. In the answer booklet you must clearly identify the question number you are attempting.

Use **blue** or **black** ink.

Before leaving the examination room you must give your answer booklet to the Invigilator; if you do not, you may lose all the marks for this paper.

SECTION 1 — SCOTTISH TEXT — 20 marks

Choose ONE text from Drama, Prose or Poetry.

Read the text extract carefully and then attempt ALL the questions for your chosen text.

You should spend about 45 minutes on this Section.

PART A — SCOTTISH TEXT — DRAMA

Text 1 — Drama

If you choose this text you may not attempt a question on Drama in Section 2.

Read the extract below and then attempt the following questions.

The Slab Boys by John Byrne

This extract is taken from Act 2 of the play. Phil has been dismissed from his job.

(*Enter PHIL.*)

	SPANKY:	I thought you were away?
	PHIL:	I went along for my wages . . . doll said she gave them to Jack.
	JACK:	The monkey's got them . . .
5	SPANKY:	Catch. (*Flings packet to PHIL.*) 'S that you off, Jack-knife? Not fancy a hot poultice before you go?
	JACK:	If you need a lift home, Alan, let me know . . . I'll try and arrange something . . .
	ALAN:	Thanks.
10	(*Exit JACK.*)	
	SPANKY:	(*To PHIL, who is opening his wage packet*) Your books?
	PHIL:	Yeh . . . P45, the lot . . . (*Reads document:*) "Non-Contributory Pension Scheme" . . . what's that?
	ALAN:	It means you haven't paid directly into . . .
15	PHIL:	Shuttit, you! I'm talking to my friend. Well?
	SPANKY:	How should I know? I've got all these dishes to wash! Can you not give us a hand? There's hundreds of them.
	PHIL:	You're forgetting something, Spanky. I don't work here any more.
	SPANKY:	You never did, Phil.
20	PHIL:	Less of the sarcasm . . . (*Sarcastically*) Slab Boy.
	SPANKY:	At least I still am one.
	PHIL:	Yeh . . . how come? Me and Hector get the heave and you're still here washing dishes safe and secure. How d'you manage it, eh?
	SPANKY:	Going to get out of my road? I've got work to do . . .
25	PHIL:	Work? Has Noddy there been getting to you?
	SPANKY:	Why don't you can it, Phil? Me and the boy wants to get cleared up.

	PHIL:	Aw . . . it's "me and the boy" now, is it?
	SPANKY:	Yeh . . . what of it?
	PHIL:	I think I'm going to be sick.
30	SPANKY:	Well, don't hang over the shades, there's gum in them already . . .
		(*PHIL grabs him. They confront one another. Enter CURRY.*)
	CURRY:	Still here, McCann? You can go any time, you know.
	PHIL:	I'm waiting for a phone call.
	CURRY:	Only urgent personal calls allowed . . .
35	PHIL:	This is urgent. I'm waiting for word from the hospital.
	CURRY:	What's up . . . someone in the family ill?
	PHIL:	It's my maw.
	CURRY:	Oh, yes, of course. Were the lacerations severe? It can do a great deal of damage, plate glass . . .
40	PHIL:	What?
	CURRY:	Plate glass . . . the stuff they have in shop windows.
	PHIL:	What d'you know about shop windows? Who told you about it?
	CURRY:	There was a bit in today's *Paisley Express* . . . "Ferguslie Park Woman in Store Window Accident" . . .
45	PHIL:	It wasn't an accident. She meant to do it.
	CURRY:	Eh? But the paper said your mother was thrown through the window by a passing car . . .
	PHIL:	Well, they got it wrong, didn't they? There was a car there but it wasn't passing . . . it was parked. What she done was take a header off the roof . . .
50		straight through the Co. window . . . simple.
	CURRY:	From the roof of a car? She must've been badly injured.
	PHIL:	Not a scratch. They say it was the angle she jumped off the roof of the motor.
	CURRY:	Good God, it must've been a miracle.
55	PHIL:	Nope . . . a Ford Prefect.

Questions

1. Look at lines 1—15.

   Explain fully the contrast in these lines between the attitude of Jack and Phil towards Alan.   **2**

2. Look at lines 16—31.

   By referring to at least two examples, analyse how the tension between Phil and Spanky is made clear.   **4**

3. Look at lines 32—55.

   By referring to at least two examples, analyse how language is used to convey the feelings of Phil and/or Curry.   **4**

4. In this extract, various aspects of Phil's character are revealed through humour. By referring to this extract and elsewhere in the play, discuss how humour is used to develop Phil's character.   **10**

Page five

[OPEN OUT FOR QUESTIONS]

DO NOT WRITE ON THIS PAGE

OR

Text 2 — Drama

If you choose this text you may not attempt a question on Drama in Section 2.

Read the extract below and then attempt the following questions.

***The Cheviot, the Stag and the Black, Black Oil* by John McGrath**

DUKE: The Queen needs men, and as always, she looks to the North. My Commissioner, Mr Loch, informs me that the response so far has been disappointing.

Enter LOCH, *now an old man.*

5   LOCH: Disappointing? A disgrace. In the whole county of Sutherland, not one man has volunteered.

DUKE: I know you to be loyal subjects of the Queen. I am prepared to reward your loyalty. Every man who enlists today will be given a bounty of six golden sovereigns from my own private purse. Now if you will all step up in an
10   orderly manner, Mr Loch will take your names and give you the money.

The DUKE *sits. Silence. Nobody moves. The* DUKE *stands angrily.*

DUKE: Damn it, do you want the Mongol hordes to come sweeping across Europe, burning your houses, driving you into the sea? (LOCH *fidgets.*) What are you fidgeting for Loch? Have you no pride in this great democracy that we
15   English — er — British have brought to you? Do you want the cruel Tsar of Russia installed in Dunrobin Castle? Step forward.

Silence. Nobody moves.

DUKE: For this disgraceful, cowardly conduct, I demand an explanation.

Short silence. OLD MAN *stands up in audience.*

20   OLD MAN: I am sorry for the response your Grace's proposals are meeting here, but there is a cause for it. It is the opinion of this country that should the Tsar of Russia take possession of Dunrobin Castle, we could not expect worse treatment at his hands than we have experienced at the hands of your family for the last fifty years. We have no country to fight for. You robbed us of our country and
25   gave it to the sheep. Therefore, since you have preferred sheep to men, let sheep now defend you.

ALL: Baa-aa.

The DUKE *and* LOCH *leave.* SOLDIER *beats retreat.*

MC: One man only was enlisted at this meeting. No sooner was he away at Fort
30   George than his house was pulled down, his wife and family turned out, and put in a hut from which an old female pauper was carried a few days before to the churchyard.

Out of thirty-three battalions sent to the Crimea, only three were Highland.

But this was only a small set-back for the recruiters. These parts were still
35   raided for men; almost as fast as they cleared them off the land, they later recruited them into the Army. The old tradition of loyal soldiering was fostered and exploited with careful calculation.

MARKS

Questions

5. Look at lines 1—18.

   The Duke uses a variety of tones in his speeches to the people in these lines. By referring to at least two examples, analyse how language is used to create different tones.

   4

6. Look at lines 17—27.

   Analyse how both the stage directions and dialogue convey the local people's defiance of the Duke.

   4

7. Look at lines 29—37.

   Explain how the MC's speech brings this section of the play to an ironic conclusion.

   2

8. Discuss how McGrath develops the theme of change in this extract and elsewhere in the play.

   10

[Turn over

OR

Text 3 — Drama

If you choose this text you may not attempt a question on Drama in Section 2.

Read the extract below and then attempt the following questions.

Men Should Weep by Ena Lamont Stewart

In this extract from Act 3, Jenny is paying a visit to Maggie and John's tenement home after a period of absence.

	Lily:	Jenny, whit're ye getting at?
	Jenny:	Mammy seems tae think they're letting Bertie hame; but they're no. *No here.* No tae this. Mammy, ye've tae see the Corporation for a Cooncil hoose.
5	Maggie:	A Cooncil house! A Cooncil hoose! Yer daddy's been up tae that lot til he's seek scunnert. Ye've tae wait yer turn in the queue.
	Jenny:	But if they kent aboot Bertie . . .
	Lily:	Is this whit brought ye back, Jenny?
10	Jenny:	It's whit gied me the courage tae come. Least . . . it was ma daddy's face . . . in the water; (*more to herself than the others*) there wis lights shimmerin on the blackness . . . it kind o slinks alang slow, a river, in the night. I was meanin tae let it tak me alang wi it.

Maggie gives a gasp.

	Maggie:	Whit kind o talk is this, Jenny? Did ye no think o us. Yer daddy an me?
15	Jenny:	Think o ye? Oh aye, Mammy, I thought o ye. But thinkin jist made me greet. I was that ashamed o masel . . . Isa and me, we were that rotten tae ye, the things we said.
	Maggie:	That's a bye, Jenny.
20	Jenny:	Naethin's ever *bye*, Mammy; it's a there, like a photy-album in yer heid . . . I kept seein ma daddy, the way he used tae sing tae me when I wis wee; I seen him holdin ma bare feet in his hands tae warm them, an feedin me bread an hot milk oot o a blue cup. (*Pause*) I don't know where you were, Mammy.
	Lily:	Ben the back room wi the midwife, likely. (*Pause*) It's as weel ye came tae yer senses; yon's no the way tae tak oot o yer troubles; a river. But ye're daein fine noo? Ye merriet?
25	Jenny:	No.
	Lily:	Oh. Livin in sin, as they ca it these days, eh?
	Jenny:	(*suddenly flaring up*) Aye, if ye want tae ca it sin! I don't. The man I'm livin wi is kind, an generous.
	Lily:	Oh aye. We can see that. We've had an eye-fu o yer wages o sin.
30	Maggie:	(*mournful*) Aw Jenny. I wisht ye'd earned it.
	Lily:	(*coarse laugh*) Oh, she'll hae earned it, Maggie. On her back.
	Maggie:	*Lily!*
	Lily:	So the Bible's a wrang, is it? The wages o sin's nae deith, it's fancy hair-dos an a swanky coat an pur silk stockins.

35 Jenny: You seem tae ken yer Bible, Auntie Lily. I never pretended tae. But I'm happy, an I'm makin *him* happy. We've a nice wee flat in a clean district, wi trees an wee gardens.

   Lily: A wee love-nest oot west! Great! Juist great — till yer tired business man gets tired o you an ye're oot on yer ear.

40 Jenny: Well, ye hevnae changed, Auntie Lily. I've got tae laugh at you.

   Lily: Laugh awa. I'm no mindin. I've kept ma self-respect.

   Jenny: Aye. An that's aboot a ye've got.

   Maggie: Oh, stop it! Stop it! (*Her hands to her head*) I wis that happy . . .

45 Jenny: Mammy, I'm sorry. We'll sit doon properly an talk. (*She draws a couple of chairs together, deliberately excluding Lily who moves off a little, but keeps within ear-shot and stands, back resting against the table — or the sideboard — watching.*) I've got plans for you.

   Maggie: Plans?

   Jenny: Aye. For getting yous a oot o this.

50 Maggie: Och Jenny, pet; you wis aye fu o dreams.

   Lily: Aye. Dreams. Fairy-tales. She went awa an impident wee bizzom an she's come back on Christmas Eve, kiddin on she's a fairy wi a magic wand.

   Jenny: (*She doesn't even look at Lily*) Listen, Mammy. We canna wait for a hoose frae the cooncil, it'll tak too lang; but mind! Ye've tae get ma daddy tae speak tae
55   them. (*Maggie nods*) So, while ye're waitin, ye're goin tae flit tae a rented hoose.

   Maggie: Jenny, ye need a lot o money tae flit!

   Jenny: I've got that. (*She opens her handbag and produces a roll of notes that makes Maggie's eyes bulge. She gasps.*) There's plenty for the flittin and the key
60   money forbye.

John comes in. He stops at the sight of Jenny and at first his face lights up: then his lips tighten.

MARKS

Questions

9. Look at lines 1—21.

   Explain two of Jenny's reasons for visiting the family home. 2

10. Look at lines 22—42.

    Analyse how Lily and Jenny's differing attitudes are shown. 4

11. Look at lines 43—62.

    Analyse the dramatic impact of at least two of the stage directions in these lines. 4

12. By referring to this extract and elsewhere in the play, discuss how Jenny's growing maturity is made clear. 10

[OPEN OUT FOR QUESTIONS]

DO NOT WRITE ON THIS PAGE

SECTION 1 — SCOTTISH TEXT — 20 marks

Choose ONE text from Drama, Prose or Poetry.

Read the text extract carefully and then attempt ALL the questions for your chosen text.

You should spend about 45 minutes on this Section.

PART B — SCOTTISH TEXT — PROSE

Text 1 — Prose

If you choose this text you may not attempt a question on Prose in Section 2.

Read the extract below and then attempt the following questions.

Mother and Son by Iain Crichton Smith

"It isn't my fault I haven't." He spoke wearily. The old interminable argument was beginning again: he always made fresh attacks but as often retired defeated. He stood up suddenly and paced about the room as if he wanted to overawe her with his untidy hair, his thick jersey, and long wellingtons.

5 "You know well enough," he shouted, "why I haven't my day's work. It's because you've been in bed there for ten years now. Do you *want* me to take a job? I'll take a job tomorrow . . . if you'll only say!" He was making the same eternal argument and the same eternal concession: "If you'll only say." And all the time he knew she would never say, and she knew that he would never take any action.

10 "Why, you'd be no good in a job. The manager would always be coming to show you what you had done wrong, and you'd get confused with all those strange faces and they'd laugh at you." Every time she spoke these words the same brutal pain stabbed him. His babyish eyes would be smitten by a hellish despair, would lose all their hope, and cloud over with the pain of the mute, suffering animal. Time and time again he would say to

15 her when she was feeling better and in a relatively humane mood: "I'm going to get a job where the other fellows are!" and time and time again, with the unfathomable and unknowable cunning of the woman, she would strike his confidence dead with her hateful words. Yes, he was timid. He admitted it to himself, he hated himself for it, but his cowardice still lay there waiting for him, particularly in the dark nights of his mind when

20 the shadow lay as if by a road, watching him, tripping behind him, changing its shape, till the sun came to shine on it and bring its plausible explanations. He spoke again, passing his hand wearily over his brow as if he were asking for her pity.

"Why should anybody laugh at me? They don't laugh at the other chaps. Everybody makes mistakes. I could learn as quickly as any of them. Why, I used to do his lessons for

25 Norman Slater." He looked up eagerly at her as if he wanted her to corroborate. But she only looked at him impatiently, that bitter smile still upon her face.

"Lessons aren't everything. You aren't a mechanic. You can't do anything with your hands. Why don't you hurry up with that tea? Look at you. Fat good you'd be at a job."

He still sat despairingly leaning near the fire, his head on his hands. He didn't even hear

30 the last part of her words. True, he wasn't a mechanic. He never could understand how things worked. This ignorance and inaptitude of his puzzled himself. It was not that he wasn't intelligent: it was as if something had gone wrong in his childhood, some lack of interest in lorries and aeroplanes and mechanisms, which hardened into a wall beyond which he could not go through — paradise lay yonder.

MARKS

35 He reached up for the tea absent-mindedly and poured hot water into the tea-pot. He watched it for a while with a sad look on his face, watched the fire leaping about it as if it were a soul in hell. The cups were white and undistinguished and he felt a faint nausea as he poured the tea into them. He reached out for the tray, put the tea-cup and a plate with bread and jam on it, and took it over to the bed. His mother sat up and took the
40 tray from him, settling herself laboriously back against the pillows. She looked at it and said:

"Why didn't you wash this tray? Can't you see it's all dirty round the edges?" He stood there stolidly for a moment, not listening, watching her frail, white-clad body, and her spiteful, bitter face. He ate little but drank three cups of tea.

Questions

13. Look at lines 1—22.

  By referring to at least two examples, analyse how language reveals the nature of the relationship between mother and son.   4

14. Look at lines 27—28.

  Identify the tone of the mother's words and analyse how this tone is created.   3

15. Look at lines 29—38.

  By referring to at least two examples, analyse how language is used to convey the son's reaction to his mother's words.   3

16. By referring to this extract and to at least one other story, discuss how Iain Crichton Smith uses contrasting characters to explore theme.   10

[Turn over

OR

Text 2 — Prose

If you choose this text you may not attempt a question on Prose in Section 2.

Read the extract below and then attempt the following questions.

The Wireless Set **by George Mackay Brown**

One afternoon in the late summer of that year the island postman cycled over the hill road to Tronvik with a yellow corner of telegram sticking out of his pocket.

He passed the shop and the manse and the schoolhouse, and went in a wavering line up the track to Hugh's croft.   The wireless was playing music inside, Joe Loss and his
5   orchestra.

Betsy had seen him coming and was standing in the door.

"Is there anybody with you?" said the postman.

"What way would there be?" said Betsy. "Hugh's at the lobsters."

"There should be somebody with you," said the postman.

10   "Give me the telegram," said Betsy, and held out her hand. He gave it to her as if he was a miser parting with a twenty-pound note.

She went inside, put on her spectacles, and ripped open the envelope with brisk fingers. Her lips moved a little, silently reading the words.

Then she turned to the dog and said, "Howie's dead." She went to the door. The
15   postman was disappearing on his bike round the corner of the shop and the missionary was hurrying towards her up the path.

She said to him, "It's time the peats were carted."

"This is a great affliction, you poor soul," said Mr. Sinclair the missionary. "This is bad news indeed. Yet he died for his country. He made the great sacrifice. So that we could
20   all live in peace, you understand."

Betsy shook her head. "That isn't it at all," she said. "Howie's sunk with torpedoes. That's all I know."

They saw old Hugh walking up from the shore with a pile of creels on his back and a lobster in each hand. When he came to the croft he looked at Betsy and the missionary
25   standing together in the door. He went into the outhouse and set down the creels and picked up an axe he kept for chopping wood.

Betsy said to him, "How many lobsters did you get?"

He moved past her and the missionary without speaking into the house. Then from inside he said, "I got two lobsters."

30   "I'll break the news to him," said Mr. Sinclair.

From inside the house came the noise of shattering wood and metal.

"He knows already," said Betsy to the missionary. "Hugh knows the truth of a thing generally before a word is uttered."

Hugh moved past them with the axe in his hand.

35   "I got six crabs forby," he said to Betsy, "but I left them in the boat."

He set the axe down carefully inside the door of the outhouse. Then he leaned against the wall and looked out to sea for a long while.

MARKS

"I got thirteen eggs," said Betsy. "One more than yesterday. That old Rhode Islander's laying like mad."

40 The missionary was slowly shaking his head in the doorway. He touched Hugh on the shoulder and said, "My poor man — "

Hugh turned and said to him, "It's time the last peats were down from the hill. I'll go in the morning first thing. You'll be needing a cart-load for the Manse."

The missionary, awed by such callousness, walked down the path between the cabbages
45 and potatoes. Betsy went into the house. The wireless stood, a tangled wreck, on the dresser. She brought from the cupboard a bottle of whisky and glasses. She set the kettle on the hook over the fire and broke the peats into red and yellow flame with a poker. Through the window she could see people moving towards the croft from all over the valley. The news had got round. The mourners were gathering.

50 Old Hugh stood in the door and looked up at the drift of clouds above the cliff. "Yes," he said, "I'm glad I set the creels where I did, off Yesnaby. They'll be sheltered there once the wind gets up."

"That white hen," said Betsy, "has stopped laying. It's time she was in the pot, if you ask me."

Questions

17. Look at lines 1—5.

    Explain how Mackay Brown creates both a sense of community life and the role of the wireless set within it.   2

18. Look at lines 6—22.

    (a) By referring to lines 6—15, analyse how the postman's attitude to Betsy is revealed.   2

    (b) By referring to lines 16—22, analyse how language is used to convey the different reactions of the missionary and Betsy to the news.   2

19. In lines 23—54, Mackay Brown reveals a contrast between the couple's real feelings and the missionary's perception of how they feel.

    By referring to at least two examples from these lines, analyse how the contrast is revealed.   4

20. In his writing, Mackay Brown explores the relationship between the island/small mainland community and the outside world. By referring to this extract and at least one other story by Mackay Brown, discuss how he does this.   10

[Turn over

OR

Text 3 — Prose

If you choose this text you may not attempt a question on Prose in Section 2.

Read the extract below and then attempt the following questions.

The Trick Is To Keep Breathing by Janice Galloway

In this extract, Joy is struggling to cope after the death of her partner, Michael.

Look

all I wanted was to be civilised and polite. I wanted to be no trouble. I wanted to be brave and discreet. This had to be the final stage of the endurance test and all I had to do was last out. I thought I was Bunyan's Pilgrim and Dorothy in The Wizard of Oz. But
5 the lasting out was terrible. I made appointments with the doctor and he gave me pills to tide me over when I got anxious. I got anxious when they didn't tide me over into anything different. He gave me more pills. I kept going to work. I was no nearer Kansas or the Celestial City. Then

I started smelling Michael's aftershave in the middle of the night. I would go to bed and
10 there it was, in a cloud all round my head. I thought if I could smell his aftershave he must be around somewhere. I saw him in cars, across the street, in buses, roaring past on strange motorbikes, drifting by the glass panel of my classroom door. I read his horoscope. How could he be having a difficult phase with money if he was dead? Of course he wasn't *dead*: just hiding. At night I sunk my face into his clothes and howled
15 at the cloth. A magazine article said it was fairly common and not as unhealthy as you'd think. Then I would go to bed and wait for the slow seep of aftershave through the ether. I knew he wasn't just a carcass liquefying in a wooden box but an invisible presence hovering in a cloud of Aramis above my bed. I also suspected I was lying. When I found the bottle, tipped on its side and leaking along the rim I knew for sure. I had put it there
20 myself ages ago so I could reach for it and smell his neck when I wanted to feel like hell in the middle of the night. Then I must have knocked it over and been too wilful to admit to what it was later. My own duplicity shocked me. I held onto the bottle for a week or so then threw it out.

My mother was right. I have no common sense. I don't know a damn thing worth
25 knowing.

THE CHURCH	THE MARRIED
THE LAW	WHAT'S WHAT

I haven't a clue.

The clock ticks too loud while I lie still, shrinking.

30 Please god make boulders crash through the roof. In three or four days when the Health Visitor comes she will find only mashed remains, marrowbone jelly oozing between the shards like bitumen. *Well*, she'll say, *We're not doing so well today, are we?* It's too cold. The hairs on my legs are stiff. I shiver and wish the phone would ring.

Needing people yet being afraid of them is wearing me out. I struggle with the paradox
35 all the time and can't resolve it. When people visit I sam distraught trying to look as if I can cope. At work I never speak but I want to be spoken to. If anyone does I get anxious and stammer. I'm scared of the phone yet I want it to ring.

MARKS

Questions

21. Look at lines 1—8.

    Analyse how Galloway makes the reader aware of Joy's efforts to cope with her situation.   2

22. Look at lines 9—23.

    By referring to at least two examples, analyse how the writer conveys Joy's desperation for Michael's presence.   4

23. Look at lines 29—37.

    By referring to at least two examples, analyse how Galloway conveys Joy's feelings of despair.   4

24. By referring to this extract and elsewhere in the novel, discuss how Galloway demonstrates Joy's fear and/or anxiety in relating to other people.   10

[Turn over

OR

Text 4 — Prose

If you choose this text you may not attempt a question on Prose in Section 2.

Read the extract below and then attempt the following questions.

Sunset Song by Lewis Grassic Gibbon

This extract is from the beginning of Part II (Drilling). In this extract Chris reflects on the death of her mother.

Lying down when her climb up the cambered brae was done, panting deep from the rate she'd come at — skirt flying and iron-resolute she'd turn back for nothing that cried or called in all Blawearie — no, not even that whistle of father's! — Chris felt the coarse grass crackle up beneath her into a fine quiet couch. Neck and shoulders and hips and
5 knees she relaxed, her long brown arms quivered by her side as the muscles slacked away, the day drowsed down an aureal light through the long brown lashes that drooped on her cheeks. As the gnomons of a giant dial the shadows of the Standing Stones crept into the east, snipe called and called —

Just as the last time she'd climbed to the loch: and when had that been? She opened her
10 eyes and thought, and tired from that and closed down her eyes again and gave a queer laugh. The June of last year it had been, the day when mother had poisoned herself and the twins.

So long as that and so near as that, you'd thought of the hours and days as a dark, cold pit you'd never escape. But you'd escaped, the black damp went out of the sunshine and
15 the world went on, the white faces and whispering ceased from the pit, you'd never be the same again, but the world went on and you went with it. It was not mother only that died with the twins, something died in your heart and went down with her to lie in Kinraddie kirkyard — the child in your heart died then, the bairn that believed the hills were made for its play, every road set fair with its warning posts, hands ready to snatch
20 you back from the brink of danger when the play grew over-rough. That died, and the Chris of the books and the dreams died with it, or you folded them up in their paper of tissue and laid them away by the dark, quiet corpse that was your childhood.

So Mistress Munro of the Cuddiestoun told her that awful night she came over the rain-soaked parks of Blawearie and laid out the body of mother, the bodies of the twins that
25 had died so quiet in their crib. She nipped round the rooms right quick and pert and uncaring, the black-eyed futret, snapping this order and that, it was her that terrified Dod and Alec from their crying, drove father and Will out tending the beasts. And quick and cool and cold-handed she worked, peeking over at Chris with her rat-like face. *You'll be leaving the College now, I'll warrant, education's dirt and you're better clear of it.*
30 *You'll find little time for dreaming and dirt when you're keeping house at Blawearie.*

And Chris in her pit, dazed and dull-eyed, said nothing, she minded later; and some other than herself went searching and seeking out cloths and clothes. Then Mistress Munro washed down the body that was mother's and put it in a nightgown, her best, the one with blue ribbons on it that she hadn't worn for many a year; and fair she made her and
35 sweet to look at, the tears came at last when you saw her so, hot tears wrung from your eyes like drops of blood. But they ended quick, you would die if you wept like that for long, in place of tears a long wail clamoured endless, unanswered inside your head *Oh mother, mother, why did you do it?*

And not until days later did Chris hear why, for they tried to keep it from her and the
40 boys, but it all came out at the inquest, mother had poisoned herself, her and the twins,

MARKS

because she was pregnant again and afraid with a fear dreadful and calm and clear-eyed. So she had killed herself while of unsound mind, had mother, kind-eyed and sweet, remembering those Springs of Kildrummie last of all things remembered, it may be, and the rooks that cried out across the upland parks of Don far down beyond the tunnels of
45   the years.

Questions

25. Look at lines 1—8.

Explain fully how Chris feels in these lines.   2

26. Look at lines 9—22.

By referring to at least two examples, analyse how the writer conveys the impact her mother's death has had on Chris.   4

27. Look at lines 23—45.

By referring to at least two examples, analyse how the writer conveys the horror of Chris's memory of her mother's death.   4

28. Discuss how Grassic Gibbon presents Chris's growing to maturity in this extract and elsewhere in the novel.   10

[Turn over

OR

Text 5 — Prose

If you choose this text you may not attempt a question on Prose in Section 2.

Read the extract below and then attempt the following questions.

The Cone-Gatherers by Robin Jenkins

This extract is taken from Chapter Four.   Duror has gone to the Big House to see Lady Runcie-Campbell.

Lady Runcie-Campbell was in the office at the front of the house writing letters. When he knocked, she bade him enter in her clear courteous musical voice.

A stranger, hearing her, would have anticipated some kind of loveliness in so charming a speaker; he might not, however, have expected to find such outstanding beauty of face
5 and form married to such earnestness of spirit; and he would assuredly have been both startled and impressed.

Duror, who knew her well, had been afraid that in her presence he might be shamed or inspired into abandoning his scheme against the cone-gatherers. In spite of her clothes, expensive though simple, of her valuable adornments such as earrings, brooches, and
10 rings, and of her sometimes almost mystical sense of responsibility as a representative of the ruling class, she had an ability to exalt people out of their humdrum selves. Indeed, Duror often associated religion not with the smell of pinewood pews or of damp Bibles, but rather with her perfume, so elusive to describe.   Her father the judge had bequeathed to her a passion for justice, profound and intelligent; and a determination to
15 see right done, even at the expense of rank or pride. Her husband Sir Colin was orthodox, instinctively preferring the way of a world that for many generations had allowed his family to enjoy position and wealth.   Therefore he had grumbled at his wife's conscientiousness, and was fond of pointing out, with affection but without sympathy, the contradiction between her emulation of Christ and her eminence as a baronet's wife.

20 She would have given the cone-gatherers the use of the beach-hut, if Duror had not dissuaded her; and she had not forgotten to ask him afterwards what their hut was like. He had had to lie.

Now, when he was going to lie again, this time knowing it would implicate her in his chosen evil, he felt that he was about to commit before her eyes an obscene gesture,
25 such as he had falsely accused the dwarf of making.   In the sunny scented room therefore, where the happy voices of the cricket players on the lawn could be heard, he suddenly saw himself standing up to the neck in a black filth, like a stags' wallowing pool deep in the wood. High above the trees shone the sun and everywhere birds sang; but this filth, as he watched, crept up until it entered his mouth, covered his ears, blinded
30 his eyes, and so annihilated him. So would he perish, he knew; and somewhere in the vision, as a presence, exciting him so that his heart beat fast, but never visible, was a hand outstretched to help him out of that mire, if he wished to be helped.

He saw her hand with its glittering rings held out to invite him to sit down.

"Good morning, Duror," she said, with a smile. "Isn't it just splendid?"

35 "Yes, my lady."

She looked at him frankly and sympathetically: it was obvious she attributed his subdued tone to sorrow over his wife. If at the same time she noticed with surprise that he hadn't shaved, it did not diminish her sympathy, as it would have her husband's.

MARKS

"How is Mrs. Duror?" she asked gently.

40 "Not too well, I'm sorry to say, my lady. This spell of fine weather has upset her. She asked me to thank you for the flowers."

She was so slim, golden-haired, and vital, that her solicitude for Peggy gripped him like a fierce cramp in his belly.

She noticed how pale he had turned, how ill he looked.

45 "I often think of your poor wife, Duror," she said.

She glanced at her husband's portrait in uniform on the desk in front of her.

Duror could not see the photograph from where he sat, but he could see clearly enough in his imagination the original, as gawky as she was beautiful, as glum as she was gay, and as matter-of-fact as she was compassionate.

50 "This war," she went on quickly, "with its dreadful separations has shown me at least what she has missed all these years. Something has come between us and the things we love, the things on which our faith depends: flowers and dogs and trees and friends. She's been cut off so much longer."

Questions

29. Look at lines 1—19.

By referring to at least two examples, analyse how Jenkins's use of language creates a positive impression of Lady Runcie-Campbell.   4

30. Look at lines 23—43.

By referring to two examples, analyse how the writer uses language to convey the contrast between Duror and Lady Runcie-Campbell.   4

31. Look at lines 50—53.

Explain why Lady Runcie-Campbell now feels more able to identify with Peggy's situation.   2

32. In the novel, Duror is presented not just as an evil character, but one who might be worthy of some sympathy.

With reference to this extract and elsewhere in the novel, explain how both aspects of Duror's character are portrayed.   10

[Turn over

SECTION 1 — SCOTTISH TEXT — 20 marks

Choose ONE text from Drama, Prose or Poetry.

Read the text extract carefully and then attempt ALL the questions for your chosen text.

You should spend about 45 minutes on this Section.

PART C — SCOTTISH TEXT — POETRY

Text 1 — Poetry

If you choose this text you may not attempt a question on Poetry in Section 2

Read the poem below and then attempt the following questions.

***To a Mouse, On turning her up in her Nest, with the Plough, November 1785* by Robert Burns**

    Wee, sleekit, cowrin, tim'rous beastie,
    O, what a panic's in thy breastie!
    Thou need na start awa sae hasty,
           Wi' bickering brattle!
5 I wad be laith to rin an' chase thee,
           Wi' murd'ring pattle!

    I'm truly sorry Man's dominion
    Has broken Nature's social union,
    An' justifies that ill opinion,
10   Which makes thee startle,
    At me, thy poor, earth-born companion,
           An' fellow-mortal!

    I doubt na, whyles, but thou may thieve;
    What then? poor beastie, thou maun live!
15 A daimen icker in a thrave
          'S a sma' request:
    I'll get a blessin wi' the lave,
          And never miss't!

    Thy wee bit housie, too, in ruin!
20 It's silly wa's the win's are strewin!
    An' naething, now, to big a new ane,
          O' foggage green!
    An' bleak December's winds ensuin,
          Baith snell and keen!

25 Thou saw the fields laid bare an' waste,
    An' weary Winter comin fast,
    An' cozie here, beneath the blast,
          Thou thought to dwell,
    Till crash! the cruel coulter past
30   Out thro' thy cell.

MARKS

That wee bit heap o' leaves an' stibble,
Has cost thee monie a weary nibble!
Now thou's turn'd out, for a' thy trouble,
     But house or hald,
35 To thole the Winter's sleety dribble,
      An' cranreuch cauld!

But Mousie, thou art no thy lane,
In proving foresight may be vain:
The best-laid schemes o' Mice an' Men
40   Gang aft agley,
An' lea'e us nought but grief an' pain,
     For promis'd joy!

Still thou are blest, compar'd wi' me!
The present only toucheth thee:
45 But, Och! I backward cast my e'e,
     On prospects drear!
An' forward, tho' I canna see,
     I guess an' fear!

Questions

33. Look at lines 1—18.

Analyse how Burns establishes at least two aspects of the speaker's personality in these lines.   4

34. Look at lines 19—36.

By referring to at least two examples, analyse how Burns creates pity for the mouse and its predicament.   4

35. Look at lines 37—48.

Explain how the final two verses highlight the contrast between the speaker and the mouse.   2

36. Discuss how Burns uses a distinctive narrative voice to convey the central concerns of this poem and at least one of his other poems.   10

[Turn over

OR

Text 2 — Poetry

If you choose this text you may not attempt a question on Poetry in Section 2.

Read the poem below and then attempt the following questions.

War Photographer by Carol Ann Duffy

In his dark room he is finally alone
with spools of suffering set out in ordered rows.
The only light is red and softly glows,
as though this were a church and he
5 a priest preparing to intone a Mass.
Belfast. Beirut. Phnom Penh. All flesh is grass.

He has a job to do. Solutions slop in trays
beneath his hands, which did not tremble then
though seem to now. Rural England. Home again
10 to ordinary pain which simple weather can dispel,
to fields which don't explode beneath the feet
of running children in a nightmare heat.

Something is happening. A stranger's features
faintly start to twist before his eyes,
15 a half-formed ghost. He remembers the cries
of this man's wife, how he sought approval
without words to do what someone must
and how the blood stained into foreign dust.

A hundred agonies in black and white
20 from which his editor will pick out five or six
for Sunday's supplement. The reader's eyeballs prick
with tears between the bath and pre-lunch beers.
From the aeroplane he stares impassively at where
he earns his living and they do not care.

MARKS

Questions

37. Look at lines 1—6.

    Analyse how imagery is used to create a serious atmosphere.   2

38. Look at lines 7—12.

    Analyse how Duffy conveys the photographer's perception of the difference between
    life in Britain and life in the war zones abroad.   4

39. Look at lines 13—18.

    Analyse the use of poetic technique to convey the distressing nature of the
    photographer's memories.   2

40. Look at lines 19—24.

    Analyse how the use of poetic technique highlights the British public's indifference
    to the suffering shown in the newspapers they read.   2

41. Referring closely to this poem and to at least one other poem by Duffy, discuss how
    she explores the link between the past and the present.   10

[Turn over

OR

Text 3 — Poetry

If you choose this text you may not attempt a question on Poetry in Section 2.

Read the poem below and then attempt the following questions.

My Rival's House by Liz Lochhead

is peopled with many surfaces.
Ormolu and gilt, slipper satin,
lush velvet couches,
cushions so stiff you can't sink in.
5   Tables polished clear enough to see distortions in.

We take our shoes off at her door,
shuffle stocking-soled, tiptoe — the parquet floor
is beautiful and its surface must
be protected. Dust-
10 cover, drawn shade,
won't let the surface colour fade.

Silver sugar-tongs and silver salver,
my rival serves us tea.
She glosses over him and me.
15 I am all edges, a surface, a shell
and yet my rival thinks she means me well.
But what squirms beneath her surface I can tell.
Soon, my rival
capped tooth, polished nail
20 will fight, fight foul for her survival.
Deferential, daughterly, I sip
and thank her nicely for each bitter cup.

And I have much to thank her for.
This son she bore —
25 first blood to her —
never, never can escape scot free
the sour potluck of family.
And oh how close
this family that furnishes my rival's place.

30 Lady of the house.
Queen bee.
She is far more unconscious,
far more dangerous than me.
Listen, I was always my own worst enemy.
35 She has taken even this from me.

She dishes up her dreams for breakfast.
Dinner, and her salt tears pepper our soup.
She won't
give up.

MARKS

Questions

42. Look at lines 1—11.

    Explain why the speaker feels uncomfortable in her rival's house.   **2**

43. Look at lines 12—22.

    By referring to at least two examples, analyse how the poet creates a tense atmosphere in these lines.   **4**

44. Look at lines 23—39.

    By referring to at least two examples, discuss how the speaker's resentment of her rival is made clear.   **4**

45. Discuss how Lochhead uses descriptive detail to explore personality in this and at least one other poem.   **10**

[Turn over

OR

Text 4 — Poetry

If you choose this text you may not attempt a question on Poetry in Section 2.

Read the poem below and then attempt the following questions.

***Visiting Hour* by Norman MacCaig**

The hospital smell
combs my nostrils
as they go bobbing along
green and yellow corridors.

5   What seems a corpse
is trundled into a lift and vanishes
heavenward.

I will not feel, I will not
feel, until
10   I have to.

Nurses walk lightly, swiftly,
here and up and down and there,
their slender waists miraculously
carrying their burden
15   of so much pain, so
many deaths, their eyes
still clear after
so many farewells.

Ward 7. She lies
20   in a white cave of forgetfulness.
A withered hand
trembles on its stalk. Eyes move
behind eyelids too heavy
to raise. Into an arm wasted
25   of colour a glass fang is fixed,
not guzzling but giving.
And between her and me
distance shrinks till there is none left
but the distance of pain that neither she nor I
30   can cross.

She smiles a little at this
black figure in her white cave
who clumsily rises
in the round swimming waves of a bell
35   and dizzily goes off, growing fainter,
not smaller, leaving behind only
books that will not be read
and fruitless fruits.

MARKS

Questions

46. Look at lines 1—7.

   Analyse how the poet's use of language conveys his response to his surroundings.   2

47. Look at lines 8—18.

   Analyse how MacCaig uses language to highlight his own sense of inadequacy.   4

48. Look at lines 19—38.

   Analyse how the poet's use of language emphasises the painful nature of the situation for both patient and visitor.   4

49. By referring to this poem, and at least one other by MacCaig, discuss how he explores the theme of loss in his work.   10

[Turn over

OR

Text 5 — Poetry

If you choose this text you may not attempt a question on Poetry in Section 2.

Read the poem below and then attempt the following questions.

An Autumn Day by Sorley MacLean

On that slope
on an autumn day,
the shells soughing about my ears
and six dead men at my shoulder,
5   dead and stiff — and frozen were it not for the heat —
as if they were waiting for a message.

When the screech came
out of the sun,
out of an invisible throbbing,
10   the flame leaped and the smoke climbed
and surged every way:
blinding of eyes, splitting of hearing.

And after it, the six men dead
the whole day:
15   among the shells snoring
in the morning,
and again at midday
and in the evening.

In the sun, which was so indifferent,
20   so white and painful;
on the sand which was so comfortable,
easy and kindly;
and under the stars of Africa,
jewelled and beautiful.

25   One Election took them
and did not take me,
without asking us
which was better or worse:
it seemed as devilishly indifferent
30   as the shells.

Six men dead at my shoulder
on an Autumn day.

MARKS

Questions

50. Look at lines 1—12.

By referring to at least two examples, analyse how the poet's use of language emphasises the impact of this experience.

4

51. Look at lines 13—24.

By referring to at least two examples, analyse how the poet uses language to highlight how meaningless the men's deaths were.

4

52. Look at lines 25—32.

Explain what the speaker finds puzzling when he reflects on the men's deaths.

2

53. Nature is a significant aspect in MacLean's poetry. Discuss how he uses nature to convey the central concern(s) of this poem and those of at least one other poem.

10

[Turn over

OR

Text 6 — Poetry

If you choose this text you may not attempt a question on Poetry in Section 2.

Read the poem below and then attempt the following questions.

Two Trees by Don Paterson

One morning, Don Miguel got out of bed
with one idea rooted in his head:
to graft his orange to his lemon tree.
It took him the whole day to work them free,
5   lay open their sides, and lash them tight.
For twelve months, from the shame or from the fright
they put forth nothing; but one day there appeared
two lights in the dark leaves. Over the years
the limbs would get themselves so tangled up
10 each bough looked like it gave a double crop,
and not one kid in the village didn't know
the magic tree in Miguel's patio.

The man who bought the house had had no dream
so who can say what dark malicious whim
15 led him to take his axe and split the bole
along its fused seam, and then dig two holes.
And no, they did not die from solitude;
nor did their branches bear a sterile fruit;
nor did their unhealed flanks weep every spring
20 for those four yards that lost them everything
as each strained on its shackled root to face
the other's empty, intricate embrace.
They were trees, and trees don't weep or ache or shout.
And trees are all this poem is about.

MARKS

Questions

54. Look at lines 1—12.

    By referring to at least two examples, analyse how the poet's use of poetic technique emphasises the importance of the story of the trees.

    4

55. Look at lines 13—16.

    By referring to at least two examples, analyse how the poet's use of language creates an impression of "the man".

    4

56. Explain the irony of the final two lines.

    2

57. Discuss how Paterson develops the theme of relationships in this and at least one other poem.

    10

[END OF SECTION 1]

[Turn over

SECTION 2 — CRITICAL ESSAY — 20 marks

Attempt ONE question from the following genres — Drama, Prose Fiction, Prose Non-fiction, Poetry, Film and Television Drama, or Language.

Your answer must be on a different genre from that chosen in Section 1.

You should spend approximately 45 minutes on this Section.

PART A — DRAMA

Answers to questions on Drama should refer to the text and to such relevant features as characterisation, key scene(s), structure, climax, theme, plot, conflict, setting . . .

1. Choose a play in which a major character's actions influence the emotions of others.

   Briefly explain how the dramatist presents these emotions and actions and discuss how this contributes to your understanding of the play as a whole.

2. Choose a play in which there is a scene involving a moment of conflict or of resolution to conflict.

   By referring to details of the scene, explain how the dramatist presents this moment and discuss how this contributes to your appreciation of the play as a whole.

3. Choose a play which explores an important issue or issues within society.

   Briefly explain the nature of the issue(s) and discuss how the dramatist's presentation of the issue(s) contributed to your appreciation of the play as a whole.

PART B — PROSE FICTION

Answers to questions on Prose Fiction should refer to the text and to such relevant features as characterisation, setting, language, key incident(s), climax, turning point, plot, structure, narrative technique, theme, ideas, description . . .

4.   Choose a novel **or** short story in which the method of narration is important.

    Outline briefly the writer's method of narration and explain why you feel this method makes such a major contribution to your understanding of the text as a whole.

5.   Choose a novel **or** short story in which there is a moment of significance for one of the characters.

    Explain briefly what the significant moment is and discuss, with reference to appropriate techniques, its significance to the text as a whole.

6.   Choose a novel **or** short story which has a satisfying ending.

    Discuss to what extent the ending provides a successful conclusion to the text as a whole.

PART C — PROSE NON-FICTION

Answers to questions on Prose Non-fiction should refer to the text and to such relevant features as ideas, use of evidence, stance, style, selection of material, narrative voice . . .

Non-fiction texts can include travel writing, journalism, autobiography, biography, essays . . .

7.   Choose a non-fiction text which recreates a moment in time.

    Discuss how the description effectively recreates this moment and show how important this is to your appreciation of the text as a whole.

8.   Choose a non-fiction text which is structured in a particularly effective way.

    Explain how the structure enhances the impact of the writer's message.

9.   Choose a non-fiction text which made you consider your views about a social or political or ethical issue.

    Explain what the issue is and how the writer uses language effectively to engage you.

[Turn over

PART D — POETRY

> *Answers to questions on Poetry should refer to the text and to such relevant features as word choice, tone, imagery, structure, content, rhythm, rhyme, theme, sounds, ideas . . .*

10. Choose a poem which takes as its starting point a memorable experience.

    Discuss how the poet's presentation of the experience helps you to appreciate its significance.

11. Choose a poem which encourages you to think differently or to understand something in a new way.

    Discuss how the poet's ideas and techniques led you to change your thinking or understanding.

12. Choose a poem which is written in a particular poetic form or which has a particularly effective structure.

    Discuss how the poet's use of form or structure contributes to the impact of the poem's central concern(s).

PART E — FILM AND TELEVISION DRAMA

> *Answers to questions on Film and Television Drama* should refer to the text and to such relevant features as use of camera, key sequence, characterisation, mise-en-scène, editing, music/sound, special effects, plot, dialogue . . .*

13. Choose a film **or** television drama in which the setting in time or place is important.

    Explain how the film or programme makers use media techniques effectively to create this setting.

14 Choose a film **or** television drama where the hero is not completely good and/or the villain is not completely bad.

    Explain how the film or programme makers use media techniques to develop the hero and/or villain.

15. Choose a film **or** television drama in which lighting and/or sound makes an important contribution to the impact of a particular sequence.

    Explain how the film or programme makers use lighting and/or sound to enhance your appreciation of the sequence.

* "television drama" includes a single play, a series or a serial.

PART F — LANGUAGE

Answers to questions on Language should refer to the text and to such relevant features as register, accent, dialect, slang, jargon, vocabulary, tone, abbreviation . . .

16. Choose the language associated with a particular vocational or interest group.

    Identify some examples of the language used within the group and discuss to what extent this shared language contributes to the effectiveness of the group's activities.

17. Choose the language of radio or television reporting on a topic such as sport, films, nature, science . . .

    Identify some of the features of this language and discuss to what extent they are effective in communicating with the target audience.

18. Choose a commercial advertising campaign which makes use of persuasive language.

    By examining specific examples, evaluate their effectiveness in achieving the purpose of the campaign.

[END OF SECTION 2]

[END OF QUESTION PAPER]

[BLANK PAGE]

DO NOT WRITE ON THIS PAGE

HIGHER

2016

National Qualifications 2016

X724/76/11

**English
Reading for Understanding,
Analysis and Evaluation — Text**

THURSDAY, 5 MAY
9:00 AM – 10:30 AM

Total marks — 30

Read the passages carefully and then attempt ALL questions, which are printed on a separate sheet.

The following two passages consider whether or not 16-year-olds should be allowed to vote.

Passage 1

Read the passage below and then attempt questions 1 to 7.

In the first passage, Catherine Bennett puts forward the case for allowing 16-year-olds to vote.

Rude, impulsive, sulky . . . still, let our 16-year-olds vote.

There are hugely important questions to address before 16-year-olds can be invited into the complicated UK electoral process. Are they sufficiently mature? Can they tell one party from another? Are they too preoccupied by a combination of exams and hectic social lives to be bothered? Even worrying about their appearance has been cited as a reason why under-18s might
5 struggle to give adequate thought to the political and economic issues facing Britain today.

There was a long period, between being sixteen myself and then, decades later, getting to know some present-day teenagers, including the one in my own house, when I would have agreed with champions of the status quo. I presumed — without knowing any — that these 16-year-olds were as clueless as my younger self, but with an increased obsession with their peer group, a result of
10 unpatrolled access to social media, greater affluence, and being subject to a constant barrage of entertainment.

If these factors were not enough to guarantee extreme teen disengagement with the political process, scientists have supplied biological reasons to question the efficiency of teenagers' smartphone-fixated brains. The last time there was a significant move to reduce the voting age,
15 the biologist Richard Dawkins set out the potential risks posed by the undeveloped teenage brain to our current epistocracy. An epistocracy — as of course all older voters will know — is government by wise people, that is, those with fully developed grey matter. In the article, Dawkins cited evidence from neuroscientists that "the brain undergoes major reconstruction from the onset of puberty which continues until 20 or beyond". Crucial, if I understand them
20 correctly, is the importance of this continuing development to the frontal lobes. This is the area at the front of the brain which "enables us to think in the abstract, weigh moral dilemmas and control our impulses". It was not even clear, the author said, that teenagers are developed enough to "be making life-changing decisions for themselves".

If we simply accept this argument, what does it mean in practice? It means that a grown-up who
25 believes in wizardry or unicorns or vampires can become a Member of Parliament, but a school pupil the age of, say, Malala Yousafzai, has yet to acquire the intellectual credentials to vote. Malala had been the victim of a terrorist attack in Pakistan as a result of her blog advocating education for girls, had recovered and continued to campaign tirelessly for equal educational opportunities for all children. This led to her becoming, in 2014, at the age of seventeen, the
30 youngest recipient of the Nobel Peace Prize.

Of course, it would be naïve to suggest that all teenagers can be as accomplished as Malala. However, there is, in fact, considerable evidence that the "unfinished" brain can be pretty good at sport, music, creating computer software and raising thousands of pounds for charity. True, 16-year-olds can be rude, sulky, reckless and unreliable. But the adult world is scarcely exempt
35 from these characteristics. Perhaps — as politicians must hope — most teenagers know too little about politics to make self-congratulatory comparisons between themselves and the at times limited brain power on show during parliamentary debates. The evidence of their own eyes confirms that, when considering normal behaviour, 16-year-olds barely compete in terms of incivility, tantrums, profanity, impulsivity, prejudice, time-wasting and an unedifying
40 dependency on tabloid websites, when compared to millions of fully enfranchised grown-ups. If law-makers ever think of restricting voting by the inadequately brained, illiterate, non-taxpaying or ignorant, the consequences for some adults would be chilling.

Indeed, recent research suggests that those who have been emphasising the negative effects of
social media and modern technology on the developing brain may have got it all wrong. Sixteen
45 and seventeen-year-olds are part of the iGeneration, the first generation who have grown up
with the digital innovations of the 21st century. They are flexible enough mentally to develop
their political worldview from the wide range of sources to be found on the Internet, too media
aware to be taken in by spin doctors and manipulative politicians.

Our teenagers do have their flaws. No, they don't always evince much money sense, although
50 they do, as consumers, pay sales tax. Yes, if voting booths were bedrooms they would probably
leave wet towels all over them. But having now witnessed some of the more loveable teenage
qualities — idealism, energy, a sense of injustice, open-mindedness — these seem to be exactly
the ones of which modern politics is starved. Even a limited turnout by young voters, minus all
the ones who are supposedly too apathetic or too busy insulting police officers or attending
55 Ibiza-themed foam parties, might inject some life into the next election.

Naturally, engaged teenagers would want answers on stuff that directly affects them such as
unpaid internships, exams, student debt, the minimum wage, benefits and perhaps any military
engagements in which they might be invited to serve. However, it might lead to a fresh look at
policies that affect future generations, by voters who will actually be around to experience the
60 consequences. If voting has to be rationed, maybe it should be elderly citizens — who may not
see the impact of, say, political inaction on climate change or carelessness about fuel
sustainability — who should give way to 16-year-olds.

We could compromise: make it seventeen. Then 16-year-olds would only have a year to wait —
after they have already married, donated an organ, bought fireworks, and signed up to fight for
65 their country — before they would be allowed to choose, alone in an exposed voting booth,
between competing political visions. Judging by the current resistance of adults who believe
they know so much better, you'd think we were doing our young people a great big favour.

Passage 2

**Read the passage below and attempt question 8. While reading, you may wish to make notes
on the main ideas and/or highlight key points in the passage.**

*In the second passage, Julia Hartley-Brewer puts forward her arguments for not allowing 16-year-
olds to vote.*

Letting 16-year-olds vote would be a disaster.

I have decided that it is only right and fair that my 8-year-old daughter should be allowed to
vote. She knows her politics and can name the party leaders on sight, which is more than can be
said for a large proportion of voters — and she pays tax. Every time she saves up her pocket
money to buy a new toy or game, it comes with a price tag that includes a hefty 20 per cent of
5   VAT. On all these grounds, she has just as much of a claim to have her say about Britain's future
as do the   16 and 17-year-olds of this country. And yet no one is demanding that she is given
the vote because, well, she's an 8-year-old. She's a child; she doesn't have the intellectual and
emotional development of an adult so she doesn't get to have the rights of adults.

So why is it that so many people — including prominent politicians — believe that we should be
10 giving 16 and 17-year-olds the right to vote? The call for the voting age to be lowered to sixteen
is as absurd an idea as you'll hear.

Yes, 16 and 17-year-olds were allowed to vote in the Scottish referendum. And what did they achieve? The turn-out for that tiny age group was a lot higher than among most other younger voters (largely, it is thought, because they were encouraged to turn out to vote by their parents)
15 but it did not enthuse the 18 to 20 age bracket, which as per usual largely didn't bother at all. Wouldn't our democracy be better served if we spent more time, effort and resources on engaging the people who already have the right to vote, rather than just adding on a few million voters who will never vote again after their first trip to the polling station?

Ah, but that's not the point, the protagonists claim. We should allow 16 and 17-year-olds to vote
20 because they are legally allowed to do other, far more important, life-changing or life-risking things than put a cross on a ballot paper, so why not let them vote as well? And that would be a really good argument, if it were true. Because, in actual fact, we don't allow our 16 and 17-year-olds to do very much. They can't legally drink alcohol or smoke, for starters. We don't trust them to be sensible with a pint of lager so why trust them with a stubby pencil in a polling
25 booth?

Okay, but they can get a job and pay income tax and that's not fair if they don't have a say in the government that sets those taxes, right? But income tax isn't the only tax we pay so why should that be the crucial decider? We all pay VAT on many of the goods we purchase from a very young age so, on that argument, my 8-year-old should be eligible to vote too.

30 Allowing 16 and 17-year-olds to vote would be a disaster. Voting is, after all, not a privilege like receiving pocket money or being permitted to stay out past your usual curfew on a Saturday night. It's a right. And a hard-won right at that.

When politicians say they want 16 and 17-year-olds to vote, what they really mean is that they want 16 and 17-year-olds to vote for them. This is not about empowering young people or
35 shifting the focus of debate to issues more relevant to 16 and 17-year-olds. Mainstream politics will continue to focus on issues important to adults, such as the economy and the state of the health service. It is simply calculated electioneering on the part of cynical politicians to retain power.

Don't believe the nonsense being spouted in the name of democracy. There is absolutely nothing wrong with making people wait until they are eighteen to vote.

[END OF TEXT]

X724/76/21

English
Reading for Understanding, Analysis
and Evaluation — Questions

THURSDAY, 5 MAY

9:00 AM – 10:30 AM

Total marks — 30

Attempt ALL questions.

Write your answers clearly in the answer booklet provided. In the answer booklet, you must clearly identify the question number you are attempting.

Use **blue** or **black** ink.

Before leaving the examination room you must give your answer booklet to the Invigilator; if you do not, you may lose all the marks for this paper.

MARKS

Attempt ALL questions
Total marks — 30

1. Read lines 1–5.

    Analyse **two** ways in which the writer attempts to engage the reader's interest in the opening paragraph.

    2

2. Read lines 6–23.

    (a) By referring to **either** the writer's viewpoint **or** to scientific research, explain why some people think teenagers should not be allowed to vote. Use your own words as far as possible in your answer.

    2

    (b) By referring to **at least two** examples, analyse how language is used to suggest that young people are not capable of voting.

    4

3. Read lines 24–30.

    Explain how the writer uses the example of Malala Yousafzai to develop her argument.

    2

4. Read lines 31–42.

    By referring to both word choice **and** sentence structure, analyse how the writer creates a negative impression of adults.

    4

5. Read lines 43–48.

    Explain why those who emphasise "the negative effects of social media and modern technology . . . may have got it all wrong". Use your own words in your answer.

    3

6. Read lines 49–55.

    By referring to **at least two** examples, analyse how the writer uses language to emphasise the positive contribution which teenage voters could make.

    4

7. Read lines 56–67.

    By referring to both tone **and** use of contrast, analyse how the writer emphasises her support of teenagers being allowed to vote.

    4

Question on both passages

8. Look at both passages.

    The writers disagree about whether or not 16 and 17-year-olds should be allowed to vote.

    Identify **three** key areas on which they disagree. You should support the points by referring to important ideas in both passages.

    You may answer this question in continuous prose or in a series of developed bullet points.

    5

[END OF QUESTION PAPER]

National Qualifications 2016

X724/76/12

English Critical Reading

THURSDAY, 5 MAY

10:50 AM – 12:20 PM

Total marks — 40

SECTION 1 — Scottish Text — 20 marks

Read an extract from a Scottish text you have previously studied and attempt the questions.

Choose ONE text from either

Part A — Drama   Pages 02–07

or

Part B — Prose   Pages 08–17

or

Part C — Poetry   Pages 18–28

Attempt ALL the questions for your chosen text.

SECTION 2 — Critical Essay — 20 marks

Attempt ONE question from the following genres — Drama, Prose Fiction, Prose Non-Fiction, Poetry, Film and Television Drama, or Language.

Your answer must be on a different genre from that chosen in Section 1.

You should spend approximately 45 minutes on each Section.

Write your answers clearly in the answer booklet provided. In the answer booklet you must clearly identify the question number you are attempting.

Use **blue** or **black** ink.

Before leaving the examination room you must give your answer booklet to the Invigilator; if you do not, you may lose all the marks for this paper.

SECTION 1 — SCOTTISH TEXT — 20 marks

Choose ONE text from Drama, Prose or Poetry.

Read the text extract carefully and then attempt ALL the questions for your chosen text.

You should spend about 45 minutes on this Section.

PART A — SCOTTISH TEXT — DRAMA

Text 1 — Drama

If you choose this text you may not attempt a question on Drama in Section 2.

Read the extract below and then attempt the following questions.

The Slab Boys by John Byrne

In this extract, from Act 2 of the play, Jack Hogg is looking for Phil, who has received a phone call.

	JACK:	I'm looking for your chum.
	SPANKY:	What're you wanting him for?
	JACK:	There's a phone call in Mr Barton's office . . . sounded rather urgent. Girl said it was the hospital.
5	SPANKY:	That's all right, I'll take it.
	JACK:	No, no . . . she was most insistent she speak to McCann himself . . .
	SPANKY:	I'll take it, I said . . .
	JACK:	No, I don't think . . .
	SPANKY:	I'm authorised! (*Exits.*)
10	JACK:	Hey . . . (*Exits.*)
		(*Pause. Enter SADIE.*)
	SADIE:	Too bloody soft, that's my trouble . . . He's not getting off with it, this time. Fifteen shillings? Not on your nelly . . . (*Sits down. Eases shoes off.*) Oooooooohhhhh . . . I should trade these in for a set of casters . . .
15		(*Enter LUCILLE. Crosses to sink.*)
		Any Epsom salts, hen?
	LUCILLE:	Waaahh! God, it's you! What're you playing at, Sadie?
	SADIE:	Have you seen that shy boy McCann on your travels?
	LUCILLE:	Shy?
20	SADIE:	Aye . . . fifteen bob shy. He still owes us for that dance ticket he got.
	LUCILLE:	Not again? When're you going to wise up? You'll just need to wait and grab him at the Town Hall . . .
	SADIE:	Oh, no . . . I'll not be seeing any Town Hall the night, sweetheart. If I thought these had to burl me round a dance floor . . . (*Cradles feet.*)

MARKS

25 LUCILLE: Are you not going? Aw, Sadie, it was a right scream last year.

SADIE: I know, flower . . .

LUCILLE: That man of yours was a howl.

SADIE: Aye . . . hysterical. Who else would sprint the length of the hall with a pint of Younger's in their fist and try leapfrogging over the top of Miss Walkinshaw
30   with that beehive hairdo of hers . . . eh? Only that stupid scunner I've got . . .

LUCILLE: How long was he off his work with the leg?

SADIE: Too long, sweetheart. He had my heart roasted, so he did. Sitting there with the bloody leg up on the fender shouting at me to put his line on at the bookie's for him. "See that?" I says. "If you're not up and back at your work
35   tomorrow I'll draw this across your back!" I had the poker in my hand . . . and I would've done it and all. Had me up to high doh. Couldn't get the stookie down the dungarees quick enough. Men? I wouldn't waste my time, hen.

LUCILLE: Come off it, Sadie . . .

SADIE: I'd to take the first one that came along. I'd've been better off with a lucky bag.

40 LUCILLE: They're not all like that, for God's sake.

SADIE: You'll learn, flower . . . you're young yet. You can afford to sift through the dross . . . till you come to the real rubbish at the bottom.

LUCILLE: Not this cookie. Lucille Bentley . . . Woman of the World . . . Fling Out Your Men!

45 SADIE: Wait till you get to my age and all you've got to show's bad feet and a display cabinet . . .

LUCILLE: Who wants to get to your age?

Questions

1. Look at lines 1–10.

    Explain how dialogue and/or stage directions are used to convey Spanky's attitude to Jack.   2

2. Look at lines 12–31.

    By referring to at least **two** examples in these lines, analyse how humour is created.   4

3. Look at lines 32–47.

    By referring to at least **two** examples, analyse how language is used to convey the different attitudes of Sadie and Lucille towards men.   4

4. By referring to this extract and to elsewhere in the play, discuss the role played by women.   10

[Turn over

OR

Text 2 — Drama

If you choose this text you may not attempt a question on Drama in Section 2.

Read the passage below and then attempt the following questions.

The Cheviot, the Stag and the Black, Black Oil by John McGrath

In this extract, Patrick Sellar is standing trial for murder.

MC:		Of all the many evictors, Mr Patrick Sellar was the only one who did not escape the full majesty of the law. He was charged with the murder of three people and numerous crimes at — Inverness High Court.

The Company become a murmuring JURY.

5   *Enter the JUDGE. They stand, then sit silently.*

Enter PATRICK SELLAR.

SELLAR: Re the charge of culpable homicide, my Lord — can you believe, my good sir, that I, a person not yet cognosed or escaped from a madhouse, should deliberately, in open day, by means of an officer who has a wife and family,

10   burn a house with a woman in it? Or that the officer should do so, instead of ejecting the tenant? The said tenant and woman being persons of whom we have no felonious intent, no malice, no ill-will.

JUDGE: Therefore, I would ask you (the jury) to ignore all the charges except two. One of these concerns the destruction of barns. In this case, Mr Sellar has

15   ignored a custom of the country, although he has not infringed the laws of Scotland. And the second case concerns the burning of the house of Chisholm. And here we are reminded of the contradictory nature of the testimony. Now if the jury are at all at a loss on this part of the case, I would ask them to take into consideration the character of the accused, for this is always of value in

20   balancing contradictory testimony. For here there is, in the first place, real evidence as regards Mr Sellar's conduct towards the sick — which in all cases has been proved to be most humane. And secondly, there are the letters of Sir George Abercrombie, Mr Fenton and Mr Brodie — which, although not evidence, must have some weight with the jury. And there are the testimonies

25   of Mr Gilzean, and Sir Archibald Dunbar — (*Sees him in the audience, waves.*) — hello, Archie. All of them testifying to Mr Sellar's humanity of disposition. How say you?

JURY: Oh, not guilty, no, no, no, etc.

JUDGE: My opinion completely concurs with that of the jury.

30   *JURY applaud PATRICK SELLAR.*

SELLAR: Every reformer of mankind has been abused by the established errors, frauds and quackery. But where the reformers have been right at bottom, they have, by patience, and by their unabating zeal and enthusiasm, got forward, in spite of every opposition. And so, I trust, will Lord and Lady Stafford, in their

35   generous exertions to better the people in this country.

More applause. Distant humming of "Land of Hope and Glory".

SELLAR: (*pointing to the mountains, from behind which a giant statue slowly emerges — eventually dwarfing the entire hall.*)

40   In lasting memorial of George Granville, Duke of Sutherland, Marquess of Stafford, K.G., an upright and patriotic nobleman, a judicious, kind and liberal landlord; who identified the improvement of his vast estates with the prosperity of all who cultivated them; a public yet unostentatious benefactor, who, while he provided useful employment for the active labourer, opened wide his hands to the distresses of the widow, the sick and the traveller: a
45   mourning and grateful tenantry, uniting with the inhabitants of the neighbourhood, erected *this pillar* . . .

Questions

5. Look at lines 7–12.

    Identify **one** tone used by Sellar in these lines and analyse how language is used to create this tone.   2

6. Look at lines 13–27.

    By referring to at least **two** examples, analyse how the language of the speech suggests the Judge's bias in favour of Sellar.   4

7. Look at lines 31–46.

    By referring to at least **two** examples, analyse how Sellar attempts to present "the reformers" and/or the Duke of Sutherland in a positive light.   4

8. Discuss how McGrath presents authority in this scene and elsewhere in the play.   10

[Turn over

OR

Text 3 — Drama

If you choose this text you may not attempt a question on Drama in Section 2.

Read the extract below and then attempt the following questions.

Men Should Weep by Ena Lamont Stewart

In this extract from Act 1, scene 1, John comes in to find Maggie talking to her sister, Lily.

John comes in carrying books under his arm. He is a big, handsome man. He puts down his books, gives Maggie a pat: they exchange warm smiles. He goes to sink and has a glass of water.

5	Maggie:	Ye dry, John? I'll pit the kettle on. I've jist minded I promised yer auld lady a cup in her bed.
	John:	She a right?
	Maggie:	Oh aye. Jist as usual . . . greetin an eatin.
	John:	(*turning to Lily with as much of a smile as he can muster*) An how's Lil?
	Lily:	I wish you'd leave aff cryin me Lil. Ma name's Lily.
10	John:	An it couldna suit ye better.
	Lily:	Whit d'ye mean by that, eh?
	Maggie:	Don't you two stert up! I've had enough the day. (*To Lily*) He didna mean onythin.
	Lily:	Well if he didna mean onythin he shouldna say onythin!
15	John:	Goad help us!
	Lily:	(*to Maggie*) Whit aboot yon ironin?
	Maggie:	Och, never heed. I'm that tired it wad kill me tae watch ye.
	Lily:	It'll be steamie day again afore ye've got that lot done.
	Maggie:	Well, I canna help it.
20	John:	Yous women! Ye've nae system!
	Lily:	Oh, I suppose if *you* was a wumman you'd hae everythin jist perfect! The weans a washed and pit tae bed at six, an everythin a spick an span. Naethin tae dae till bedtime but twiddle yer thumbs. Huh!
	John:	I'd hae a system . . .
25	Lily and Maggie:	(*together*) He'd hae a system!
	John:	Aye, I'd hae a *system*. Ony man wull tell ye, ye can dae naethin properly wi'oot ye hae a *system*.
	Lily:	And ony wumman'll tell ye that there's nae system ever inventit that disnae go tae Hell when ye've a hoose-fu o weans and a done aul granny tae look efter.
30	Maggie:	Never heed him, Lily. Ye should see him tryin tae mak the breakfast on a Sunday; ye'd get yer kill! If he's fryin bacon, he's fryin bacon, see? He's no keepin an eye on the toast an on the kettle, an breakin the eggs intae the pan a at the same time.

MARKS

	John:	Well, it's no ma job. If it *wis* ma job . . .
35	Maggie:	We ken: ye'd hae a system.
	Lily:	Well, if you're sure there's naethin I can dae, Maggie, I'll awa.
	Maggie:	Och no, wait and hae a wee cup wi us.
	Lily:	Naw . . . I'll mak yin at hame and hae something tasty tae it. A rarebit, mebbe.
	John:	(*winking at Maggie*) Aye, you dae that Lily; nae use hintin for ony rarebits here.
40	Lily:	(*not having seen the wink*) I like that! Hint! The cheek! It was me brung yon tin o baked beans that's sittin up on your dresser this minute, John Morrison!
	Maggie:	Och, he's only pullin yer leg, Lily.
	Lily:	If that's a sense o humour I'm glad I hevna got one. Yous men! I wouldna see one o you in ma road.
45	John:	Oh ho! If a man jist crep ontae your horizon, ye'd be efter him like a cock at a grosset.
50	Lily:	(*hauling on her coat*) I'm no stayin here tae be insultit. Ye can keep the beans, Maggie, but that's the last ye're getting frae me till ye learn some folks their manners. Aye. And ye can tell yon precious Alec o yours that the next time he maks enough at the dugs, tae get fleein drunk in the middle o Argyle Street, he can pay me back ma ten shillingy note.
		She stamps out of the room, slamming the door
	Maggie:	Ye shouldna tease Lily, John. Yin o they days she'll tak the huff and no come back, and whaur'll I be then?

Questions

9. Look at lines 1–15.

   Analyse how dialogue and/or stage directions are used to convey John's relationship with Maggie, **and** John's relationship with Lily in these lines.   4

10. Look at lines 20–35.

    By referring to at least **two** examples, analyse how both Maggie and Lily try to undermine John's opinion that women have "nae system".   4

11. Look at lines 39–52.

    Explain any **two** reasons for Lily's negative feelings when she leaves.   2

12. By referring to this extract and to elsewhere in the play, discuss John's role within the family.   10

[Turn over

SECTION 1 — SCOTTISH TEXT — 20 marks

Choose ONE text from Drama, Prose or Poetry.

Read the text extract carefully and then attempt ALL the questions for your chosen text.

You should spend about 45 minutes on this Section.

PART B — SCOTTISH TEXT — PROSE

Text 1 — Prose

If you choose this text you may not attempt a question on Prose (Fiction or Non-Fiction) in Section 2.

Read the extract below and then attempt the following questions.

The Crater by Iain Crichton Smith

"All present and correct, sir," said Sergeant Smith.

"All right, let's go then," said Lieutenant Mackinnon.

Down the trench they went, teeth and eyes grinning, clattering over the duckboards with their Mills bombs and their bayonets and their guns. "What am I doing here?" thought
5   Robert, and "Who the hell is making that noise?" and "Is the damned wire cut or not?" and "We are like a bunch of actors," and "I'm leading these men, I'm an officer."

And he thought again, "I hope the guns have cut that barbed wire."

Then he and they inched across No Man's Land following the line of lime which had been laid to guide them. Up above were the stars and the air was cool on their faces. But there
10   were only a few stars, the night was mostly dark, and clouds covered the moon. Momentarily he had an idea of a huge mind breeding thought after thought, star after star, a mind which hid in daylight in modesty or hauteur but which at night worked out staggering problems, pouring its undifferentiated power over the earth.

On hands and knees he squirmed forward, the others behind him. This was his first raid
15   and he thought, "I am frightened." But it was different from being out in the open on a battlefield. It was an older fear, the fear of being buried in the earth, the fear of wandering through eternal passageways and meeting grey figures like weasels and fighting with them in the darkness. He tested the wire. Thank God it had been cut. And then he thought, "Will we need the ladders?" The sides of the trenches were so deep sometimes
20   that ladders were necessary to get out again. And as he crawled towards the German trenches he had a vision of Germans crawling beneath British trenches undermining them. A transparent imagined web hung below him in the darkness quivering with grey spiders.

He looked at his illuminated watch. The time was right. Then they were in the German trenches. The rest was a series of thrustings and flashes. Once he thought he saw or
25   imagined he saw from outside a dugout a man sitting inside reading a book. It was like looking through a train window into a house before the house disappears. There were Mills bombs, hackings of bayonets, scurryings and breathings as of rats.

MARKS

A white face towered above him, his pistol exploded and the face disappeared. There was a terrible stink all around him, and the flowing of blood. Then there was a long silence.
30 Back. They must get back. He passed the order along. And then they wriggled back again avoiding the craters which lay around them, created by shells, and which were full of slimy water. If they fell into one of these they would be drowned. As he looked, shells began to fall into them sending up huge spouts of water. Over the parapet. They were over the parapet. Crouched they had run and scrambled and were over. Two of them were
35 carrying a third. They stumbled down the trench. There were more wounded than he had thought. Wright . . . one arm seemed to have been shot off. Sergeant Smith was bending over him. "You'll get sent home all right," he was saying. Some of the men were tugging at their equipment and talking feverishly. Young Ellis was lying down, blood pouring from his mouth. Harris said, "Morrison's in the crater."

40 He and Sergeant Smith looked at each other. They were both thinking the same: there is no point, he's had it. They could see each other's eyes glaring whitely through the black, but could not tell the expressions on the faces. The shells were still falling, drumming and shaking the earth. All these craters out there, these dead moons.

Questions

13. Look at lines 1–13.

    Analyse how language is used to convey Robert's state of mind.   2

14. Look at lines 14–22.

    By referring to at least **two** examples, analyse how language is used to create a sense of threat.   4

15. Look at lines 23–43.

    By referring to at least **two** examples, analyse how language is used to highlight the tense nature of the soldiers' situation.   4

16. By referring to this and to at least one other short story by Iain Crichton Smith, discuss the impact of extreme situations on his characters.   10

[Turn over

OR

Text 2 — Prose

If you choose this text you may not attempt a question on Prose (Fiction or Non-Fiction) in Section 2.

Read the extract below and then attempt the following questions.

The Whaler's Return by George Mackay Brown

He put his head through the door and saw a few farmers sitting round the fire drinking. The barmaid was standing at a mirror twisting her yellow hair at the back of her head. At last she got a fine burnished knot on it and drove a pin through to hold it in place.

Flaws hadn't seen a woman for six months. He went in and asked for a mug of ale.

5 "We only sell whisky here," said the girl, "threepence a glass."

"A glass of whisky then," said Flaws.

He thought it might be the last chance he would ever have to speak to a pretty girl. Peterina was good and hard-working, but rather ugly.

Flaws stood at the bar and drank his whisky. The four farmers sat round the fire saying 10 little. It was Wednesday in Hamnavoe, the day they drove in their beasts to sell at the mart.

"Do you do much trade in the White Horse?" said Flaws to the barmaid.

"We welcome only the better sort of person here," said the girl, "the quiet country men, not the ruffians and tramps from the herring boats and the whalers. And of course the office workers too, and business people. We're always very busy in the evening after the 15 shops and offices close. No fighting scum from the boats ever cross the threshold of the White Horse." Out of her pretty mouth she spat on the stone floor.

Flaws was glad he was wearing his decent suit of broadcloth, the one his old mother always packed in mothballs at the bottom of his chest for departures and home-comings.

He ordered two glasses of whisky, one for the barmaid. She smiled at him sweetly. They 20 touched rims till the glasses made a small music and the whisky trembled into yellow circles. Flaws was transported. He longed to touch her burnished head. Given time, solitude, and another dram or two, he could well imagine himself kissing her across the bar.

"I haven't seen you in the White Horse before," said the barmaid. "What is your occupation, 25 sir?"

"God forgive me for telling a lie," said Flaws to himself. Then he squared his shoulders and said, "I only visit the islands now and then. I'm a commercial traveller. I travel for earthenware and china."

The barmaid glittered at him with eyes, teeth, hair, rings.

30 The door opened and Small the lawyer's clerk tiptoed in, his drunken nose (Flaws thought) redder than ever. He went up to the bar slowly, eyeing Flaws the way a hunter eyes his quarry. "If it isn't Flaws!" he cried at last. "If it isn't my old friend! And did you catch many whales at Greenland, eh? I can smell the blubber and the oil with you. I warrant you have a fine pile of sovereigns in your pocket. You're the first seaman ever to get into the White 35 Horse."

Flaws could have killed the little drunken clerk at that moment. The barmaid was suddenly looking at him with eyes as cold as stones.

MARKS

40 Flaws hoisted his box on his shoulder and made for the door without a word. His pocket was heavy with more silver and copper; he had broken another sovereign in the White Horse. He stood, hot with shame and resentment, on the road outside.

"A commercial traveller!" cried Small the lawyer's clerk at the bar. Suddenly the interior of the White Horse was loud with merriment, the deep bass laughter of the farmers mingling with the falsetto mirth of the lawyer's clerk and the merry tinkle of the barmaid.

Flaws walked on towards Birsay, red in the face.

Questions

17. Look at lines 1–16.

   By referring to at least **two** examples, analyse how language is used to create a striking impression of the barmaid.   **4**

18. Look at lines 17–29. `

   By referring to at least **two** examples, analyse how language is used to indicate the significance of this moment for Flaws.   **4**

19. "He stood, hot with shame and resentment . . ." (line 40)

   From your reading of the whole extract, explain why Flaws felt "shame" and "resentment" at this point.   **2**

20. By referring to this extract and to at least one other short story, discuss the use of literal and metaphorical journeys in Mackay Brown's stories.   **10**

[Turn over

OR

Text 3 — Prose

If you choose this text you may not attempt a question on Prose (Fiction or Non-Fiction) in Section 2.

Read the extract below and then attempt the following questions.

***The Trick Is To Keep Breathing* by Janice Galloway**

In this extract, Joy describes her home and the early days of her relationship with Michael.

The cottage was tiny but cheap. There was a bus stop right outside the door and people with no sense used to look in while they were waiting for the bus, as though I was TV. But it also meant travel: buses stopping and starting right outside my door for whenever I needed to go somewhere. It made me feel free. I papered every wall myself and built shelves,
5   wired my own plugs and painted the place fresh. A kind of damp smell hung on in the kitchen but it was my own place, my home now. Paul helped move my things. The parting wasn't bitter. We wanted to be civilised and polite. Unexplained bouts of weeping disturbed the quiet some evenings but I figured they were good signs. Everybody needs to cry now and then. I was there less than six months when Michael phoned his two word call.

10   *She knows.*

He moved in the same night with three carrier bags. There was nowhere else for him to go. He missed the kids but we were OK. Some nights we'd stay awake right through on the pleasure of holding the other warm body in the dark we never expected would be there. We got up red-eyed for work to go to the same place in the same car, came home together
15   at night. When we washed the dishes, we'd watch our reflections in the night-blacked window, kissing.

One night, he got out of bed and didn't come back for a while. It was 2am. I got uneasy about it. I found him in the kitchenette, right at the back of the cottage, turning lilac in the cold. He was kneeling on the concrete looking at something. I kneeled down too and tried
20   to see what it was. There was a mushroom growing out of the skirting. **LOOK** he said, **LOOK**. We didn't know what to think. I poked it with a fork and it broke off. We went back to bed and tried to forget about it.

We were in the kitchen cooking: I was throwing spaghetti onto the roughcast to see if it was ready while he was stirring sauce. The spaghetti landed awkwardly and I saw another
25   mushroom right next to where it had settled on the wall. **LOOK** I said and we both looked again. This one was more securely attached. It didn't break first time so Michael got a knife and cut it away from the side of the window. It left a little pink trail like anaemic blood where it had been growing. After a month there were little shoots all along the hallway. Mould drew lines round the tops of walls and baby mushrooms appeared overnight. I
30   wouldn't let him touch them because I thought they were dangerous or something. I didn't know where they were coming from and preferred just to let them alone in case. In case. Maybe I thought they would go away if we pretended hard enough. Every so often, I would find him in the hall or the kitchen, peering down and scratching with a penknife, then trying to hide it when he saw me coming. I would hear him in the bathroom, running the
35   taps and washing his hands. He got a book from the library and read up about mushrooms.

MARKS

Dry rot, he said, matter-of-factly.

Dry rot. He gave me the book so I could read about it too. It was more sinister than the name. The house was being eaten from the inside by this thing. The spores could pass through concrete and plaster and multiply by the thousand thousand as we slept. They
40 could take over the whole structure if they wanted. I lay awake at night wondering what was going on out there in the hall while we were in our beds. The estimates for fixing it were unbelievable. I started having trouble sleeping. I avoided looking at the walls or skirting during the day.

Meantime Michael's council application paid off. The place was too big but he took it. It
45 was cheerful, bright, full of windows. Yellow walls and white woodwork. It was important he had his own place so he needn't feel dependent. Besides I didn't want anyone staying with me out of necessity. People gave us bits of things to fill it with. We shipped in the clothes from the cottage during the night, away from the silent spores, the creeping red clouds.

Questions

21. Look at lines 1–9.

    By referring to at least examples, analyse how the writer's use of language conveys Joy's attempts to be optimistic about her new life.   3

22. Look at lines 17–35.

    By referring to at least examples, analyse how the writer's use of language conveys Joy's growing sense of anxiety.   3

23. Look at lines 36–49.

    Analyse how the writer's use of language highlights the contrast between the cottage and Michael's council house. You should refer to both sides of the contrast in your answer.   4

24. By referring to this extract, and to elsewhere in the novel, discuss how Galloway conveys the impact of Joy's relationship with Michael.   10

[Turn over

OR

Text 4 – Prose

If you choose this text you may not attempt a question on Prose (Fiction or Non-Fiction) in Section 2.

Read the extract below and then attempt the following questions.

Sunset Song **by Lewis Grassic Gibbon**

In this extract, which is from Part III (Seed-Time), Chris's father has just died.

And out she went, though it wasn't near kye-time yet, and wandered away over the fields; it was a cold and louring day, the sound of the sea came plain to her, as though heard in a shell, Kinraddie wilted under the greyness. In the ley field Old Bob stood with his tail to the wind, his hair ruffled up by the wind, his head bent away from the smore of it. He heard
5   her pass and gave a bit neigh, but he didn't try to follow her, poor brute, he'd soon be over old for work. The wet fields squelched below her feet, oozing up their smell of red clay from under the sodden grasses, and up in the hills she saw the trail of the mist, great sailing shapes of it, going south on the wind into Forfar, past Laurencekirk they would sail, down the wide Howe with its sheltered glens and its late, drenched harvests, past Brechin
10 smoking against its hill, with its ancient tower that the Pictish folk had reared, out of the Mearns, sailing and passing, sailing and passing, she minded Greek words of forgotten lessons, Παντα ρεί, *Nothing endures*. And then a queer thought came to her there in the drookèd fields, that nothing endured at all, nothing but the land she passed across, tossed and turned and perpetually changed below the hands of the crofter folk since the oldest of
15 them had set the Standing Stones by the loch of Blawearie and climbed there on their holy days and saw their terraced crops ride brave in the wind and sun. Sea and sky and the folk who wrote and fought and were learnéd, teaching and saying and praying, they lasted but as a breath, a mist of fog in the hills, but the land was forever, it moved and changed below you, but was forever, you were close to it and it to you, not at a bleak remove it held
20 you and hurted you. And she had thought to leave it all!

She walked weeping then, stricken and frightened because of that knowledge that had come on her, she could never leave it, this life of toiling days and the needs of beasts and the smoke of wood fires and the air that stung your throat so acrid, Autumn and Spring, she was bound and held as though they had prisoned her here. And her fine bit plannings!
25 — they'd been just the dreamings of a child over toys it lacked, toys that would never content it when it heard the smore of a storm or the cry of sheep on the moors or smelt the pringling smell of a new-ploughed park under the drive of a coulter. She could no more teach a school than fly, night and day she'd want to be back, for all the fine clothes and gear she might get and hold, the books and the light and learning.

30 The kye were in sight then, they stood in the lithe of the freestone dyke that ebbed and flowed over the shoulder of the long ley field, and they hugged to it close from the drive of the wind, not heeding her as she came among them, the smell of their bodies foul in her face — foul and known and enduring as the land itself. Oh, she hated and loved in a breath! Even her love might hardly endure, but beside it the hate was no more than the
35 whimpering and fear of a child that cowered from the wind in the lithe of its mother's skirts.

MARKS

And again that night she hardly slept, thinking and thinking till her head ached, the house quiet enough now without fairlies treading the stairs, she felt cool and calm, if only she could sleep. But by morning she knew she couldn't go on with Uncle and Auntie beside her,
40 they smothered her over with their years and their canny supposings. Quick after breakfast she dressed and came down and Auntie cried out, real sharplike, *Mighty be here, Chris, where are you going?* as though she owned Blawearie stick and stone, hoof and hide. And Chris looked at her coolly, *I'm away to Stonehaven to see Mr Semple, can I bring you anything?* Uncle Tam rose up from the table then, goggling, with his medals clinking, *Away*
45 *to Stonehive? What are you jaunting there for? I'll transact any business you have.* Their faces reddened up with rage, she saw plain as daylight how near it lay, dependence on them, she felt herself go white as she looked at them.

Questions

25. Look at lines 1–20.

    By referring to at least **two** examples, analyse how the writer creates a sense of Chris's physical surroundings **and/or** her awareness of Scotland's past.   4

26. Look at lines 21–36.

    By referring to at least **two** examples, analyse how the writer reveals Chris's feelings about staying on the land **and/or** her previous plans to leave.   4

27. Look at lines 37–47.

    Analyse how dialogue is used to convey the attitude of at least **one** of the characters.   2

28. By referring to this extract and to elsewhere in the novel, discuss how Grassic Gibbon develops the idea that *"Nothing endures"*.   10

[Turn over

OR

Text 5 — Prose

If you choose this text you may not attempt a question on Prose (Fiction or Non-Fiction) in Section 2.

Read the extract below and then attempt the following questions.

The Cone-Gatherers by Robin Jenkins

In this extract, Roderick is on his way to visit the cone-gatherers in their hut.

By the time the hut came in sight he was exhausted, in body and spirit; sweat of exertion and of fear drenched him. Near some yew trees whose branches reached the ground, forming dark caverns, he halted, to look into his bag to make sure that the cake, the symbol of reconciliation, had not been made to vanish by the evil presences he had just
5 defied. Reassured, he stood breathing in the woodsmoke drifting up so peacefully out of the rusted chimney.

If his senses had not been so preternaturally alert, and if from the dirty hut had not irradiated a light illuminating every leaf on all the trees about it, he would never have noticed the lurker under the cypress, entangled in the thin green bony arms that curled
10 out like an octopus's. No sunshine struck there, and even the luminance from the hut seemed to fail. At first he could not tell who it was, although he was sure it was not one of the cone-gatherers. He felt cold, and frightened, and sick at heart. Here at the very hut was the most evil presence of all, and it was visible.

When he realised that the motionless figure under the cypress was Duror, he crept in
15 dismay into a cave of yew. It was his first retreat, and it was cowardly. Yet he could not force himself to complete the pilgrimage and knock on the door. Duror was a barrier he could not pass.

As he crouched in the earthy darkness like an animal, he wondered what Duror's purpose could be in lurking there. The gamekeeper hated the men in the hut and wished to have
20 them expelled from the wood. Was he now spying on them in the hope that he would find them engaged in some wrong-doing, such as working today, which was Sunday? By their agreement with his mother they were not to work on Sundays. But Duror himself shot deer on Sundays; he did not often go to church, and when he did he sat with his arms folded and a smile of misery on his lips. Why then did he hate the cone-gatherers and wish to
25 drive them away? Was it because they represented goodness, and himself evil? Coached by his grandfather, Roderick knew that the struggle between good and evil never rested: in the world, and in every human being, it went on. The war was an enormous example. Good did not always win. So many times had Christian been overcome and humiliated; so long had Sir Galahad searched and suffered. In the end, aye, in the bitter end, the old judge
30 had said, with a chuckle, good would remain alone in the field, victorious.

The minutes passed. Nothing had changed. The blue smoke still rose from the chimney. Duror had not moved. In his den of yew Roderick grew cramped; and in an even darker, narrower den of disillusionment his mind whimpered.

Half an hour, at insect's pace, crept by. Only a leaf or two had fallen from a tree, as a
35 breeze stirred. Far away, over the loch, a gull had screamed.

MARKS

Had Duror gone mad? Was this the change his mother had asked Mrs. Morton about? Again Roderick recalled the scene at the deer drive with Duror embracing as if in love the screaming deer and hacking at its throat with a knife. Mrs. Morton, who was Duror's friend, had talked about the perils of the wood; she had mentioned the cone-gatherers, but
40 perhaps in her heart she had been meaning Duror. If he was mad, then, was he now waiting with a gun to commit murder?

Peeping through the yew needles, Roderick saw in imagination the door of the hut open, and the cone-gatherers come out, the tall one who slightly limped and always frowned, and the small one who stooped and smiled. Then in the cypress the gun cracked, and the
45 two men lay dead on the grass.

Questions

29. Look at lines 1–13.

    By referring to at least **two** examples, analyse how the writer uses language effectively to create a sinister atmosphere.   4

30. Look at lines 18–45.

    By referring to at least **two** examples, analyse how Roderick is presented as a mature character despite his youth.   4

31. Duror is important in this extract, although he actually does very little. With reference to the extract as a whole, explain why he is important.   2

32. With reference to this extract, and to elsewhere in the novel, discuss how the writer develops the theme of conflict between good and evil.   10

[Turn over

SECTION 1 — SCOTTISH TEXT — 20 marks

Choose ONE text from Drama, Prose or Poetry.

Read the text extract carefully and then attempt ALL the questions for your chosen text.

You should spend about 45 minutes on this Section.

PART C — SCOTTISH TEXT — POETRY

Text 1 — Poetry

If you choose this text you may not attempt a question on Poetry in Section 2

Read the poem below and then attempt the following questions.

A Poet's Welcome to His Love-Begotten Daughter; The First Instance that entitled him to the Venerable Appellation of Father **by Robert Burns**

Thou's welcome, wean, mishanter fa' me,
If thought of thee, or of thy mammy,
Shall ever daunton me or awe me,
       My sweet wee lady!
5   Or if I blush when thou shalt ca' me
       Ti-ta or daddy.

Tho' now they ca' me fornicator,
An' tease my name in kintry clatter,
The mair they talk, I'm kent the better,
10   E'en let them clash;
An auld wife's tongue's a feckless matter
       To gie ane fash.

Welcome! my bonnie, sweet, wee dochter,
Tho' ye come here a wee unsought for,
15 And tho' your comin' I hae fought for,
       Baith kirk and queir;
Yet, by my faith, ye're no unwrought for
       That I shall swear!

Sweet fruit o' monie a merry dint,
20   My funny toil is now a' tint,
Sin' thou came to the warl' asklent,
       Which fools may scoff at;
In my last plack thy part's be in 't
       The better ha'f o't.

25   Tho' I should be the waur bestead,
Thou's be as braw and bienly clad,
And thy young years as nicely bred
       Wi' education,
As onie brat o' wedlock's bed,
30   In a' thy station.

MARKS

Wee image o' my bonnie Betty,
I, fatherly, will kiss and daut thee,
As dear, an' near my heart I set thee
        Wi' as guid will
35 As a' the priests had seen me get thee
        That's out o' hell.

Lord grant that thou may ay inherit
Thy mither's person, grace an' merit,
An' thy poor, worthless daddy's spirit,
40   Without his failins,
'Twill please me mair to see thee heir it,
        Than stockit mailens.

For if thou be what I wad hae thee,
And tak the counsel I shall gie thee,
45 I'll never rue my trouble wi' thee,
        The cost nor shame o't,
But be a loving father to thee,
        And brag the name o't.

Questions

33. Look at lines 1–6.

    Analyse how the speaker conveys his feelings about his newly born child.   2

34. Look at lines 7–18.

    By referring to at least **two** examples, analyse how the poet's language makes clear the speaker's response to his critics.   4

35. Look at lines 25–48.

    By referring to at least **two** examples, analyse how the poet's language effectively reveals aspects of the speaker's personality.   4

36. Discuss Burns' treatment of the religious **and/or** moral concerns of his time in this, and at least one other, poem.   10

[Turn over

OR

Text 2 — Poetry

If you choose this text you may not attempt a question on Poetry in Section 2.

Read the extract below and then attempt the following questions.

Mrs Midas by Carol Ann Duffy

It was late September. I'd just poured a glass of wine, begun
to unwind, while the vegetables cooked. The kitchen
filled with the smell of itself, relaxed, its steamy breath
gently blanching the windows. So I opened one,
5   then with my fingers wiped the other's glass like a brow.
He was standing under the pear tree snapping a twig.

Now the garden was long and the visibility poor, the way
the dark of the ground seems to drink the light of the sky,
but that twig in his hand was gold. And then he plucked
10   a pear from a branch — we grew Fondante d'Automne —
and it sat in his palm like a light bulb. On.
I thought to myself, Is he putting fairy lights in the tree?

He came into the house. The doorknobs gleamed.
He drew the blinds. You know the mind; I thought of
15   the Field of the Cloth of Gold and of Miss Macready.
He sat in that chair like a king on a burnished throne.
The look on his face was strange, wild, vain. I said,
What in the name of God is going on? He started to laugh.

I served up the meal. For starters, corn on the cob.
20   Within seconds he was spitting out the teeth of the rich.
He toyed with his spoon, then mine, then with the knives, the forks.
He asked where was the wine. I poured with shaking hand,
a fragrant, bone-dry white from Italy, then watched
as he picked up the glass, goblet, golden chalice, drank.

25   It was then that I started to scream. He sank to his knees.
After we had both calmed down, I finished the wine
on my own, hearing him out. I made him sit
on the other side of the room and keep his hands to himself.
I locked the cat in the cellar. I moved the phone.
30   The toilet I didn't mind. I couldn't believe my ears:

how he'd had a wish. Look, we all have wishes; granted.
But who has wishes granted? Him. Do you know about gold?
It feeds no one; aurum, soft, untarnishable; slakes
no thirst. He tried to light a cigarette; I gazed, entranced,
35   as the blue flame played on its luteous stem. At least,
I said, you'll be able to give up smoking for good.

MARKS

Questions

37. Look at lines 1–12.

    By referring to at least **two** examples, analyse how the poet's language conveys the contrast in atmosphere between stanza 1 and stanza 2.

    4

38. Look at lines 13–24.

    Analyse how the poet's language in these lines creates an unsettling mood.

    2

39. Look at lines 25–36.

    By referring to at least **two** examples, analyse how the poet's language presents the character of Mrs Midas.

    4

40. By referring closely to this poem, and to at least one other poem by Duffy, discuss how the poet explores the attempts of characters to cope with life-changing situations.

    10

[Turn over

OR

Text 3 — Poetry

If you choose this text you may not attempt a question on Poetry in Section 2.

Read the extract below and then attempt the following questions.

***The Bargain* by Liz Lochhead**

The river in January is fast and high.
You and I
are off to the Barrows.
Gathering police-horses twitch and fret
5   at the Tron end of London Road and Gallowgate.
The early kick-off we forgot
has us, three thirty, rubbing the wrong way
against all the ugly losers
getting ready to let fly
10 where the two rivers meet.

    January, and we're
looking back, looking forward,
don't know which way

    but the boy
15 with three beautiful Bakelite
Bush radios for sale in Meadow's Minimarket is
buttonpopping stationhopping he
doesn't miss a beat   sings along   it's easy
to every changing tune

20 Yes today we're in love aren't we?
with the whole splintering city
its big quick river   wintry bridges
its brazen black Victorian heart.
So what if every other tenement
25 wears its hearth on its gable end?
All I want
is my glad eye to catch
a glint in your flinty Northern face again
just once.   Oh I know it's cold
30 and coming down
and no we never lingered long among
the Shipbank traders.
Paddy's Market   underneath the arches
stank too much today
35 the usual wetdog reek rising
from piles of old damp clothes.

MARKS

Questions

41. Look at lines 1–13.

    By referring to at least **two** examples, analyse how the language in these lines introduces the deterioration of the speaker's relationship.   **4**

42. Look at lines 14–19.

    Analyse how the poet's language creates a change of mood.   **2**

43. Look at lines 20–36.

    By referring to at least **two** examples, analyse how the poet uses setting to reflect the current state of the speaker's relationship.   **4**

44. By referring to this poem, and at least one other poem by Lochhead, discuss how she explores the theme of difficult relationships.   **10**

[Turn over

OR

Text 4 — Poetry

If you choose this text you may not attempt a question on Poetry in Section 2.

Read the poem below and then attempt the following questions.

Memorial **by Norman MacCaig**

Everywhere she dies. Everywhere I go she dies.
No sunrise, no city square, no lurking beautiful mountain
but has her death in it.
The silence of her dying sounds through
5 the carousel of language, it's a web
on which laughter stitches itself. How can my hand
clasp another's when between them
is that thick death, that intolerable distance?

She grieves for my grief. Dying, she tells me
10 that bird dives from the sun, that fish
leaps into it. No crocus is carved more gently
than the way her dying
shapes my mind. — But I hear, too,
the other words,
15 black words that make the sound
of soundlessness, that name the nowhere
she is continuously going into.

Ever since she died
she can't stop dying. She makes me
20 her elegy. I am a walking masterpiece,
a true fiction
of the ugliness of death.
I am her sad music.

MARKS

Questions

45. Look at lines 1–8.

By referring to at least **two** examples, analyse how the language emphasises the devastating impact of the loved one's death on the speaker's life.

3

46. Look at lines 9–17.

By referring to at least **two** examples, analyse how the language conveys the close bond between the loved one and the speaker.

4

47. Look at lines 18–23.

By referring to at least **two** examples, analyse how the language emphasises the fact that the subject's death remains ever present in the speaker's mind.

3

48. Discuss how reaction to suffering is explored in this, and at least one other, poem by MacCaig.

10

[Turn over

OR

Text 5 — Poetry

If you choose this text you may not attempt a question on Poetry in Section 2.

Read the poem below and then attempt the following questions.

***Shores* by Sorley MacLean**

If we were in Talisker on the shore
where the great white mouth
opens between two hard jaws,
Rubha nan Clach and the Bioda Ruadh,
5 I would stand beside the sea
renewing love in my spirit
while the ocean was filling
Talisker bay forever:
I would stand on the bareness of the shore
10 until Prishal bowed his stallion head.

And if we were together
on Calgary shore in Mull,
between Scotland and Tiree,
between the world and eternity,
15 I would stay there till doom
measuring sand, grain by grain,
and in Uist, on the shore of Homhsta
in presence of that wide solitude,
I would wait there forever
20 for the sea draining drop by drop.

And if I were on the shore of Moidart
with you, for whom my care is new,
I would put up in a synthesis of love for you
The ocean and the sand, drop and grain.
25 And if we were on Mol Stenscholl Staffin
when the unhappy surging sea dragged
the boulders and threw them over us,
I would build the rampart wall
against an alien eternity grinding (its teeth).

MARKS

Questions

49. Look at lines 1–14.

    By referring to at least **two** examples, analyse how language is used to convey the powerful impact of the landscape on the speaker.   4

50. Look at lines 15–24.

    By referring to at least **two** examples, analyse how language is used effectively to convey the intensity of the speaker's love.   4

51. Look at lines 25–29.

    By referring to ideas **and/or** language, evaluate the effectiveness of these lines as a conclusion to the poem.   2

52. Referring closely to this and to at least one other poem, discuss how MacLean explores the impact of time on human experience.   10

[Turn over

MARKS

OR

Text 6 — Poetry

If you choose this text you may not attempt a question on Poetry in Section 2.

Read the poem below and then attempt the following questions.

The Thread **by Don Paterson**

Jamie made his landing in the world
so hard he ploughed straight back into the earth.
They caught him by the thread of his one breath
and pulled him up. They don't know how it held.
5 And so today I thank what higher will
brought us to here, to you and me and Russ,
the great twin-engined swaying wingspan of us
roaring down the back of Kirrie Hill

and your two-year-old lungs somehow out-revving
10 every engine in the universe.
All that trouble just to turn up dead
was all I thought that long week. Now the thread
is holding all of us: look at our tiny house,
son, the white dot of your mother waving.

Questions

53. Look at lines 1–4.

By referring to at least **two** examples, analyse how the poet's use of language suggests the difficulties surrounding Jamie's birth.

4

54. Look at lines 5–10.

Analyse how the poet's use of language conveys the present circumstances of the family.

2

55. Look at lines 11–14.

By referring to at least **two** examples, evaluate the effectiveness of these lines as a conclusion to the poem.

4

56. Discuss how the poet explores the fragility of human life in this, and at least one other, poem.

10

[END OF SECTION 1]

SECTION 2 — CRITICAL ESSAY — 20 marks

Attempt ONE question from the following genres — Drama, Prose Fiction, Prose Non-fiction, Poetry, Film and Television Drama, or Language.

Your answer must be on a different genre from that chosen in Section 1.

You should spend approximately 45 minutes on this Section.

PART A — DRAMA

Answers to questions on Drama should refer to the text and to such relevant features as characterisation, key scene(s), structure, climax, theme, plot, conflict, setting . . .

1. Choose a play in which a central character is in conflict with **or** rejects another character.

   Briefly explain the circumstances of the conflict or rejection and go on to discuss the consequences of this conflict or rejection for the play as a whole.

2. Choose a play in which the historical **and/or** geographical **and/or** social setting is important to your understanding of the play.

   Explain how the dramatist presents the setting and discuss why it is important to your understanding of the play as a whole.

3. Choose a play which has an effective opening scene **or** concluding scene.

   By briefly referring to details of the scene, explain how the dramatist made it effective and discuss how it contributes to your appreciation of the text as a whole.

[Turn over

PART B — PROSE FICTION

Answers to questions on Prose Fiction should refer to the text and to such relevant features as characterisation, setting, language, key incidents(s), climax, turning point, plot, structure, narrative technique, theme, ideas, description . . .

4. Choose a novel **or** short story in which there is a central character to whom you react with mixed feelings.

   With reference to appropriate techniques, briefly explain why you react to the character in this way and discuss how this reaction adds to your understanding of the text as a whole.

5. Choose a novel **or** short story that deals with a theme of moral **or** social significance.

   With reference to appropriate techniques, explain how the writer develops this theme and discuss why its development adds to your appreciation of the text as a whole.

6. Choose a novel **or** short story in which the choice of setting is central to your appreciation of the text.

   Briefly explain how the writer effectively creates setting and, with reference to appropriate techniques, discuss how the writer's presentation of the setting is central to your appreciation of the text as a whole.

PART C — PROSE NON-FICTION

Answers to questions on Prose Non-Fiction should refer to the text and to such relevant features as ideas, use of evidence, stance, style, selection of material, narrative voice . . .

Non-fiction texts can include travel writing, journalism, autobiography, biography, essays . . .

7. Choose a non-fiction text in which the writer engages your interest in a place **or** culture.

   Discuss, with reference to appropriate techniques, how the writer successfully engages your interest in this place or culture.

8. Choose a non-fiction text in which the writer describes a traumatic **or** rewarding experience.

   Discuss, with reference to appropriate techniques, how the writer conveys the traumatic or rewarding nature of the experience.

9. Choose a non-fiction text in which the writer attempts to influence the reader's opinion on a person **or** an issue.

   Discuss, with reference to appropriate techniques, how the writer attempts to influence the reader's opinion on the person or the issue.

PART D — POETRY

Answers to questions on Poetry should refer to the text and to such relevant features as word choice, tone, imagery, structure, content, rhythm, rhyme, theme, sounds, ideas . . .

10. Choose a poem in which the poet creates a vivid sense of a particular time **or** a particular place.

    Discuss how the poet's vivid depiction of time or place adds to your appreciation of the central concern(s) of the poem.

11. Choose a poem with a moral **or** social **or** political theme.

    Discuss, with reference to appropriate techniques, how the poet's presentation of the theme deepens your understanding of the poem as a whole.

12. Choose a poem in which the poet effectively creates a character **or** persona.

    Discuss, with reference to appropriate techniques, how the poet's effective creation of the character or persona enhances your appreciation of the poem as a whole.

[Turn over for next question

PART E — FILM AND TELEVISION DRAMA

Answers to questions on Film and Television Drama* should refer to the text and to such relevant features as use of camera, key sequence, characterisation, mise-en-scène, editing, music/sound, special effects, plot, dialogue . . .

13. Choose a film **or** television drama in which there is a particularly tense or dramatic sequence.

    Explain how the film or programme makers use media techniques to achieve this effect.

14. Choose a film **or** television drama which concerns an individual **or** a group of characters facing a significant challenge.

    Explain how the film or programme makers use media techniques to convey the significance of this challenge.

15. Choose a film **or** television drama which is targeted at a specific audience.

    Explain how the film or programme makers use media techniques to target this audience.

* "television drama" includes a single play, a series or a serial.

PART F — LANGUAGE

Answers to questions on Language should refer to the text and to such relevant features as register, accent, dialect, slang, jargon, vocabulary, tone, abbreviation . . .

16. Choose a particular area of language associated with mass communication, eg advertising, broadcasting, technology.

    Identify specific examples and discuss to what extent they are effective.

17. Choose language used in a specific work setting such as hospital, courtroom, garage, school, parliament . . .

    Identify specific examples of the language used and evaluate their effectiveness within the work setting.

18. Choose the language associated with pressure groups (multi-cultural organisations, environmental agencies, faith groups, campaigners for equality . . .)

    By referring to specific examples, discuss what makes the language of one such group successful in achieving its purpose to persuade.

[END OF SECTION 2]

[END OF QUESTION PAPER]

SQA HIGHER
ENGLISH 2016

HIGHER ENGLISH
2014 SPECIMEN QUESTION PAPER

PAPER 1 — READING FOR UNDERSTANDING, ANALYSIS AND EVALUATION

Marking Instructions for each question

Passage 1

Question		Expected Response	Max mark	Additional Guidance
1.	(a)	Candidates should identify two of the writer's feelings in the first paragraph. Candidates must use their own words. No marks are awarded for verbatim quotations from the passage. *1 mark for each point from the "Additional Guidance" column.*	2	Possible answers include: • she felt troubled, as though watching an illegal/senseless act • she felt responsible/guilty for a terrible act • she felt morally uncertain; questioned whether or not she was justified in doing this or any other acceptable answer
	(b)	Candidates should analyse how the language emphasises the importance of trees. Marks will depend on the quality of comment on appropriate language feature(s). 2 marks may be awarded for reference plus detailed/insightful comment; 1 mark for reference plus more basic comment; 0 marks for reference alone. *Possible answers shown in the "Additional Guidance" column.*	4	Possible answers include: *Word choice* • "ever more (precious)" suggests trees' increasing value • "precious" suggests trees are valuable, to be cherished • "a rebuke to built-in obsolescence": trees effectively criticise/stand in opposition to a world where products are designed to have only a limited life • "remnants" suggests precious remains from the past • "mammoth (limb)" suggests something on a massively impressive scale • "reassuring" suggests they offer comfort • "they will endure" suggests permanence, continuity, resilience • "the ancients" suggests trees have been considered valuable throughout the ages • "gods" suggests their almost religious significance • "ring by ring" suggests trees' natural, organic, unhurried growth • "worship" suggests our attitude should be respectful, reverent, devotional • "worse...worship": candidates might argue that the use of alliteration adds to the impact of the concluding statement • use in general of "religious" language ("God's arm", "cathedrals", "gods", "worship") heightens trees' spiritual significance • "our living past": trees connect us to our heritage *Imagery* • "a steady point in a churning world": trees offer steadfast permanence in a fast-changing, impermanent, turbulent world • (personification of) "reaches out", "mammoth limb" suggests a majestic living creature • "like God's arm...Rome": simile suggests majesty, beauty, spiritual significance, awesome impact • "calming like cathedrals": simile suggests their scale, majesty, spiritual quality, that they should be treated with reverence, that they are good for our inner well-being

Question		Expected Response	Max mark	Additional Guidance
	(b)	*(continued)*		**Punctuation/sentence structure** • structure of opening sentence "I'm…world": the two phrases at the end of the sentence (heightened by the parallel structure) serve as a powerful development of the "precious" idea • balanced nature of final sentence: the artful juxtaposition of the near-reverent tone of the first part of the sentence, followed by the more matter-of-fact, modern tone of the second half brings the paragraph to a quietly effective conclusion or any other acceptable answer
2.		Candidates should demonstrate understanding of how the protesters differ from what might have been expected. Candidates must use their own words. No marks are awarded for verbatim quotations from the passage. *1 mark for each point from the "Additional Guidance" column.*	2	Possible answers include: • we might have expected the protesters to be (over) zealous environmental activists/(ultra)dedicated conservationists (explanation of "eco-warriors")/people who have rejected the conventional values of society (explanation of "hippies") • instead they are just normal people/a typical cross-section of the community/people of all ages and from all walks of life or any other acceptable answer
3.		Candidates should analyse how the writer's use of language conveys her feelings of unhappiness. Marks will depend on the quality of comment. For full marks there must be comment on at least two features. 2 marks may be awarded for reference plus detailed/insightful comment; 1 mark for reference plus more basic comment; 0 marks for reference alone. *Possible answers shown in the "Additional Guidance" column.*	3	Possible answers include: *Sentence structure* • series of three short, simple, matter-of-fact sentences at start of paragraph suggest the inevitable fate that awaits the trees and the irresistible march of the developers • positioning of "By March" at start of sentence suggests fixed, immovable timeline to destruction • structure of fourth sentence ("Local…benefits."): initial praise for efforts of local community is offset immediately by pessimistic recognition of government power; the sentence then reaches a climax with her attack on government policy • use of parenthesis "as new roads do" to emphasise the inevitable futility of government transport policy *Word choice:* • "last stand" (could be dealt with as imagery) suggests a defensive position facing inevitable defeat against insuperable odds • "only" suggests defeat itself is inevitable • "determined" suggests inflexible, unyielding nature of government policy • "market" suggests her scepticism about government policy: they are "selling" it as progress but "market" suggests this is more image than reality; suggests government is being unscrupulous, deceitful, conniving • "short-term" suggests transient, limited nature (of benefits) • "dubious" suggests deep uncertainty, unreliability (of benefits) • "fill up" suggests saturation, full to overflowing • "spanking new": hyperbole of her apparent enthusiasm could be argued to betoken her fundamental antipathy • "boarded-up" suggests the development will be to the continued detriment of an already rundown Hastings; suggests that Hastings itself needs attention *Contrast* • "spanking new" versus "boarded-up" emphasises the pointlessness of building new premises when existing ones lie empty and abandoned

Question		Expected Response	Max mark	Additional Guidance
3.		*(continued)*		**Tone** • some candidates may recognise and discuss the changing tone of this paragraph, in particular the somewhat defeated, hopeless tone of the first three sentences which changes to an angry, scathing, sceptical tone in the rest of the paragraph. or any other acceptable answer
4.	(a)	Candidates should identify two claims the government makes about the protesters. For full marks there must be understanding demonstrated of two claims. Any two points from the "Additional Guidance" column for 1 mark each.	2	Possible answers include: the government claims the protesters: • are not interested in protecting the environment • are only interested in looking after their own (advantaged) interests • have no interest in the fate of people less well-off/less fortunate than themselves or any other acceptable answer
	(b)	Candidates should analyse how at least two features of language convey the strength of the writer's belief in tree conservation. Marks will depend on the quality of understanding shown of key ideas and the quality of comment on appropriate language features. 2 marks may be awarded for detailed/insightful comments; one mark for more basic comments; 0 marks for reference alone. *Possible answers shown in the "Additional Guidance" column.*	4	Possible answers include: **Word choice** • "special kind" suggests people who don't care about trees are particularly awful • "arrogance" suggests the insufferable conceit of those who don't care about trees • "bigger than history" suggests arrogance on a grand scale • (repeated) use of violent language when describing trees – felling (ie "cutting down" suggests something akin to an act of murder; "slicing into" suggests a savage, violent attack; "brutal" suggests a ruthless, crude, cruel, vicious attack; "grotesque" suggests a strange, distorted, unnatural, outrageous act; "chopping down" suggests a categorical, definitive act). • "fine" suggests the majesty, worthiness of the tree • "aching (poignancy)" suggests how deeply hurt she is when trees are cut down • writer's use of "shock tactics" in making a developed, quite visceral comparison between killing living creatures and cutting down trees: some candidates may recognise that the writer shows the strength of her feeling by developing an argument that many readers will find shocking or extreme **Imagery** • by comparing (in a very visual way) the fate of trees to the fate of whales and elephants ("mightiest mammal") the writer is associating trees with elevated concepts such as the awesome wonder of the natural world, beauty, majesty, conservation... • "enormous creature" suggests epic scale of what is being destroyed **Punctuation/sentence structure** • use of colon (line 31) introduces explanation of what this "special kind of arrogance" involves • punchy conclusion to paragraph ("Not so a tree") emphasises just how different the trees' situation is to even the most impressive or endangered of our natural creatures or any other acceptable answer

Question		Expected Response	Max mark	Additional Guidance
5.	(a)	Candidates should identify any four reasons given for cutting down trees. Candidates should use their own words as far as possible. No marks are awarded for verbatim quotations from the passage. *Any four points from the "Additional Guidance" column for 1 mark each.*	4	Possible answers include: • they may contribute to land sinking (which would affect buildings on that land) • they are regarded as potentially damaging to vehicles • they are regarded as potentially a danger to young people • they shed (twigs and leaves) and that leaves things (public spaces, houses or vehicles) looking dirty and untidy • some trees are considered unfashionable (and people want to replace them with something more popular) • selling trees makes money, can boost a country's economy • they are converted into timber for commercial purposes or any other acceptable answer
	(b)	Candidates should analyse how their chosen image emphasises the writer's opposition to cutting down trees. Marks will depend on the quality of comment. A detailed/insightful comment will be worth 2 marks; a more basic comment will be worth 1 mark. Mere identification of an image will be 0 marks. When dealing with imagery, answers must show recognition of the literal root of the image and then explore how the writer is extending it figuratively. *Possible answers shown in the "Additional Guidance" column.*	2	Possible answers include: • "butchers": just as a butcher is involved in carving up animals into large-scale pieces, so the writer is suggesting that municipal workers are cutting back the trees to a significant degree. It also suggests that the nature of the work performed is rather brutal and indiscriminate • "embarrassed stumps": just as an embarrassed person feels self-conscious and exposed, so the writer is suggesting that trees look vulnerable after the work has been carried out on them • "autumnal hell": just as hell is seen as a place of eternal damnation, so the writer is using this hyperbolic term to ridicule the wild over-reaction of those who find trees a problem at particular times of the year • "like a beautiful girl being forced to sell her hair": just as the girl exchanges a personal asset, an attractive feature for financial gain, so the writer suggests Burma gave away part of the country's natural beauty for money or any other acceptable answer
6.		Candidates should evaluate the final paragraph's effectiveness as a conclusion to the passage as a whole. Marks will depend on the quality of comment. For full marks there must be appropriate attention to the idea of a conclusion. A more basic comment may be awarded 1 mark. *Possible answers shown in the "Additional Guidance" column.*	2	Possible answers include: • the writer concedes that inevitably trees will be cut down to make way for developments, a point she has already made in relation to the Hastings development and government policy in general • the writer returns to an argument which she has discussed throughout the passage: economic growth versus the innate value of trees. The Hastings development is an example of economic growth (very short-term in the writer's opinion), while the writer stresses at several points the value of preserving trees (for example, establishing the majesty and wonder of trees in the opening paragraphs; showing how much they mean to ordinary people protesting against the Hasting development; suggesting they are more important than creatures great and small) • the writer concludes by re-asserting how important a part of our heritage trees are: they are a link to our past ("they are our history inscribed in the natural world") and a means by which people leave their mark on society ("which rich men, planting beautiful orchards to their own glorious memory"). The link to the past idea has already been developed, for example in lines 10-11, while the idea of planting trees for posterity is explicitly discussed in lines 38-39 ("planting...loved ones").

Question	Expected Response	Max mark	Additional Guidance
6.	*(continued)*		• some candidates will recognise the elevated quality of the writing in the final paragraph (quite different in tone to some of the almost brutally graphic sections of the passage) and link it to the persuasively idealistic message the writer has been trying to convey in much of the passage or any other acceptable answer
7.	Candidates should identify key areas of agreement in the two passages by referring in detail to both passages. There may be some overlap among the areas of agreement. Markers will have to judge the extent to which a candidate has covered two points or one. Candidates can use bullet points in this final question, or write a number of linked statements. Evidence from the passage may include quotations, but these should be supported by explanations. *Approach to marking shown in the "Additional Guidance" column.* *Key areas of agreement shown in grid below. Other answers are possible.*	5	The mark for this question should reflect the quality of response in two areas: • identification of the key areas of agreement in attitude/ideas • level of detail given in support The following guidelines should be used: **Five marks** — comprehensive identification of three or more key areas of agreement with full use of supporting evidence **Four marks** — clear identification of three or more key areas of agreement with relevant use of supporting evidence **Three marks** — identification of three or more key areas of agreement with supporting evidence **Two marks** — identification of two key areas of agreement with supporting evidence **One mark** — identification of one key area of agreement with supporting evidence **Zero marks** — failure to identify any key area of agreement and/or total misunderstanding of task

	Area of Agreement	Janice Turner	Colin Tudge
1.	awe/wonder/majesty	spiritual, almost religious significance; comparison to whales, elephants	magnificence of the kauri
2.	heritage/permanence	link to previous centuries; certain feature in an uncertain world; will outlive us all	have outlasted the moa; now treated with reverence in New Zealand
3.	trees as teachers	we should question our assumption of superiority	we can learn from trees
4.	ordinary people see trees' importance	Hastings protesters; gift to posterity	New Zealand conservationists; Kenyan women (impact on quality of life)
5.	government and businesses' misguided economic priorities	government short-termism (Britain, Burma, Iceland, etc); trees considered expendable in the interests of "progress"	opposition to tree-based farming; profit-driven outlook of big businesses
6.	lack of respect	councils, officialdom, some homeowners	historical clearing; governments; companies; western desire to control nature
7.	brutality	trees are cut down or cut back quite brutally	hacking and racking continues

PAPER 2 — CRITICAL READING

SECTION 1 — Scottish Text

SCOTTISH TEXT (DRAMA)

Text 1 — Drama — *The Slab Boys* by John Byrne

Question	Expected response	Max mark	Additional guidance
1.	Candidates should make reference to two appropriate examples of dialogue with appropriate comment on what is suggested about Phil. 1 mark for each appropriate reference with comment. 0 marks for reference/quotation alone.	2	Possible answers include: **Aggressive personality** — reference and comment on: *"If he catches you going through his stuff, he'll break your jaw", "Shut the folder or I'll get the blame. I get the blame for everything around here…" "Which is exactly how your features are going to look if Phil comes back"* **He doesn't accept responsibility** — reference and comment on: *"I get the blame for everything around here…"* **Artistic talents** — *reference and comment on:* *"God, they are good, aren't they? There's one of Elvis…'s dead like him, isn't it?"* **Difficult relationship with mother:** *"And there's one of his maw. Christ, you can tell, can't you?"*
2.	Candidates should make reference to two appropriate examples of dialogue with appropriate comment on what is suggested about Curry. 1 mark for each appropriate reference with comment. 0 marks for reference/quotation alone.	2	Possible answers include: *"I remember when Bob Downie used to work here he was always…"* suggests a fondness for telling stories *"Jimmy Robertson and I used to go up to Saturday morning classes together…"* suggests he is keen to learn/is sociable. *"I showed Bob Downie a few tricks while he was with us. Expect he told you, eh?"* suggests he enjoys being looked up to/can be overbearing/is looking for approval.
3.	Candidates should identify the contrasting attitudes which Curry shows. 1 mark for each side of the contrast. 1 additional mark will be awarded for comment on appropriate textual evidence which supports each side of the contrast. 0 marks for reference/quotation alone.	4	Possible answers include: **Curry to the Slab Boys** Curry's attitude is negative, eg, dismissive, unsympathetic, severe, intolerant… Comment could be made on: *"They aren't yours, Farrell, that's for sure. You've got trouble trying to draw water from that tap over there."* *"And they can't be Hector's. Too bold for him…"* *"You're not going to tell me they're McCann's"* Curry refers to Phil in derogatory terms — *"loafer", "flyman", "crony", "miserable carcase"* There is an implication of challenge/conflict in *"Well, we'll soon see about this…"* Commanding tone used in *"…Farrell!"* Use of imperatives — *"Get a move on!", "Tell him…", "Get those…", "Will you gee yourself up a bit!"* Refers to Spanky as *"Bloody corner boy."* Mockery implied by *"You'd think it was a damned bath you were having!"* Aggressive questioning of Spanky. **Curry to Alan** Curry's attitude is positive, eg ingratiating, sycophantic, obsequious Comment could be made on: *"You never let on Bob Downie was your father…see you young fellows…Chief Designer at Templars…Some of your artwork… Let's have a butcher's."*

Question	Expected response	Max mark	Additional guidance
3.	*(continued)*		Curry is now interested in the artwork, mistaking it for Alan's.
			"A right talented pair of buggers."
			Use of derogatory term in an attempt at humour/familiarity.
			"Now Alan, where were we…I dare say your dad's covered some of this ground with you…I showed Bob Downie a few tricks… Right. Alan…what's the first thing we do when we're starting a charcoal sketch?"
			Curry is now taking an interest, keen to engage with Alan.
			Reference could be made to the use of Alan's first name rather than the surnames with which Curry addresses the Slab Boys.
4.	Candidates should include an acceptable piece of humorous dialogue and should then show how this evokes sympathy for Spanky.	2	Possible answers include:
	0 marks for quotation/reference alone.		*"Yeh, you have a word with him, kiddo…I'm sure he'll appreciate it."*
	A detailed/insightful comment plus reference will score 2 marks; a more basic comment plus reference will be worth 1 mark.		Spanky's use of sarcasm following Alan's rather derogatory comment on the Slab Room (*"He's wasting his time in here."*)
			"And just leave the rest of his body down there?"
	Quotation is likely but not necessary. Candidates can illustrate their understanding by referring to the content of the extract.		Spanky's joke shows that he is able to retaliate with wit in the face of Curry's anger.
			"They aren't yours Farrell, that's for sure. You've got trouble trying to draw water from that tap over there."
			Curry's sneering joke seems particularly nasty in contrast to the fawning treatment of Alan — unequal treatment makes us sympathetic to Spanky.
5.	Candidates should discuss how the theme of frustrated ambition is developed in the text and should refer to appropriate textual evidence to support their discussion.	10	Up to 2 marks can be achieved for identifying elements of commonality as identified in the question, ie the theme of frustrated ambition.
			A further 2 marks can be achieved for reference to the extract given.
	0 marks for reference/quotation alone.		6 additional marks can be awarded for discussion of similar references to at least one other part of the text by the writer.
	Candidates can answer in bullet points in this final question, or write a number of linked statements.		<u>In practice this means:</u>
			Identification of commonality (2) (eg: theme, characterisation, use of imagery, setting, or any other key element…)
			from the extract:
			1 x relevant reference to technique/idea/feature (1) 1 x appropriate comment (1) (maximum of 2 marks only for discussion of extract)
			from at least one other text/part of the text:
			as above (x3) for up to 6 marks
			OR
			more detailed comment x2 for up to 6 marks
			Thus, the final 6 marks can be gained by a combination of 3, 2 and 1 marks depending on the level of depth/detail/insight. The aim would be to encourage quality of comment, rather than quantity of references.
			In comments on the rest of the play, possible references include:
			• The Art School's rejection of Phil's application for entry • Hector's failed attempts to take Lucille to the staff dance • The length of time which Slab Boys have to wait before getting a desk
			Many other references are possible.

Text 2 — Drama — *The Cheviot, the Stag and the Black, Black Oil* by John McGrath

Question	Expected response	Max mark	Additional guidance
6.	Candidates should explain how the minister's speech reveals that he regards himself as a force of authority and control. Marks can be awarded for three appropriate references or quotations with suitable commentary. OR a reference with more detailed/insightful comment may be awarded 2 marks, plus reference with more basic comment can receive 1 mark. 0 marks for reference/quotation alone.	3	Candidates should show how the language used reveals that, rather than attending to his congregation's pastoral needs or speaking up as a spokesman or teacher for his community, the minister represents the powers of authority and control, reprimanding and criticizing those resistant to change. Possible references include: Repeated warnings of "wickedness" suggest that immorality in this life shall not go unpunished in the next one. "the wrath of the Almighty" suggests that because of their wrong-doing , they should fear what awaits them. "For I will repay, saith the Lord" suggests that vengeance awaits those who are seen to have been wrongdoers in their current life. "the troubles that are visiting you are a judgement")/"a warning of the final judgement that is to come" infers a conflation between the secular authorities (landlords) and divine authority, and that this is a foretaste of what is still to come "some of you … are so far from the fold" suggests the wickedness of this life shall not go unpunished in the next one. "wailing and gnashing of teeth" suggests the divine torment that is awaiting for offences committed in this life. "dignity of your womanhood" suggests that their actions are an attack on women in general and therefore worse because they have been committed by women. "risen up to curse your masters"/"violate the laws of the land"/"burning of the writs" all suggest revolting acts or rebellion against their betters or the accepted order or status quo.
7.	Candidates should include one example of humorous dialogue or stage direction and analyse how it is used. 1 mark should be awarded for the reference or quotation plus appropriate analysis. 0 marks for quotation/reference alone. A detailed/insightful comment plus reference will score 2 marks; a more basic comment plus reference will be worth 1 mark. Quotation is likely but not necessary. Candidates can illustrate their understanding by referring to the content of the extract.	2	Through the use of bracketed directions (Big cheer), (Groan) and (More groans), the rest of the cast act as a chorus, reminiscent of humorous, pantomime-like responses. The cast substitute for the audience's reactions producing a dialogue with the First Girl, similar to audience participation between performers and audience, integral to the light-hearted manner of a ceilidh. Humour is evident in the ridiculing and deflating of the figures of authority by ducking the law officers "in a neighbouring pool". These farcical methods (as above) involve role reversal in that it was men, historically, who meted this punishment on women. Humour is also evident in the First Girl's speech when she refers to "the people made a stout resistance." It is in fact "the women" who carried out the action with the men forming "a second line of defence". This is humorously described in ironic terms by stating this defensive line was "in case the women should receive any ill-treatment."
8.	Candidates should explain what two examples of music contribute to the scene. 2 marks shall be awarded for the two examples with appropriate comments. 0 marks for reference/quotation alone.	2	Possible answers include: A fiddle and the quiet humming of a hymn set the sombre atmosphere for John to perform his role as the minister. It is ironic in these circumstances that the hymn is "The Lord is my Shepherd" — he is not acting as an appropriate leader of his flock, particularly as the sheep are displacing the tenants. After Liz's/First Girl's monologue, a fiddle "strikes up" and plays something upbeat and rousing to allow the company to dance and celebrate their victory of the women over authority, dancing being an integral part of a ceilidh. It seems appropriate that the women should lead off the dance to celebrate a female-won victory. It is also a further example of role reversal.

Question	Expected response	Max mark	Additional guidance
9.	Candidates should refer to at least two examples of financial detail, and explain how these details are relevant to the themes of the play. Candidates may be awarded 3 marks for three appropriate examples/quotations with basic suitable accompanying comment. Alternatively, 2 marks may be awarded for a more detailed/insightful comment. 0 marks for reference/quotation alone.	3	Possible answers include: Reference to the Old Man describing how the growth of the Highland population was outstripping the means to sustain it, and that for some, emigration was the only option. As a result of the Industrial Revolution and improved agricultural methods, wealth was expanding. Methods of capitalism were used to make further profits around the world as well as in the Scottish Highlands. A breed of sheep, the Cheviot, was introduced to make money and displace the inhabitants who were there. Narratively, the drama is grounded in the history of economic change in the Scottish Highlands where the people were forced to accept emigration either to poorer land, crowded industrial cities or abroad. The forces of exploitative capitalism were to prove stronger than the organisation of the people.
10.	Candidates should discuss how the theme of the role of women is developed in the play and should refer to appropriate textual evidence to support their discussion. 0 marks for reference/quotation alone Candidates can answer in bullet points in this final question, or write a number of linked statements.	10	Up to 2 marks can be achieved for identifying elements of commonality as identified in the question, ie the role of women. A further 2 marks can be achieved for reference to the extract given. 6 additional marks can be awarded for discussion of similar references to at least one other part of the text by the writer. In practice this means: Identification of commonality (2) (eg: theme, characterisation, use of imagery, setting, or any other key element…) from the extract: 1 x relevant reference to technique/idea/feature (1) 1 x appropriate comment (1) (maximum of 2 marks only for discussion of extract) from at least one other text/part of the text: as above (x3) for up to 6 marks OR more detailed comment x2 for up to 6 marks Thus, the final 6 marks can be gained by a combination of 3, 2 and 1 marks depending on the level of depth/detail/insight. The aim would be to encourage quality of comment, rather than quantity of references. In comments on the rest of the play, possible references include: • Over the different periods women have taken the initiative and led others. • Women have displayed solidarity as well as community spirit, while their male counterparts have responded with indifference or been absent altogether. • The female players of the drama have been given equal opportunity to express themselves through poem, song and general narration. Many other references are possible.

Text 3 — Drama — *Men Should Weep* by Ena Lamont Stewart

Question	Expected response	Max mark	Additional guidance
11.	Candidates should give a clear explanation of Maggie's differing attitudes to Isa and Alec with appropriate reference to the dialogue. 1 mark should be awarded for each reference or quotation plus appropriate analysis. 0 marks for reference/quotation alone.	2	Possible answers include: **Attitude to Isa** Resents her/has no respect for her/dislikes her/thinks she's not "good enough" for Alec/thinks she's hard-hearted. Possible references include: • "An here! You've to leave aff tormentin him" — thinks Isa is too hard on Alec; that Alec doesn't deserve such cruel treatment. • "Threatenin to leave him when ye ken he's that daft aboot ye." — thinks Isa is heartless in the face of Alec's devotion. • "Goad kens why" — thinks Isa isn't worth Alec's devotion. • "…ye're a worthless slut if ever there wis yin" — disrespects Isa; thinks she's 'common', not good enough for Alec. • "I'll learn ye tae ca me a bitch!" — sees herself as superior to Isa, is ready to teach her a lesson. **Attitude to Alec** Protective of Alec/loving/loyal/sees him as the victim/blind to Alec's weakness/molly-coddles him/treats him like a child. Possible references include: • "Alec's shiverin; he can hardly staun on his feet" — Maggie worries about his health/is protective of him. **and/or** • "An get a packet o Woodbine tae" — indulges him • "Ye ken he's that daft aboot ye" — has sympathy for Alec's devotion and sees him as the victim of Isa's hard-heartedness.
12.	Candidates should exemplify and explain one example each of Maggie, John and Isa's attitudes to how a man is expected to behave. 1 mark should be awarded for each reference or quotation plus appropriate analysis. 0 marks for reference/quotation alone.	3	**Maggie** Maggie believes, to an extent, that a husband and wife are equal partners and therefore a man should pull his weight around the house and respect his wife. Men need to talk less about putting the world to rights and should take more decisive action to find employment. A man should support his wife and present a united front against outsiders. Possible references include: "Ye couldna even wash up a dish for me. It's me that aye has tae dae twa jobs when you get the sack!" "Aye, I've seen yous men lookin for work. Haudin up the street corners, ca'in doon the Government…" "(Pause) Whit a meant wis…" "And I like a man…tae stand up for his wife." **Isa** For all her hard, calculating ways, Isa sees her identity as an extension of her man's. She wants men to be men — to take the traditional dominant role — which is why she finds Alec's personality so disappointing. Possible references include: "Quite right. A woman disnae respect a man that's *nae* a man." "That's the stuff! He's needin somebody tae tak him in haun. He's beyond me. I cannae dae naethin with him." "Aye, he's jist a great big baby. If he disnae get whit he wants, he greets…" "I like a man tae *be* a man. Staun up for hissel."

Question	Expected response	Max mark	Additional guidance
12.	*(continued)*		**John** He believes himself to be the man of the house and, as such, women should submit to his superiority. His traditional working class male chauvinism means he believes housework is beneath him, he can treat his wife disrespectfully and his word is final. Possible references include: "Aw, shut up harpin on that string." "Tae Hell wi this Jessie business every time I'm oot o a job!" "I'm no turnin masel intae a bloomin skivvy! I'm a man!" "There's nae drink comin intae this hoose!" "Shut yer mouth or I'll shut it for ye!"
13.	Candidates should make reference to the stage directions to support discussion about John's character. A single detailed/insightful comment about John's character, supported by reference to the stage directions, could score 2 marks. Alternatively, two more basic comments on two examples could score 1 mark each. 0 marks for reference/quotation alone.	3	Candidates should identify John's utter defeat when reminded of his failure to provide for his family. His bravado is quickly extinguished in the face of the truth, revealing the vulnerability which lies just under the surface of his macho posturing. Possible references: "*John, as if he had been shot…*" – suggests the instant blow to his pride when reminded that he does not provide for his family. "*…drops Alec…*" – suggests the instant blow to his pride, to the extent that he doesn't feel he has the right to have any authority over even the weakest member of his family. "*…slumps…puts his head in his hands.*" – suggests how defeated and hopeless he feels. "*demoralised*" suggests how his identity as a man is based on his pride as head of the house.
14.	Candidates should explain two examples of John's behaviour that Maggie finds disappointing. 0 marks for reference/quotation alone.	2	Possible answers include: Maggie is disappointed by John blaming her for not keeping the house in order. "Ma Goad! Whit a hell o a hoose tae come hame tae!" Maggie is disappointed by the aggressive/bullying/disrespectful way John speaks to her. "Aw, shut up harpin on that string" "Shut yer mouth or I'll shut it for ye!" Maggie is disappointed by John's lack of support for her. "Well, ye're certainly actin like yin." (a "bitch") Maggie is disappointed by John's sympathy/understanding for Isa. "Maggie! That's no fair. She's upset" "Don't cry, Isa; he's nae worth it." Maggie is disappointed by John blaming her for the way Alec has turned out. "It's *your* fault. You spoiled him frae the day he wis born." Maggie is disappointed by John's lack of compassion for Alec. "ye're getting nae whisky. D'ye understan?" Maggie is disappointed by John's betrayal in not taking her side. "And I like a man…tae stand up for his wife."

Question	Expected response	Max mark	Additional guidance
15.	Candidates should discuss to what extent this scene is important to Maggie's character development and should refer to appropriate textual evidence to support their discussion. 0 marks for reference/quotation alone. Candidates can choose to answer in bullet points in this final question, or write a number of linked statements.	10	Up to 2 marks can be achieved for identifying elements of commonality as identified in the question, ie Maggie's development as a character. A further 2 marks can be achieved for reference to the extract given. 6 additional marks can be awarded for discussion of similar references to at least one other part of the text by the writer. In practice this means: Identification of commonality (2) (eg: theme, characterisation, use of imagery, setting, or any other key element…) from the extract: 1 x relevant reference to technique/idea/feature (1) 1 x appropriate comment (1) (maximum of 2 marks only for discussion of extract) from at least one other text/part of the text: as above (x3) for up to 6 marks OR more detailed comment x2 for up to 6 marks Thus, the final 6 marks can be gained by a combination of 3, 2 and 1 marks depending on the level of depth/detail/insight. The aim would be to encourage quality of comment, rather than quantity of references. In comments on the rest of the play, possible references include: Maggie's portrayal in the opening scenes of the play: down-trodden; exhausted; oppressed by poverty and running a chaotic home; accepting of her lot; loyal to John. Maggie's continued development as the play progresses, eg reaches breaking point with the children and her situation in general. Maggie is driven by her determination to do what she wants and by what is best for her family; takes control of her life. Many other references are possible.

Text 1 – Prose – *In Church* by Iain Crichton Smith

Question	Expected response	Max mark	Additional guidance
16.	Candidates should cover both (i) futility and (ii) cruelty, and both language features of word choice and sentence structure. Points on futility are more likely to be found in the first paragraph; and on cruelty in the second. 0 marks for reference/quotation alone.	4	Possible answers include: **Futility** Sentence structure • Repetition of "over and over" to little point • Climactic sentence ending emphasising relentlessness Word choice • "continuously revised" • "scribbled over endlessly" **Cruelty** Sentence structure • Short, harsh sentences • Mostly climactic sentences, emphasising, eg "the beaks", "going for the head" • Sentence patterning using violent description in participial clauses, eg "probing upwards from below", "pecking and jabbing"

Question	Expected response	Max mark	Additional guidance
16.	*(continued)*		Word choice • Emphasis on violent action, eg "attacked…probing" • Emphasis on persistence, eg "synchronise their movements", "zeroing in on it" • The single bird's vulnerability, eg "upwards from below", "was weakening"
17.	Candidates should explain how the anecdote about the dogfight develops the theme of the futility of war. Marks may be awarded for a comment with supporting evidence. 2 marks may be awarded for one detailed/insightful comment; 1 mark for a more basic point. Detailed reference or quotation may be used, plus comment. 0 marks for reference/quotation alone.	2	Candidates may focus on the pointlessness of victory in which the victor is also killed; the noble and human qualities displayed by the German pilot (which do not save him); the parallel of the birds fighting to the death = nature "at war" and the human conflict supposedly about ideals Possible references include: • "long duel/…in turn/…shot down/…/bullet…penetrated his back…out at the chest" • "pilot seated at the controls", "upright', "disciplined", "aristocratic", "eyes staring straight ahead", and perfectly dead"
18.	Candidates should discuss how the writer conveys the narrator's unfamiliarity with his surroundings. 2 marks can be awarded for reference plus detailed/insightful comment; 1 mark for reference plus more basic comment. 0 marks for reference/quotation alone.	4	Possible answers include: • "staring" — the verb conveys his focused attention on the church • "never been in a church like this before" — the phrase "like this" conveys his unfamiliarity • "either a helpless or a welcoming gesture" — use of "either" shows his lack of familiarity with the imagery in the stained glass window • "which he thought might be a confessional" — use of "might be" conveys his unfamiliarity • "gazed for a long time at the… cross" — conveys his interest in his surroundings • "silence was oppressive" — conveys his sense of unease in an unfamiliar setting • "not at all like the churches at home" — "not at all" shows that everything is different • "there was more ornament, it was less bare, more decorated" — list of phrases conveys the unfamiliar details he notices
19.	Candidates should discuss how the writer develops the theme of the destructive nature of war and should refer to appropriate textual evidence to support their discussion. 0 marks for reference/quotation alone. Candidates can answer in bullet points in this final question, or write a number of linked statements.	10	Up to 2 marks can be achieved for identifying elements of commonality as identified in the question, ie the destructive nature of war. A further 2 marks can be achieved for reference to the extract given. 6 additional marks can be awarded for discussion of similar references to at least one other short story by the writer. <u>In practice this means:</u> Identification of commonality (2) (eg: theme, characterisation, use of imagery, setting, or any other key element…) From the extract: 1 x relevant reference to technique/idea/feature (1) 1 x appropriate comment (1) (maximum of 2 marks only for discussion of extract) From at least one other text/part of the text: As above (x3) for up to 6 marks

Question	Expected response	Max mark	Additional guidance
19.	*(continued)*		OR
			More detailed comment x2 for up to 6 marks
			Thus, the final 6 marks can be gained by a combination of 3, 2 and 1 marks depending on the level of depth/detail/insight. The aim would be to encourage quality of comment, rather than quantity of references.
			In comments on other texts, possible references include:
			• The raid in *The Crater* — insignificant in itself but leads to horrifying deaths • Morrison turned into a "monster" in the green slime of the crater • In *The Telegram* — focus on the suffering of those left back home, fearing but not understanding the war
			Many other references are possible.

Text 2 — Prose — *A Time to Keep* by George Mackay Brown

Question	Expected response	Max mark	Additional guidance
20.	For full marks, answers should cover the topics of both "poverty of the land" and "inadequacy as a farmer", using both reference and comment. 2 marks may be awarded for reference plus detailed/insightful comment; 1 mark for reference plus more basic comment. 0 marks for reference/quotation alone.	4	Possible answers include: **Poverty of the land** • "Stones and clumps of heather" — simple description illustrating land unsuitable for cultivation • "squelch into a sudden bit of bog" — alliteration emphasising the difficulties faced in tilling the land • "no-one on God's earth could plough such a wilderness" — exaggeration emphasising the narrator's pessimism and feelings of dissatisfaction • "my spade rang against stones" —onomatopoeia emphasising poor quality of the land **Inadequacy as a farmer** • "They lay, red bits of rag …" — impressionistic description/basic symbolism/sentence structure illustrating the consequences of not being up to the job • "What a fool!" — use of internal monologue to give narrative viewpoint
21.	Candidates should analyse how sentence structure is used to develop the narrator's worsening mood. 2 marks may be awarded for reference plus detailed/insightful comment; 1 mark for reference plus more basic comment. 0 marks for references alone.	4	Possible answers include: • "It was Good Friday" — short, terse sentence illustrating the narrator's rationalist unwillingness to accept the religiosity of his neighbours • "There was one stone … tearing the sharp bits out of the ground" — climactic sentences illustrating the difficulty of the task and the increasing ferocity of his response to it • "The house was dead. The pot sat black …" — sparse, severe sentence structure illustrating the bleakness of his mood • "I closed my eyes" — economy/brevity of sentence structure to suggest the blankness and nihilism of his attitude(s)
22.	Candidates may choose to concentrate on Ingi's attempts to lighten his mood or to show how she worsens it. Either will be acceptable. Reference plus detailed/insightful comment will be awarded 2 marks; 1 mark for reference plus more basic comment. 0 marks for reference/quotation alone.	2	Possible answers include: • "She rose up quickly … put her cold hand on my forehead" — Ingi shows sympathy and solicitude; she attempts to tend to his physical weakness • Ingi tries to cheer him up by telling him about the new lambs "such bonny peedie things!" • "Ingi was at the service with the laird …" — her religiosity, and acceptance of her neighbours' communal worship, worsens his antipathy towards religion and the community

Question	Expected response	Max mark	Additional guidance
23.	Candidates should discuss how the writer creates flawed but engaging characters and should refer to appropriate textual evidence to support their discussion. 0 marks for reference/quotation alone. Candidates can answer in bullet points in this final question, or write a number of linked statements.	10	Up to 2 marks can be achieved for identifying elements of commonality as identified in the question, ie characters who are flawed but nonetheless engage the reader's sympathy. A further 2 marks can be achieved for reference to the extract given. 6 additional marks can be awarded for discussion of similar references to at least one other short story by the writer. In practice this means: Identification of commonality (2) (eg: theme, characterisation, use of imagery, setting, or any other key element...) from the extract: 1 x relevant reference to technique/idea/feature (1) 1 x appropriate comment (1) (maximum of 2 marks only for discussion of extract) from at least one other text/part of the text: as above (x3) for up to 6 marks OR more detailed comment x2 for up to 6 marks Thus, the final 6 marks can be gained by a combination of 3, 2 and 1 marks depending on the level of depth/detail/insight. The aim would be to encourage quality of comment, rather than quantity of references. In comments on other stories, possible references include: • The character of Flaws in *The Whaler's Return* — well intentioned and compassionate but naïve and easily distracted • In *Tartan the Vikings*, sparing the children while raiding the village (Kol murdered) • In *The Eye of the Hurricane*, Captain Stevens' drunkenness, yet he is respected by comrades for courage and decency Many other references are possible.

Text 3 — Prose — *The Trick is to Keep Breathing* by Janice Galloway

Question	Expected response	Max mark	Additional guidance
24.	Candidates should explain how Galloway makes the reader aware of Joy's attitude towards the psychiatrist. Attitude should be clear, but may be implicit. 2 marks may be awarded for reference plus detailed/insightful comment, showing contribution to understanding of attitude. 1 mark for reference plus more basic comment. 2 marks may be awarded in this way. 0 marks for reference/quotation alone.	2	Candidates should recognise that Joy is dismissive of the psychiatrist/mocking/expects visit to be a waste of time. Possible answers include: • Use of humour, eg "Lesson1", "Lesson2" undermines seriousness of her situation/listing her expectations of the visit/as though she has prepared herself for the worthlessness of the visit • Opening line states emphatically that she "knew" it would be a "disappointment". • Dismissive tone in "psychiatrists aren't as smart as you'd think"/"not mind-readers...look as though they are." • Refers to him as "Dr One" — not worthy of a name/suggests they are all the same. • Disappointed in his question "So ... Why ...?" — exactly as predicted in her list. Adds to humour • "He thought I wasn't trying" — suggests she believes he does not understand her

Question	Expected response	Max mark	Additional guidance
25.	Candidates should analyse how the writer's use of language is effective in conveying Joy's state of mind. Candidates' understanding of Joy's mood should be clear but may be implicit. Two examples of references plus detailed/insightful explanation awarded 2 marks each = 4. Or four examples with more basic explanation. Marks may be awarded for combinations of above. 0 marks for reference/quotation alone.	4	Candidates should refer to: state of mind: panic/loss of control/confusion/sense of panic. Word choice: "my throat was contracting" — difficulty in breathing Metaphor: "I was about to short-circuit" — suddenly shut down/break down Sentence structure: repetition of "I hadn't" emphasises her sense of panic at what she hadn't prepared for Separates parts of herself to emphasise her feeling of disembodiment: brain and body feel separate Personification: "My mouth knew more…"/"The voice didn't need me….like me" — as if she has no control over the voice — it is an entity on its own. Reinforces this with "I let…out of harm's way." She wants to try to co-operate but sees the whole thing as pointless — emphasised by the voices in italics Repetition of "whispered" — makes voices seem alive
26.	Candidates should analyse how the writer highlights the significance of Michael's death. For full marks, different techniques should be exemplified and commented on in terms of effectiveness. Reference plus detailed/insightful comment = 2 marks. Reference plus more basic comment = 1 mark. Marks may be awarded for combination of the above. 0 marks for reference/quotation alone.	4	Possible answers include: **Structure:** Indented sections represent Joy's spoken words. Contrast between matter of matter of fact tone, achieved by short sentences, and final part of sentence "and he drowned" puts emphasis on this point; short sentences leading up to this summarise the many contributing factors in her breakdown, but emphasis on "he drowned" shows this is the most significant factor; sentence does not end with a full stop suggesting she continues to think about this/puts emphasis on this part of the sentence. Repetition of "he drowned" — emphasises significance of this. "He drowned" — short sentence in paragraph of its own — emphasises significance of the point. Flashback to Michael's accident: "side of the pool….and the sky" — emphasises the reality of her situation; this is what she fears. **Contrast:** Between inner feelings and what she says "I heard the last bit twisting out of kilter…" **Word choice:** "out of kilter" — suggests loss of balance perhaps caused by panic/fear; "eerie" — suggests something sinister/something terrifying **Imagery:** Simile: "like the Bates Motel in Psycho" — comparison to horror movie makes her terror about remembering the accident clear; Personification: furniture seems to be alive — "liver-coloured furniture breathing" — nightmarish image emphasises her terror

Question	Expected response	Max mark	Additional guidance
27.	Candidates should discuss how the writer develops the theme of loss and should refer to appropriate textual evidence to support their discussion. 0 marks for reference/quotation alone. Candidates may choose to answer in bullet points in this final question, or write a number of linked statements.	10	Up to 2 marks can be achieved for identifying elements of commonality as identified in the question, ie the theme of loss. A further 2 marks can be achieved for reference to the extract given. 6 additional marks can be awarded for discussion of similar references to at least one other part of the text by the writer. <u>In practice this means:</u> Identification of commonality (2) (eg: theme, characterisation, use of imagery, setting, or any other key element...) from the extract: 1 x relevant reference to technique/idea/feature (1) 1 x appropriate comment (1) (maximum of 2 marks only for discussion of extract) from at least one other text/part of the text: as above (x3) for up to 6 marks OR more detailed comment x2 for up to 6 marks Thus, the final 6 marks can be gained by a combination of 3, 2 and 1 marks depending on the level of depth/detail/insight. The aim would be to encourage quality of comment, rather than quantity of references. In comments on the rest of the novel, possible references include: • The loss of Michael — horror of holiday experience • The loss of her mother — devastating effects of bereavement • The loss of self — determination — anorexia/relationships with men Many other references are possible.

Text 4 — Prose — *Sunset Song* by Lewis Grassic Gibbon

Question	Expected response	Max mark	Additional guidance
28.	Candidates should discuss any two aspects of each character, supported by appropriate textual reference. Two aspects of John Guthrie's character with appropriate reference for 2 marks. Two aspects of Long Rob's character with appropriate reference for 2 marks. 0 marks for reference/quotation alone.	4	Possible answers include: **John Guthrie** Alert/decisive/energetic/persistent, determined/angry, religious fervour Possible references include: "first down at the ... Knapp" "ran ... banged ... cried ... smashed in" "and when he got no answer he smashed in the window" *"Damn't to hell do you want to be roasted?"* **Long Rob** Athletic/in tune with nature/brave/compassionate/calm under pressure/kind/unconcerned about his own safety Possible references include: "louping dykes like a hare" "helped Mrs Strachan with the bairns" "smoking his pipe as cool as you please" "dived in and out", "tore and rived that off a blazing wall"

Question	Expected response	Max mark	Additional guidance
29.	Candidates should analyse how the writer's use of language creates a sense of urgency. Reference and comment to show how sense of urgency is created. 2 marks may be awarded for detailed/insightful comment; 1 mark for more basic comment. 0 marks for reference/quotation alone.	2	Possible answers include: "blazing" — fire is burning strongly, creating danger "lapping" — inescapable presence of the fire which is wrapping, enfolding, surrounding "crackling" — onomatopoeic loud rustling Many very long sentences which convey the frenzied panic as one event runs on from another, eg "He was first down at the …" "the bairns scraiched" shows their inarticulate fear/panic "he'd only his breeks on" shows rush — no time to get dressed
30.	Candidates should analyse how the writer's use of language conveys the ferocity of the fire. Reference and comment to show how sense of urgency is created. 2 marks may be awarded for detailed/insightful comment; 1 mark for more basic comment. 0 marks for reference/quotation alone.	4	Possible answers include: "swithered" — suggests frightening spectacle of the barn which moved from side to side as a result of the fire "roared" — suggests the fire made a loud, ferocious sound like a wild animal "roaring alight" — as above, but again combines sight and sound "snarling" — onomatopoeic/personification, suggesting the fire is making a growling sound like an ill-natured beast "eating in to" — suggests unstoppable force which is consuming, making inroads into "charred" — reduced to carbon "screamed and screamed" — repetition emphasises the horse's fear or pain as it cried out shrilly "smell and smoke" — alliteration conveys inescapable presence of the fire's effects Frequent linking of actions with the repeated use of "and" suggests the continuous, confused activity due to danger caused by fire's ferocity, eg "And at that sound … and cried … and she screamed … and to help … and the bairns … and Long Rob …" Narrative and dialogue combined in the same sentence to indicate there is no time to pause or waste, eg "But pipe and all he dived in … *Oh my sampler!* and in Rob tore … " Rare use of a colon to split the viable rescue actions from the impossible — "He it was … another angle: but that was no good …"
31.	Candidates should discuss how the writer conveys positive aspects of the community and should refer to appropriate textual evidence to support their discussion. 0 marks for reference/quotation alone. Candidates can answer in bullet points in this final question, or write a number of linked statements.	10	Up to 2 marks can be achieved for identifying elements of commonality as identified in the question, ie positive presentation of the community. A further 2 marks can be achieved for reference to the extract given. 6 additional marks can be awarded for discussion of similar references to at least one other part of the text by the writer. In practice this means: Identification of commonality (2) (eg: theme, characterisation, use of imagery, setting, or any other key element…) from the extract: 1 x relevant reference to technique/idea/feature (1) 1 x appropriate comment (1) (maximum of 2 marks only for discussion of extract) from at least one other text/part of the text: as above (x3) for up to 6 marks OR more detailed comment x2 for up to 6 marks

Question	Expected response	Max mark	Additional guidance
31.	*(continued)*		Thus, the final 6 marks can be gained by a combination of 3, 2 and 1 marks depending on the level of depth/detail/insight. The aim would be to encourage quality of comment, rather than quantity of references.
			In comments on the rest of the novel, possible references include:
			• the threshing at Peesie's Knapp; • the visit of Long Rob and Chae to Blawaerie at New Year • the celebration of Chris's wedding
			Many other references are possible.

Text 5 — Prose — *The Cone-Gatherers* by Robin Jenkins

Question	Expected Response	Max mark	Additional guidance
32.	For full marks candidates should make reference to how both sympathy and admiration are evoked, but there is no requirement for equal coverage of the two elements. One detailed/insightful comment, supported by reference from lines 1-40, may be awarded 2 marks; a more basic comment plus reference should be awarded 1 mark. 0 marks for reference/quotation alone.	4	References could be used to support sympathy and/or admiration. **Possible answers include:** "Neil appeared like an old man…He would cautiously go down on his haunches, wait, apparently to gather strength and endurance against the pain of that posture…" — Neil's rheumatism, worsened by Lady Runcie's Campbell's thoughtless rejection of the brothers from the beach hut and their subsequent soaking, causes him great pain and yet he is stoical and perseveres with the task in hand. The alliteration in "pain of that posture" emphasises the discomfort "…and then would begin to pick up the seed-cases…if it were not." — the detailed nature of Jenkins' description emphasises the painstaking nature of the task/Neil's dogged determination to carry out the task properly despite the pain he is in. "…as ninety out of a hundred would be barren." — the statistic demonstrates Neil's perseverance in carrying out so futile a task, which adds to our admiration "crippled with rheumatism", "hobbled on his haunches" —Jenkins' detailed description(s) of the severity of Neil's physical problems adds to the sympathy we feel for him "Such fidelity to so simple but indispensible a task…magnificent trees." — Neil's stoical commitment to his work evokes the simple goodness of the common man in the face of adversity "To praise it…inadequacy of life itself." — Neil's quiet faithfulness to his task is a thing of great nobility and seems to illustrate something fundamental about man's existence "Behind him Neil began to sob", "And he began to pour out an account of the expulsion…" — Neil's burden of looking after and protecting Calum is overwhelming when he is faced with the thoughtless cruelty of others. "Sob" has connotations of childish crying, which effectively conveys the distress of Neil "I'm responsible for him, Mr. Tulloch…" — Neil's simple declaration of dedication to looking after and protecting Calum provokes great admiration "No man on earth has ever…so well." — Mr Tulloch recognises Neil's loyalty to Calum, and admires his selfless commitment to his brother's well-being "…how stooped and contorted Neil was then, by rheumatism and despair…" — Neil's problems are both physical and emotional, creating sympathy in the reader "…as if in some terrible penance, he was striving to become in shape like his brother." — the idea of Neil doing "penance" because he feels such guilt for failing to stand up to Lady Runcie-Campbell provokes sympathy for the despair he feels and the burden he carries on his own

Question	Expected Response	Max mark	Additional guidance
33.	Candidates should explain Neil's attitude to Lady Runcie-Campbell. This attitude does not have to stated separately; it can be explained through the references given. 2 marks may be awarded for a detailed/insightful comment plus reference. 1 mark should be awarded for a more basic comment plus reference. 0 marks for reference/quotation alone.	4	Neil's attitude towards Lady Runcie-Campbell: he bitterly resents her superior attitude towards the brothers, in particular Calum, and is angered and insulted by her behaviour towards them Possible answers include: "Why is it, Mr Tulloch…that the innocent have always to be sacrificed?" — Neil is bitter about the way he and Calum have been treated because they are of low social standing in the eyes of Lady Runcie-Campbell; they are not worthy so must be "sacrificed" for her comfort He is also referring to the working class man fighting at war to preserve a way of life which gives nothing to him, or people like him (but is much to the benefit of the ruling elite as symbolised by Lady Runcie-Campbell) "We were driven out like slaves…Her dog was to be saved from the storm but not my brother." — Neil is disgusted by Lady Runcie-Campbell's callous treatment of the brothers. She values animals over men, and thinks her superior social standing justifies her actions "Did she think we were monkeys that would bite her?" — Neil is angered by Lady Runcie-Campbell's ignorant prejudice towards the brothers, thinking that they are little better than uncivilised animals just because they are simple working men "Neil shook his head dourly. My brother's the shape…to despise him?" — Neil cannot agree with Mr Tulloch's more measured attitude towards Lady Runcie-Campbell. He points out Lady Runcie-Campbell's arrogance in believing herself a greater judge than God Himself, but also hints at her hypocrisy as a Christian.
34.	Candidates should explain Mr Tulloch's attitude to Lady Runcie-Campbell. This attitude does not have to be stated separately; it can be explained through the references given. 2 marks may be awarded for a detailed/insightful comment plus reference. 1 mark should be awarded for a more basic comment plus reference. 0 marks for reference/quotation alone.	2	Mr Tulloch's attitude towards Lady Runcie-Campbell: he is more measured and sympathetic, recognising the conflict she feels between being seen to do her "duty" as a member of the ruling class and reaching out to all men with Christian compassion Possible references include: "I think maybe she was taken by surprise…Maybe she got a bit of a shock." — Tulloch recognises the unexpected nature of the brothers' appearance in the beach hut, and is prepared to believe that Lady Runcie-Campbell acted out of surprise rather than malice "She's a good woman really; but she's got a code to live by." — Tulloch recognises that Lady Runcie-Campbell's decisions are driven by her need to be seen to be doing what is expected of a woman in her position. She must uphold the natural division between the classes and preserve the "code" on which society is founded
35.	Candidates should discuss the central concern of the innocent being sacrificed, and its development, and should refer to appropriate textual evidence to support their discussion. 0 marks for reference alone. Candidates can answer in bullet points in this final question, or write a number of linked statements.	10	Up to 2 marks can be achieved for identifying elements of commonality as identified in the question, ie theme of sacrifice of the innocent. A further 2 marks can be achieved for reference to the extract given. 6 additional marks can be awarded for discussion of similar references to at least one other part of the text by the writer. In practice this means: Identification of commonality (2) (eg: theme, characterisation, use of imagery, setting, or any other key element…)

Question	Expected Response	Max mark	Additional guidance
35.	*(continued)*		from the extract:
			1 x relevant reference to technique/idea/feature (1)
			1 x appropriate comment (1)
			(maximum of 2 marks only for discussion of extract)
			from at least one other text/part of the text:
			as above (x3) for up to 6 marks
			OR
			more detailed comment x2 for up to 6 marks
			Thus, the final 6 marks can be gained by a combination of 3, 2 and 1 marks depending on the level of depth/detail/insight. The aim would be to encourage quality of comment, rather than quantity of references.
			In comments on the rest of the novel, possible references include:
			• The conflict involving Duror, Calum and Neil — the weak and vulnerable at the mercy of a more powerful and malevolent force
			• The world of nature (the wood) mirrors the world of war: Jenkins' use of animal imagery suggests a world of destruction and violence, culminating in the deer hunt
			• Calum's death: the culmination of Calum's Christ-like associations
			Many other references are possible.

Text 1 — Poetry — *Holy Willie's Prayer* by Robert Burns

Question	Expected Response	Max mark	Additional guidance
36.	Candidates should explain what Holy Willie means when he calls himself a "chosen sample". 2 marks may be awarded for detailed/insightful comment plus reference; 1 mark for more basic comment plus reference.	2	Possible answers include:
			• A reference to Calvinism/predestination/the Elect
			• God has chosen Willie to be one of the Elect
			• Willie claims not to be able to understand why he has been "chosen" and demonstrates mock-modesty
37.	Candidates should comment on the contradiction between Willie's words and actions/feelings for full marks. Candidates should focus on two examples; 2 marks may be awarded for detailed/insightful comment plus reference; 1 mark for more basic comment plus reference. The contrast/contraction should be clear in the commentary. 0 marks for reference/quotation alone.	4	Possible answers include:
			Words
			• "a pillar o' thy temple" — "pillar" suggests something strong/steadfast, creating the sense that Willie sees himself as a good (moral) example to others
			• "Strong as a rock" — simile suggests strength/power of something natural — suggesting Willie sees himself as a natural choice of leader
			• "A guide, a buckler and example (/To a thy flock.)" — the list of items suggests that Willie sees himself as special and a moral leader/supporter defender of morality/faith
			• "I am keepet by Thy fear/Free frae them a'" — reference to "fear" suggests that Willie respects God's power and will live a good life; "free" suggests his life will avoid sin and he will keep the Commandments

Question	Expected Response	Max mark	Additional guidance
37.	(continued)		**Actions/feelings** • "fash'd wi' fleshly lust" — Willie admits giving in to one of the deadly sins, thus proving he is not a good example to others; "fash'd" is informal suggesting he sees his actions as trivial/bothersome rather than morally wrong • "yestreen, Thou kens, wi' Meg" — use of informal "Thou" is disrespectful, suggesting Willie views God as a friend rather than the powerful Creator of his faith; the tone of "Thou kens" suggests Willie is not really ashamed of his actions, his lust; he does not treat women with respect • "I'll ne'er lift a lawless leg/Again upon her" — use of alliteration to emphasise "lawless leg" adds to the triviality of the expression and to Willie's hypocrisy • "Wi Leezie's lass, three times I trow" — tone here is almost boastful, suggesting Willie is anything but reverent and atoning for his sins; use of alliteration again trivializes the comment; informality of the expression emphasises his lack of respect for the (unnamed) girl • "I was fou" — informal expression again suggests he treats God as a friend and is not ashamed of his behaviour • "wad never steer her" — "steer" has animalistic connotations and emphasises his lack of respect for the girl
38.	Candidates should identify the change of tone with two examples for 1 mark each. 0 marks for reference/quotation alone.	4	Possible answers include: **Tone** • "Maybe Thou lets this fleshly thorn/Buffet Thy servant e'en and morn/Lest he o'er proud and high should turn" — the tone is reflective, as Holy Willie considers that God might be tormenting him with these humiliating events to stop him becoming arrogant. • "But God confound their stubborn face/And blast their name" — the tone is of anger as Holy Willie berates his congregation for their behaviour. This emphasises his anger and contradicts his desire to pray; the lines emphasise his desire for vengeance upon his enemies.
39.	Candidates should discuss the contrast between Holy Willie and at least one other character and should refer to appropriate textual evidence to support their discussion. 0 marks for reference/quotation alone. Candidates can answer in bullet points in this final question, or write a number of linked statements.	10	Up to 2 marks can be achieved for identifying elements of commonality as identified in the question, ie the contrast between Holy Willie and another character or characters. A further 2 marks can be achieved for reference to the extract given. 6 additional marks can be awarded for discussion of similar references to at least one other poem by the poet. In practice this means: Identification of commonality (2) (eg: theme, characterisation, use of imagery, setting, or any other key element…) from the extract: 1 x relevant reference to technique/idea/feature (1) 1 x appropriate comment (1) (maximum of 2 marks only for discussion of extract) from at least one other text/part of the text: as above (x3) for up to 6 marks OR more detailed comment (x2) for up to 6 marks Thus, the final 6 marks can be gained by a combination of 3, 2 and 1 marks depending on the level of depth/detail/insight. The aim would be to encourage quality of comment, rather than quantity of references.

Question	Expected Response	Max mark	Additional guidance
39.	(continued)		In comments on other poems by Burns, possible references include: • *Tam O'Shanter* — relishing life, non-hypocritical • *A Poet's Welcome to his Love-Begotten Daughter* — non-apologetic self-awareness, warm and genuinely loving • *Address to the Deil* — ironic sense of own flaws Many other references are possible.

Text 2 — Poetry — *Originally* by Carol Ann Duffy

Question	Expected Response	Max mark	Additional guidance
40.	2 marks can be awarded for two examples which highlight the dramatic impact. A detailed/insightful comment on one example may be awarded 2 marks. Reference plus basic comment for 1 mark. 0 marks for reference/quotation alone.	2	Possible answers include: • Word choice of "we"/"our" suggests a sense of comforting group identity/defining event in family history • Repetition of "our" suggests the need for group identity in the face of new circumstances • Word choice of "fell" suggests a loss of control over event/helplessness in the face of change • Word choice of "cried"/"bawling" suggests the degree of distress caused by the move. • The sequence "the city .... rooms" suggests a poignant re-tracing of the route/desire to return • Word choice of "vacant" suggests the physical/emotional emptiness of the place that used to be home • The climactic conclusion to the sequence "city … any more." suggests the finality of the move • The word choice of "stared" suggests a stunned reaction to the move. • The contrast of the poet's reaction — "stared"— with the reactions of her brothers —"cried"/"bawling" — highlights the poet's shocked reaction • Symbolic use of "blind toy" — like the poet the toy is unfeeling and unaware of what is happening • Word choice of "holding its paw" suggests a desperate need for comfort/reassurance
41.	Candidates should explain fully what Duffy means by the image "all childhood is an emigration." Simple comment about journey to adulthood for 1 mark. A detailed/insightful comment may be awarded 2 marks. Reference to journey alone = 0 marks.	2	Possible answers include: Childhood is a journey from safety/security/the familiar OR Childhood is a journey into the unknown/to independence/potentially risky and dangerous situations.
42.	Candidates should analyse how the poet's use of poetic technique conveys the distress of the family members. 3 marks can be awarded for three examples of language highlighting the distress. Reference plus basic comment for 1 mark. Alternatively, 2 marks may be awarded for reference plus more detailed/insightful comment. 0 marks for reference/quotation alone.	3	Possible answers include: • The positioning/abruptness of the minor sentence "Your accent wrong" suggests lack of acceptance/sense of exclusion. • The parenthesis/positioning of "which seem familiar" suggest a sense of confusion/disorientation/déjà vu triggered by the new environment. • The word choice of "unimagined" suggests some unspeakable horror. • The word choice of "big boys" suggests the intimidating appearance of the boys/the vulnerability of the poet. • The detail "eating worms" suggests outlandish/disgusting behaviour. • The word choice of "shouting" suggests the intimidating nature of the way the boys are speaking.

Question	Expected Response	Max mark	Additional guidance
42.	*(continued)*		• The word choice of "you don't understand" suggests confusion/alienation. • The image "anxieties … loose tooth" suggests that a loose tooth causes annoyance but the parents' concerns about the move won't go away. • The word choice of "in my head" suggests that the parents' concerns have made a deep impression on the poet. • The italics/the phrase "*I want … country*" suggests the strength of the desire to return. • The word choice of "*want*" "*our*"/"*own*" suggests the depth of her desire for the familiar.
43.	Candidates should show understanding of the term "conclusion" and show how the content of the last stanza continues — or contrasts with — ideas and/or language from the first two stanzas. 3 marks can be awarded for three appropriate, basic comments. A detailed/insightful comment on one example may be awarded 2 marks. Other examples are acceptable. 0 marks for reference/quotation alone.	3	Possible answers include: **Ideas** • The poet has moved on in her life, and she has adapted to her new life • This move has created a sense of uncertainty as to her true origins, and sense of belonging **Language** • "But" suggests a change from her previous outsider status to becoming assimilated into the new environment. • The sequence "you forget … or change" suggests the gradual/indeterminable process of assimilation. • The idea of "brother swallow a slug" links back to "eating worms" and suggests her brother's acceptance of the local culture. • The use of the dialect word "skelf" suggests a hankering back to previous home or limited influence of previous culture on her. • The image "skelf of shame" suggests that just as a "skelf" is a splinter of wood, so is her sense of shame in betraying her past rather limited. • The image "my tongue … snake" suggests that just as a snake sheds its old skin, she is shedding her old life/adapting to suit her new life. • The idea of "my voice … like the rest" links back to "Your accent wrong" suggesting the poet's continuing assimilation into her new culture. • The list "I lost … the right place?" suggests an awareness of the amount she has lost by emigrating. • The use of the question at the end of the previous list introduces uncertainty — has she actually "lost" the items in the list? • The positioning/abruptness of "And I hesitate" suggests the poet's uncertainty about her cultural identity or where she really belongs.
44.	Candidates should discuss the use of contrast in this and other poems by Carol Ann Duffy and should refer to appropriate textual evidence to support their discussion. 0 marks for reference/quotation alone. Candidates can answer in bullet points in this final question, or write a number of linked statements.	10	Up to 2 marks can be achieved for identifying elements of commonality as identified in the question, ie use of contrast to highlight main concerns of this and other poems by Duffy. A further 2 marks can be achieved for reference to the extract given. 6 additional marks can be awarded for discussion of similar references to at least one other poem by the poet. <u>In practice this means:</u> Identification of commonality (2) (eg: theme, characterisation, use of imagery, setting, or any other key element…)

Question	Expected Response	Max mark	Additional guidance
44.	(continued)		from the extract:
			1 x relevant reference to technique/idea/feature (1)
			1 x appropriate comment (1)
			(maximum of 2 marks only for discussion of extract)
			from at least one other text/part of the text:
			as above (x3) for up to 6 marks
			OR
			more detailed comment x2 for up to 6 marks
			Thus, the final 6 marks can be gained by a combination of 3, 2 and 1 marks depending on the level of depth/detail/insight. The aim would be to encourage quality of comment, rather than quantity of references.
			In comments on other poems, possible references include:
			• Conventional romance versus realistic love in "Valentine" • Love and hate/revenge in "Havisham" • Peacefulness of darkroom versus horror of war zone in "War Photographer"
			Many other references are possible.

Text 3 – Poetry – *For My Grandmother Knitting* by Liz Lochhead

Question	Expected Response	Max mark	Additional guidance
45.	Candidates should analyse how the poet's use of poetic technique helps to clarify the main ideas of the poem. 2 marks may be awarded for detailed/insightful comment plus reference; 1 mark for more basic comment plus reference. 0 marks for reference/quotation alone.	2	Possible answers include: • "There is no need they say" – the speech makes clear that the grandmother's efforts are unappreciated/misunderstood • "the needles still move" – the present tense makes clear the persistence of the grandmother in continuing to stay busy • "their rhythms in the working of your hands" – the word choice makes clear her skill • "once again … fisher-girl." – the sibilance of "sure and skilful" makes clear her past, the way that she had to work hard to get by • Alliteration of "master of your movements then" emphasises her skill in the past • Sibilance and onomatopoeia of "slit the still-tickling quick silver fish" recreating the sound of the needles working • Imagery of "silver fish" suggesting that she makes the needles come to life/can control their movement • "Hard work … of necessity" word choice makes clear the austerity of her life/her need to work
46.	Candidates should analyse how the poet conveys what the grandmother's life was like as a younger woman. 3 marks can be awarded for reference plus detailed/insightful comment; 1 mark for reference plus more basic comment. 0 marks for reference/quotation alone.	3	Possible answers include: • Repetition of "once the hands" emphasising the number of tasks, showing stages of married life – wedding day, caring for husband, looking after children/bringing up family • Word choice of "the hand-span waist" uses the word "hand" to refer to the grandmother as slim and fragile • Word choice of "scrubbed his back" shows her performing a task for husband, working hard • Alliteration of "made do and mended" emphasising the repetitive tasks/need to scrimp and save and make the best of what they had • Onomatopoeia and sibilance of "scraped and slaved slapped" emphasising the repetitive nature of her life • Series of verbs "mended scraped … slaved slapped" emphasising the number of tasks which she had to perform • Word choice of "slapped sometimes" shows that she was capable of being harsh and strict when she felt it was necessary

Question	Expected Response	Max mark	Additional guidance
47.	Candidates should identify the grandchildren's attitude to their grandmother and explain how it has been conveyed. 2 marks can be awarded for one example with detailed/insightful comments or two examples with more basic comments. 0 marks for reference/quotation alone.	2	Possible answers include: • "But now …" — conjunction shows that despite all that their grandmother has done, her children seem ungrateful/do not understand her • "there is no need"/"no necessity" shows the children's failure to understand the grandmother's need to be busy and productive • Repetition of "too much … too many" shows that the children are extremely insistent and constantly ask her to stop • "wave them goodbye Sunday" shows how regularly they visit but that they ultimately leave the grandmother alone • Ellipsis of "there's no necessity … " suggests that they continue to protest at the amount of knitting, and consider her efforts a waste of time
48.	Candidates should show understanding of the term "conclusion" and show how the content of lines 34-45 continues — or contrasts with — ideas and/or language from the previous lines. 3 marks can be awarded for three appropriate, basic comments. A detailed/insightful comment on one example may be awarded 2 marks. Other examples are acceptable. 0 marks for reference/quotation alone.	3	Possible answers include: **Ideas** • Grandmother's aged frailty compared to younger, stronger "versions" of her • Her skills remain, though not necessarily understood/appreciated **Language** • "big on shrunken wrists" emphasises the physical damage done to the grandmother, contrasts with the "hand-span" waist earlier in the poem • Series of minor sentences/adjectives of "Swollen-jointed. Red. Arthritic. Old" emphasising the accumulated damage to her hands and wrists, climaxing with the simple conclusion that she is "old" • "But" at the beginning of the sentence and line emphasising that despite her ailment the grandmother continues to knit tirelessly • Enjambment of "But … stop" in contrast to the line "Swollen-jointed … Old." emphasising that her grandmother is in perpetual motion • Word "rhythms" from earlier in the poem emphasising the regular, faultless nature of the grandmother's knitting • Word choice of "easily" placed on a line of its own emphasises how effortless it is • Repeated structure of "as if … remembered … as if … forgotten" showing that the movement has become almost instinctive • "remembered … forgotten" refers back to her grandmother's life previously
49.	Candidates should discuss the importance of the theme of memory in Lochhead's work and should refer to appropriate textual evidence to support their discussion. 0 marks for reference/quotation alone. Candidates can answer in bullet points in this final question, or write a number of linked statements.	10	Up to 2 marks can be achieved for identifying elements of commonality as identified in the question, ie the theme of memory in other poems by Lochhead. A further 2 marks can be achieved for reference to the extract given. 6 additional marks can be awarded for discussion of similar references to at least one other poem by the poet. In practice this means: Identification of commonality (2) (eg: theme, characterisation, use of imagery, setting, or any other key element…) from the extract: 1 x relevant reference to technique/idea/feature (1) 1 x appropriate comment (1) (maximum of 2 marks only for discussion of extract) From at least one other text/part of the text: as above (x3) for up to 6 marks

Question	Expected Response	Max mark	Additional guidance
49.	(continued)		OR more detailed comment x2 for up to 6 marks Thus, the final 6 marks can be gained by a combination of 3, 2 and 1 marks depending on the level of depth/detail/insight. The aim would be to encourage quality of comment, rather than quantity of references. In comments on other poems, possible references include: • *The Bargain*: memory of perfect day in love — sense of impermanence • *View of Scotand/Love Song*: contrast and continuum — past rituals and more genuine personal Hogmanays • *Some Old Photographs*: romanticising of past undercut by sense of reality Many other references are possible.

Text 4 — Poetry — *Sounds of the Day* by Norman MacCaig

Question	Expected Response	Max mark	Additional guidance
50.	Candidates should demonstrate awareness of how the poet uses poetic technique to create a vivid sense of place. A single detailed/insightful comment may be awarded 2 marks; more basic comments will be worth 1 mark each. 0 marks for reference/quotation alone.	4	Possible answers include: • Onomatopoeia of "clatter" illustrates vivid/loud/strident sound of horses' hooves which were a familiar part of everyday life. • Alliteration in "clatter came" emphasises the expected quality/ordinariness of the sound. • Sibilance of "horses crossing" creates a soothing tone to echo his feelings of contentment in this place. • Onomatopoeia of "creaked". The high pitched sound conveys the energy of the location/the variety of sounds surrounding the narrator. • Consonance of "snuffling puff" contrasts with harsher sounds to create a sense of reassurance, establishing the blanket of sounds which were part of the environment. • Repetition of "blocking ... unblocking" to echo the cyclical order of the natural world and its continuous, everyday sounds. • Imagery of "black drums rolled". Just as a drum roll is a loud and booming sound, the poet is suggesting that the roar of the sea illustrates the strength and power of nature. Reference could be made to word choice of "black" foreshadowing the difficulty that lies ahead. • Parallel structure of "when......it was" to reinforce the familiar/customary/regular pattern of the place and its inhabitants. • Humorous/ironic reference to the "lapwing" conveys MacCaig's dislike of the attitude of self-interested landowners whose attitudes are mirrored by the bird's territorial instinct
51.	Candidates should demonstrate awareness of the intrinsic nature of the change in circumstance. This may be implicit in comments on how the poet uses poetic technique to convey the change. A single detailed/insightful comment may be awarded 2 marks; more basic comments will be awarded 1 mark each. Reference alone: 0. Mere identification of feature: 0.		Possible answers include: • Sibilance/onomatopoeia of "scraped shut" mirrors the emotional pain of the narrator as the closing door scratches the hard surface creating a harsh/unnatural/unpleasant sound. Contrasts with previous stanza which highlighted the reassuring sounds of the natural world. • Symbol of a door scraping shut to echo the fundamental nature of the change/finality of the closed door emphasises the cessation of what has gone before. • Positioning of "end" emphatically conveys the absolute/definitive nature of the change (and its implications) on the narrator. • Word choice of "all the sounds" reinforces the dramatic change. All that mattered is gone as the previously comforting effect of "all the sounds" is now lost.

Question	Expected Response	Max mark	Additional guidance
51.	*(continued)*		• Change in verb tense to present (at end of stanza) makes clear the impact of the change as the immediacy invites the reader to share their distress. • Candidates may also make valid comments on the single sentence, three line stanza contrasting with the previous stanza, to exemplify the change from the free/busy/open environment of the natural world to the confined and enclosed space in which he now finds himself.
52.	Candidates should demonstrate awareness of how the poet makes clear the impact of this incident on the narrator, through his use of language. A detailed/insightful comment may be awarded 2 marks; more basic comments will be awarded 1 mark each. 0 marks for reference/quotation alone. Mere identification of feature: 0. Be alert to answers which make valid points dealing with imagery as word choice.	4	Possible answers include: **Stanza 3** • Word choice of "You left me" creates a blunt/accusatory tone. Displays narrator's emotional response. Candidates may offer valid comments linked to feelings of shock/anger/resentment. • Reference may also be made to personal pronouns "You…me" to create intimacy and further establish the deep emotional effects of the parting. • Word choice (and positioning) of "beside" demonstrates the lack of the physical presence of the loved one, conveying feelings of isolation. • Word choice of "quietest" stands in stark contrast to life affirming sounds of stanza 1 emphasising the void of meaningful sound now the person has left. • Candidates may also comment on the short, single sentence stanza which is stripped bare to echo/mirror the raw emotions of the narrator. **Stanza 4** • Personal pronouns "I … I … my" convey the narrator's immediate reaction as being somewhat naïve/self-indulgent. • Word choice of "pride only" suggests the narrator's reaction to the shock was initially on a superficial level. • Positioning of "forgetting that" signals the dawning realisation that the emotional effects of the loss will be on a much deeper level. • Word choice/onomatopoeia of "plunge" has connotations of depth/immersion suggesting that the impact will be much greater than initially perceived. • Word choice of "freezing" creates a bleak/despairing tone highlighting his pain/distress/anguish. • Positioning of "you feel" begins to plot how the narrator's positive emotions have been overtaken and shut down as a consequence of the parting. • Extended metaphor "bangle of ice … numb". Just as a hand thrust into ice-cold water will take a moment to react, so the poet suggests that the impact of the loss moves from an initial, localised shock into a general closing down of all feeling. The blow of the person leaving has overwhelmed the narrator and isolated him from all that was previously meaningful. This clarifies the poet's message about the all-consuming nature of loss.
53.	Candidates should discuss how MacCaig uses contrast to explore theme in his work and should refer to appropriate textual evidence to support their discussion. 0 marks for reference/quotation alone. Candidates can answer in bullet points in this final question, or write a number of linked statements.	10	Up to 2 marks can be achieved for identifying elements of commonality as identified in the question, ie MacCaig's use of contrast to develop theme. A further 2 marks can be achieved for reference to the extract given. 6 additional marks can be awarded for discussion of similar references to at least one other poem by the poet. <u>In practice this means:</u> Identification of commonality (2) (eg: theme, characterisation, use of imagery, setting, or any other key element…)

Question	Expected Response	Max mark	Additional guidance
53.	*(continued)*		from the extract:
			1 x relevant reference to technique/idea/feature (1)
			1 x appropriate comment (1)
			(maximum of 2 marks only for discussion of extract)
			from at least one other text/part of the text:
			as above (x3) for up to 6 marks
			OR
			more detailed comment x2 for up to 6 marks
			Thus, the final 6 marks can be gained by a combination of 3, 2 and 1 marks depending on the level of depth/detail/insight. The aim would be to encourage quality of comment, rather than quantity of references.
			In comments on other poems, possible references include:
			• The external grotesqueness contrasting with the inner beauty in *Assisi*
			• The noisy life force that is *Aunt Julia* contrasting with the silence of death
			• The professionalism contrasting with the raw suffering in *Visiting Hour*
			Many other references are possible.

Text 5 — Poetry — *Heroes* by Sorley MacLean

Question	Expected Response	Max mark	Additional guidance
54.	Candidates should reference the use of poetic technique and explain how this contributes to the effectiveness of the opening stanza. 2 marks for detailed/insightful comment plus reference; 1 mark for more basic comment plus reference. 0 marks for reference/quotation alone.	2	Possible answers include: Repetition of names of legendary heroes effective in establishing theme of heroism in battle OR Contrast of specific Scottish names and place-names with anonymous English soldier or "everyman" effective in establishing tone of irony/theme of heroism OR "I did not see" effective in establishing poet's feelings about/attitudes towards the English soldier/tone of irony
55.	Candidates should discuss the speaker's attitude towards the English soldier. 2 marks for reference plus detailed/insightful comment; 1 mark for reference plus more basic comment. For full marks, candidates should make reference to both sections of the poem. 0 marks for reference/quotation alone.	4	Possible answers include: **From lines 5-11** • "poor little chap"/"chubby cheeks" or reference — word choice conveys sympathy towards soldier because he is young/inexperienced/childish/to be pitied • "knees grinding" or reference — word choice conveys sympathy for soldier's nervousness/anxiety • "pimply unattractive face" or reference — word choice conveys soldier is not conventionally handsome/heroic/poet is unsympathetic towards soldier/does not admire soldier • "garment of the bravest spirit" or reference — word choice conveys the poet feels the soldier's outward appearance hides/covers his bravery • He was not a hit "in the pub in the time of the fists being closed" or reference — word choice/use of inverted commas for legal jargon/formal language shows that poet dismisses the idea that soldier was typically drunk/violent • "a lion against the breast of battle" or reference — word choice (contrasting with earlier word choice) conveys poet's admiration for soldier's bravery

Question	Expected Response	Max mark	Additional guidance
55.	*(continued)*		**From lines 35-38** • "a great warrior of England" or reference — tone of irony • "a poor manikin on whom no eye would rest" or reference — metaphor conveys poet's sympathy towards soldier's youth/inexperience/inferiority • "no Alasdair of Glen Garry" or reference — irony of soldier's achievements in comparison with legendary hero • "he took a little weeping to my eyes" or reference — word choice/use of unusual verb construction/irony conveys that poet feels sadness but simultaneously undermines soldier's heroism
56.	Candidates should quote or reference at least two examples of use of poetic technique and explain fully how these convey the horror of war. 2 marks may be awarded for reference plus detailed/insightful comment; 1 mark for reference plus more basic comment. 0 marks for reference/quotation alone.	4	Possible answers include: • "morose wounding showers" or reference — word choice/personification conveys power/darkness of attack • "His hour came" or reference — word choice conveys idea that his time for glory/death has arrived/is inevitable • "notched iron splinters" or reference — consonance/word choice conveys brutality of attack • "in the smoke and flame" or reference — word choice conveys poor visibility/darkness/danger • "shaking and terror of the battlefield" or reference — word choice focuses on fear/anxiety of soldiers in face of attack/lack of heroism • "bullet shower" or reference — metaphor conveys amount and range of shots/attack • "it wasn't much time he got" or reference — structure/blunt word choice conveys speed of attack/death • "He kept his guns to the tanks" or reference — word choice conveys soldier's bravery/determination in face of attack • "bucking with tearing crashing screech" or reference — repetition of participles/consonance emphasises violence/speed/extent of attack • "that biff" or reference — informal/slang word/understatement/irony to describe fatal blow/shot conveys power of blow/shot
57.	Candidates should discuss how MacLean develops a theme or themes through his observation of people or places and should refer to appropriate textual evidence to support their discussion. 0 marks for reference/quotation alone. Candidates can answer in bullet points in this final question, or write a number of linked statements.	10	Up to 2 marks can be achieved for identifying elements of commonality as identified in the question, ie how MacLean develops theme through observation of people or places. A further 2 marks can be achieved for reference to the extract given. 6 additional marks can be awarded for discussion of similar references to at least one other poem by the poet. In practice this means: Identification of commonality (2) (eg: theme, characterisation, use of imagery, setting, or any other key element...) from the extract: 1 x relevant reference to technique/idea/feature (1) 1 x appropriate comment (1) (maximum of 2 marks only for discussion of extract) from at least one other text/part of the text: as above (x3) for up to 6 marks OR more detailed comment x2 for up to 6 marks Thus, the final 6 marks can be gained by a combination of 3, 2 and 1 marks depending on the level of depth/detail/insight. The aim would be to encourage quality of comment, rather than quantity of references.

Question	Expected Response	Max mark	Additional guidance
57.	(continued)		In comments on other poems, possible references include: • *Hallaig*: love song to place develops theme of injustice (of clearances) • *Screapadal*: beauty of area used as warning against destructive urge of humanity • *Shores*: love explored in terms of ocean/beach/rocks Many other references are possible.

Text 6 — Poetry — *The Ferryman's Arms* by Don Paterson

Question	Expected Response	Max mark	Additional guidance
58.	Candidates should discuss how the poet uses poetic technique to introduce theme in the opening. 1 mark should be awarded for one main theme introduced in the opening. 2 marks should be awarded for comment on language/literary techniques. 2 marks may be awarded for one detailed, insightful comment on one example; OR 2 marks may be awarded for two more basic comments on two examples. 0 marks for reference/quotation alone.	3	Possible answers include: **Themes** • Death • The divided self **References** • Symbolism of "Ferryman" — reference to Greek mythology, Charon ferrying souls of dead to Hades • "Arms" — suggests embrace by death • "About to sit down" — sense of life interrupted by suddenness of death/recognition of divided self • References to darkness ("Guinness", "darkened back room") = death • Symbol/simile of moth = soul taking flight/drawn towards the darkness • "ten minutes to kill" — cliché suggests opposite: time is killing us • "hell of it" — horror of life being used up/afterlife • "half-pint of Guinness": incompleteness • "took myself on" — paradox present in any challenge to self • Contrast between passive verb ("was magnetized") and active ("I took") — self as opposing antagonists
59.	For full marks, candidates should provide comments on example(s) showing both "stages" in the change of mood. This could be done through 2 marks for a detailed/insightful comment on one example OR more basic comments on two different examples. 0 marks for reference/quotation alone.	4	Possible answers include: **Examples suggesting alienation/uncertainty** • Symbolism "Slotting/a coin in the tongue" — ancient ritual of preparing dead for final journey: turns game into encounter with mortality • "stood with my back turned" — symbolic of things going on behind his back/not grasping what is happening • "rumble" — symbolic reference to thunder, approach of something ominous • "cowl" — reference to hooded figure (death) • Sound: "abrupt intestinal rumble" — suggests discomfort, lack of control • "clacked on the slate" onomatopoeia suggests alarming, discordant sound • "striplight batted awake" — intermittent sound suggests inefficiency, neglect • "dusty green cowl" creates image of slightly squalid, unnerving "trap" waiting for him • Word choice: "looked around for a cue" — sense of helplessness • "cue" double meaning ("cue" in drama) — need for hint to help in understanding • Examples suggesting confidence • Word/verb choice: "I went on to make" — dynamic verb suggesting control of world around him • Word choice/connotations: "immaculate clearance" — sense of clean, in control, powerful action

Question	Expected Response	Max mark	Additional guidance
59.	*(continued)*		<ul><li>Metaphor: "low punch" suggests confident manipulation of rules</li><li>Word choice: "low punch ... wee dab of side" suggests speaker confidently practising trickery</li><li>"vanishing trick": metaphor —sense of magical accomplishment</li><li>Word choice: "stopped/before gently rolling back": sense of poise and control reinforces mood of confidence</li><li>Enjambment: "stopped/before ... " suggests smooth movement = confidence (as above)</li><li>Personification: "shouldering its way" — white ball moving with confidence reflects the speaker's increased confidence</li></ul>
60.	Candidates should show understanding of the term "conclusion" and show how the content of the second stanza continues — or contrasts with — ideas and/or language from the first stanza. 3 marks can be awarded for three appropriate, basic comments. A detailed/insightful comment on one example may be awarded 2 marks. Other examples are acceptable. 0 marks for reference/quotation alone.	3	Possible answers include: **Ideas**<ul><li>The idea of the divided self</li><li>Our lack of choice/journey towards death, which we face alone</li></ul>**Language**<ul><li>Visual image of ferry arriving, almost unobtrusively ("without breaking the skin of the water") or 'innocently' ("chugged" is childish, non-threatening word) echoes "drawn, like a moth" and "gently rolling back" but this is the awaited ferry, bringing the idle passing of time (this life?) to an end</li><li>"Black as my stout", "somewhere unspeakable" returns us to an ominous, mysterious world (shadowed by death)</li><li>"Foaming lip mussitates endlessly ... trying to read and re-read the shoreline" is a metaphor for our lifelong, constant attempts to understand life and death (develops idea of drinking Guinness)</li><li>Poem closes on image of "losing opponent" — sense of this part of self being temporarily defeated or left behind emphasised by disrupted rhythm, short, parenthetical phrases ("stuck in his tent of light", "for practice"), enjambment (" sullenly/knocking")</li><li>Paradox of ferry possibly taking "my losing opponent" who is also himself. First clear reference to this "opponent" as separate: game can now be seen in this context — theme of divided self falls into place</li></ul>

Question	Expected Response	Max mark	Additional guidance
61.	Candidates should discuss how Paterson uses ordinary experiences to explore deeper truths about humanity and should refer to appropriate textual evidence to support their discussion. 0 marks for reference/quotation alone. Candidates can answer in bullet points in this final question, or write a number of linked statements.	10	Up to 2 marks can be achieved for identifying elements of commonality as identified in the question, ie Paterson's use of language to explore the deeper truths behind ordinary experiences. A further 2 marks can be achieved for reference to the extract given. 6 additional marks can be awarded for discussion of similar references to at least one other poem by the poet. <u>In practice this means:</u> Identification of commonality (2) (eg: theme, characterisation, use of imagery, setting, or any other key element…) from the extract: 1 x relevant reference to technique/idea/feature (1) 1 x appropriate comment (1) (maximum of 2 marks only for discussion of extract) from at least one other text/part of the text: as above (x3) for up to 6 marks OR more detailed comment x2 for up to 6 marks Thus, the final 6 marks can be gained by a combination of 3, 2 and 1 marks depending on the level of depth/detail/insight. The aim would be to encourage quality of comment, rather than quantity of references. In comments on other poems, possible references include: • Use of image of gallstone being kicked by boy; game linked to theme of death in *Nil, Nil* • The central symbol of the thread — fragility of human life in *The Thread* • Paradox used in *Waking with Russell* to explore nature of (parental) love Many other references are possible.

Section 2 – CRITICAL ESSAY
Supplementary marking grid

	Marks 20-19	Marks 18-16	Marks 15-13	Marks 12-10	Marks 9-6	Marks 5-0
Knowledge and understanding	thorough knowledge and understanding of the text	secure knowledge and understanding of the text	clear knowledge and understanding of the text	adequate knowledge and understanding of the text	limited evidence of knowledge and understanding of the text	very little knowledge and understanding of the text
The critical essay demonstrates:	perceptive selection of textual evidence to support line of argument which is fluently structured and expressed	detailed textual evidence to support line of thought which is coherently structured and expressed	clear textual evidence to support line of thought which is clearly structured and expressed	adequate textual evidence to support line of thought, which is adequately structured and expressed	limited textual evidence to support line of thought which is structured and expressed in a limited way	very little textual evidence to support line of thought which shows very little structure or clarity of expression
	perceptive focus on the demands of the question	secure focus on the demands of the question	clear focus on the demands of the question	adequate focus on the demands of the question	limited focus on the demands of the question	very little focus on the demands of the question
Analysis **The critical essay demonstrates:**	perceptive analysis of the effect of features of language/filmic techniques	detailed analysis of the effect of language/filmic techniques	clear analysis of the effect of features of language/filmic techniques	adequate analysis of features of language/filmic techniques	limited analysis of the effect of features of language/filmic techniques	very little analysis of features of language/filmic techniques
Evaluation **The critical essay demonstrates**	committed evaluative stance with respect to the text and the task	engaged evaluative stance with respect to the text and the task	clear evaluative stance with respect to the text and the task	adequate evidence of an evaluative stance with respect to the text and the task	limited evidence of an evaluative stance with respect to the text and the task	very little evidence of an evaluative stance with respect to the text and the task
Technical Accuracy **The critical essay demonstrates:**	few errors in spelling, grammar, sentence construction, punctuation and paragraphing the ability to be understood at first reading			significant number of errors in spelling, grammar, sentence construction, punctuation and paragraphing which impedes understanding		

HIGHER ENGLISH
2015

PAPER 1 — READING FOR UNDERSTANDING ANALYSIS AND EVALUATION

Marking Instructions for each question

Question	Expected Answer(s)	Max Mark	Additional Guidance
1.	Candidates should identify two positive aspects of Central Valley, California, given in lines 1–5. Candidates must use their own words. No marks for straight lifts from the passage. *Any two of the points in the "Additional Guidance" column for 1 mark each.*	2	Possible answers: • idyllic/pastoral ("almond trees", "sweet air", "orchards", "fields of ...") • perfect/attractive ("sweet air", "vision") • diverse ("pomegranates, pistachios, grapes and apricots") • bountiful/fertile/productive ("million almond trees", "Beyond the almond orchards ... fields of ...", "two million dairy cows ... six billion dollars' worth ...") • vast/expansive/scale ("a million almond trees", "Beyond ... were fields of ...", "Somewhere in the distance")
2.	Candidates should analyse how the writer's use of language creates a negative impression of Central Valley in lines 6–10. For full marks there should be comments on at least 2 examples. 2 marks may be awarded for reference plus detailed/insightful comment; 1 mark for more basic comment; 0 marks for reference alone. *Possible answers shown in the "Additional Guidance" column.*	4	Possible answers: • "deeply disturbing" suggests unsettling/unnatural nature of agriculture in Central Valley • contrast e.g. "it may sound like ... but it is ..." — emphasises the unnatural qualities of Central Valley • repetition/list of "no birds, no butterflies, no beetles" — drives home the absence of nature/lack of wildlife • "single blade of grass" suggests that the most basic elements of nature have been eradicated here/wild nature is not tolerated • "only bees" highlights the strange lack of insect life • "arrive by lorry"/"the bees are hired by the day" — highlights the artificiality of Central Valley • "multibillion-dollar"/"industry" suggests anonymity/mass-produced for profit
3.	Candidates should analyse how the writer makes clear her disapproval of dairy farming methods used in Central Valley. For full marks there must be comment on both word choice and sentence structure, but these do not need to be evenly divided. 2 marks may be awarded for reference plus detailed/insightful comment; 1 mark for more basic comment; 0 marks for reference alone. Possible answers shown in the "Additional Guidance" column.	4	Possible answers: Word Choice • "last" suggests farmers see the cows as disposable objects, to be dismissed like rubbish when no longer productive • "crammed" suggests stifling, dangerous conditions • "barren" suggests emptiness, sterility, discomfort of the pens • "tiny patches" suggests restrictive, cramped areas in which cows are housed • "listlessly" suggests lack of life, lethargy, conditions weaken cows • "artificial (diets)" — emphasises the unnatural, unhealthy treatment of these cows • "pushed" suggests forceful manipulation • "grotesquely" suggests this type of dairy farming is monstrous, hideous • "worn out" suggests this type of farming is destructive • "short lives" — poignant description emphasises the tragic and unnatural consequences

Question	Expected Answer(s)	Max Mark	Additional Guidance
3.	*(continued)*		**Sentence Structure** • positioning of "As for the cows," at the start of this paragraph creates a despairing tone and/or introduces the negative description of the cows' lives • inversion used in "Crammed … antibiotics." highlights the atrocious conditions in which the cows are kept • list "fed, milked or injected with antibiotics" emphasises the assembly line/uncaring manner of the farms, suggesting the cows are merely part of a repetitive industrial process • list of procedures ("selective breeding … hormones") highlights the seemingly scientific procedures involved, making this type of farming seem like a cold and uncaring experiment on animals • climactic final sentence ("In their short lives … grass.") emphatically/dramatically highlights the contrast between these cows and the environment with which we would normally associate them
4.	For full marks candidates should show understanding of the key point: the movement from farming methods in California to their application in the UK. 2 marks may be awarded for detailed/insightful comment supported by appropriate use of reference/quotation; 1 mark for more basic comment; 0 marks for reference alone. *Possible answers shown in the "Additional Guidance" column.*	2	Possible references include: • the writer's change of focus from the USA to UK is signalled by the question "Could the British … look like this?" • the writer's move to consider intensive farming in the UK is suggested by "Farming in Britain … intensification from America" • the writer goes on to suggest that some of the intensive farming methods used in the USA — "bees arrive by lorry"— may soon arrive in the UK — "Bees are disappearing" • the writer goes on to suggest that some intensive farming methods are already being adopted in the UK, "mega-dairies and mega-piggeries" • the writer highlights the impact of intensive farming already being witnessed in the UK "countryside too sterile … native birds"
5.	Candidates should summarise the differences between Government food policy and consumer wishes. For full marks, both sides must be dealt with but not necessarily equally divided. Candidates must attempt to use their own words. No marks for straight lifts from passage. *Any four points from the "Additional Guidance" column for 1 mark each.*	4	Possible answers include: Government food policy: • buy more British/regional produce ("urging families to buy British food") • buy less foreign food ("Choosing to buy fewer imports") • ease pressure on farmers ("churn out more for less") • be more environmentally aware ("more eco-friendly way of eating") • buy in-season/healthy food ("seasonal fruit and vegetables") Consumer wishes: • drawn to less expensive produce ("addicted to cheap meat … products") • not concerned about origins of food ("supply lines … globe") • previously exotic/expensive food now commonplace/inexpensive ("once delicacies … cheap as chips") • expectation of variety "supply lines … globe"

Question	Expected Answer(s)	Max Mark	Additional Guidance
6.	Candidates should analyse how imagery and sentence structure convey the writer's criticism of industrial farming. For full marks there should be comments on both imagery and sentence structure but these do not have to be evenly divided. 2 marks may be awarded for reference plus detailed/insightful comment; 1 mark for more basic comment; 0 marks for reference alone. *Possible answers shown in the "Additional Guidance" column.*	4	Possible answers: Imagery: • "dirty secret": suggests that the methods used in factory farming are so shocking that they cannot be revealed • "front line": suggests that industrial farming is a desperate struggle against competitors, with frequent business casualties • "treadmill": suggests that industrial farming is very hard work and consists of never-ending repetitive chores • "plummeting": suggests that proximity to an industrial farm causes a devastating drop in the value of local homes Sentence structure: • Parenthesis "to investigate … produced" makes clear the specific nature of the "truth" • List of countries "France … South America" indicates extent of intensive farming • Colon in line 38 introduces example of people directly affected • Dash in line 39 introduces example of people directly affected • Repetitive sentence openings "I talked … I also talked" emphasises the scale the problem, based on her evidence gathering/variety of people affected • List "their homes … pollution" emphasises range of stories by people affected
7.	Candidates should explain how the writer continues the idea that the Central Valley dairy farming is "nightmarish", by making 3 key points. Candidates must attempt to use their own words. No marks for straight lifts from passage. *Any three points from the "Additional Guidance" column for 1 mark each.*	3	Possible answers include: • visible contamination of air/pollution ("yellowish-grey smog") • waste products in the ground ("bovine population … people") • the animals are kept in terrible conditions ("mud, corrugated iron and concrete.") • the overpowering smell ("nauseating reek") • huge buildings are a blight on the landscape ("array of towering … muddy pens.") • (apocalyptic) sense of desolation ("human population is sparse")
8.	Candidates should evaluate the final paragraph's effectiveness as a conclusion to the writer's criticism of industrial farming. For full marks there must be appropriate attention to the idea of a conclusion but this does not have to be limited to points about structure. Candidates may make valid points about the emotive/rhetorical impact of the conclusion. 2 marks awarded for detailed/insightful comment plus reference. 1 mark awarded for a more basic comment. *Possible answers shown in the "Additional Guidance" column.*	2	Possible answers include: • by giving details of the proposed mega-dairy in Lincolnshire, the writer reminds us of her earlier point that the British countryside faces a similar fate to that of Central Valley • the writer reminds us of the ludicrous size of these factory farms by revealing the enormous number of cows planned for this mega-dairy • by including the ridiculous claim that "cows do not belong in fields" the writer forcefully reminds us that those who practise intensive farming have scant regard for nature or natural processes • the writer concludes the passage with a warning that factory farms are getting larger in a rather surreptitious way, suggesting that we are being duped by the unscrupulous owners of these farms • the writer's rather poignant final sentence reminds the readers of the unnatural nature of this transition from the outdoors to indoors

Question	Expected Answer(s)	Max Mark	Additional Guidance
9.	Candidates should identify three key areas of agreement in the two passages. Candidates can use bullet points in this final question, or write a number of linked statements. *Approach to marking shown in the "Additional Guidance" column.* *Key areas of agreement shown in grid below. Other answers are possible.*	5	The following guidelines should be used: Five marks — identification of three key areas of agreement with detailed/insightful use of supporting evidence Four marks — identification of three key areas of agreement with appropriate use of supporting evidence Three marks — identification of three key areas of agreement Two marks — identification of two key areas of agreement One mark — identification of one key area of agreement Zero marks — failure to identify any key area of agreement and/or misunderstanding of task

	Area of Agreement	Passage 1	Passage 2
1.	Intensive farming is a highly productive process.	• size and fertility of the farms in Central Valley • high yields from dairy cows in Central Valley • farmers "churn out m ore or less"	• increased productivity of farms following introduction of intensive methods after Second Word War • higher numbers of chickens raised in less space • shorter time taken for animals to reach "edible size"
2.	Intensive farming yields affordable food for everyone.	• meat, fish and dairy products from factory farms are much cheaper • whole chickens sell for ridiculously low prices • farmers are under pressure to produce cheaper food	• factory farming fulfilled post-war policy of "cheap meat, eggs and cheese for everyone" • intensive farming allowed poorer people to have a much richer diet
3.	Intensive farming has brought about a change in people's dietary habits.	• previously expensive foods are now within the reach of everyone • exotic foods are now widely available • cheap meats contain more fat	• we have switched from a diet which was based on cereals/vegetable to one which is high in animal fats
4.	Intensive farming damages the environment and wildlife.	• nature is almost absent in Central Valley • bee populations are in decline • bird populations are in decline • natural habitats are disappearing • the UK countryside is increasingly barren • "desecration" of countryside • Central Valley is heavily polluted	• traditional, attractive farms are disappearing • hedgerows and wildlife are being lost • rivers and streams are being polluted
5.	Intensive farming causes undue stress and suffering to farm animals.	• factory farm animals are treated like machines rather than living creatures • these farm animals have shorter lifespans • conditions are very poor for these animals	• too many animals crammed into small spaces • unnatural for animals to be indoors all of the time • animal growth rates are unnatural • our misguided view that farm animals and pets have different needs causes suffering
6.	People who live beside or work in factory farms are adversely affected.	• property values are affected by industrial farms • people become ill because of pollution from these farms • air quality in Central Valley is worse than that of a big city • ruined aesthetics of Central Valley • farmers are under constant pressure to produce "more with less"	• introduction of intensive farming in the UK caused thousands of job losses in rural areas • the livelihoods of many traditional farmers have been badly affected

	Area of Agreement	Passage 1	Passage 2
7.	We need to restrict/oppose this development of intensive farming in the UK.	• the writer argues that factory farming is not the only way to produce affordable food • Central Valley is presented as a warning about what could happen in the UK • the writer notes that the movement of farm animals indoors is insidious and unnatural	• in the final paragraph, the writer provides us with a set of guidelines on what "we need to" do in order to return to the "environmentally friendly, humane and healthy" farming methods of the past
8.	Intensive farming may have a negative impact on human health	• cheap meats contain more fat • meat contaminated with drugs • quality of produce is low • health problems linked to pollution produced by intensive farms	• contaminated meat enters the human food chain • degenerative diseases connected to a high fat diet
9.	The unnatural nature of intensive farming	• limited lifespan of animals • animals prevented from living naturally outdoors • natural processes subject to human intervention	• animals denied natural living conditions • farm animals' lives considerably shortened in recent years • detrimental effects of unnatural animal diets

PAPER 2 – CRITCAL READING

SECTION 1 – Scottish Text

For all Scottish Texts, marking of the final question, for 10 marks, should be guided by the following generic instruction in conjunction with the specific advice given for the question on each Scottish Text:

Candidates can answer in bullet points in this final question, or write a number of linked statements.

0 marks for reference/quotation alone.

Up to 2 marks can be achieved for identifying elements of commonality as identified in the question.
A further 2 marks can be achieved for reference to the extract given.
6 additional marks can be awarded for discussion of similar references to at least one other part of the text (or other story or poem) by the writer.

<u>In practice this means:</u>

Identification of commonality (2) (e.g.: theme, characterisation, use of imagery, settng, or any other key element …)

from the extract:

1 × relevant reference to technique/idea/feature (1)
1 × appropriate comment (1)
(maximum of 2 marks only for discussion of extract)

from at least one other text/part of the text:

2 marks for detailed/insightful comment plus quotation/reference

1 mark for more basic comment plus quotation/reference

0 marks for quotation/reference alone

(Up to 6 marks).

SCOTTISH TEXT (DRAMA)

Text 1 — Drama — *The Slab Boys* by John Byrne

Question	Expected Answer(s)	Max Mark	Additional Guidance
1.	Candidates should explain the contrast between the attitudes of Jack and Phil to Alan. For full marks both sides of contrast must be covered.	2	Possible answers include: • Jack: helpful, friendly, deferential, due to Alan's social position/family connections/youth • Phil: aggressive/hostile as he does not want to be patronised after being dismissed
2.	Candidates should analyse how the tension between Spanky and Phil is made clear in lines 16–31. 2 marks awarded for detailed/insightful comment plus quotation/reference. 1 mark for more basic comment plus quotation/reference. 0 marks for quotation/reference alone.	4	Possible answers include: • Spanky's use of questions/exclamations show his irritation with Phil eg 'How should I know? I've got all these dishes to wash! Can you not give us a hand?' • Spanky's wounding retaliation about Phil losing his job: 'At least I still am one (a Slab Boy)' • Phil's sarcastic response to Spanky's comment identifying himself with Alan: 'Aw, it's 'me and the boy' now, is it?' • Phil's disgust at Spanky's abandonment of him/conforming to the conventional work ethic 'I think I'm going to be sick'
3.	Candidates should analyse how language is used to convey the feelings of Phil and/or Curry. 2 marks awarded for detailed/insightful comment plus quotation/reference 1 mark for more basic comment plus quotation/reference. 0 marks for quotation/reference alone.	4	Possible answers include: **Curry:** • Dismissive towards Phil/gloating about his dismissal, shown in mock-helpful tone of 'Still here … any time' • Unsympathetic initially towards Phil/rules are rules attitude: formal language of 'Only urgent personal calls allowed' • Sympathetic (later) when discussing the plight of Phil's mother: 'She must've been badly injured' **Phil:** • Repeated questions demonstrating his incredulity and growing indignation that Curry is intruding into his personal life 'What … about it?' • Defiance/refusal to be an object of pity: use of blunt language/description emphasising the ludicrous visual effect rather than real pain of his mother's 'accident': 'What she done … simple'
4.	Candidates should discuss how humour is used to develop Phil's character. Candidates may choose to answer in bullet points in this final question or write a number of linked statements.	10	Up to 2 marks can be achieved for identifying elements of commonality as identified in the question, ie how humour is used to develop Phil's character. A further 2 marks can be achieved for reference to the extract given. 6 additional marks can be awarded for discussion of similar references from at least one other part of the text. In practice this means: Identification of commonality eg: Phil uses sarcasm/mockery/irony as a defence mechanism to help him cope with work or home problems From the extract: 2 marks for detailed/insightful comment plus quotation/reference; 1 mark for more basic comment plus quotation/reference; 0 marks for quotation/reference alone. eg "Nope … a Ford Prefect" use of bathos/name of car to 'correct' Curry's comment about the miracle shows his refusal to acknowledge the pain or seriousness of his mother's situation in front of Curry/humour used to protect/defend his own pride (2 marks)

Question	Expected Answer(s)	Max Mark	Additional Guidance
4.	*(continued)*		From at least one other text/part of the text: 2 marks for detailed/insightful comment plus quotation/reference; 1 mark for more basic comment plus quotation/reference; 0 marks for quotation/reference alone (Up to 6 marks). Possible answers include: • Phil and Spanky's witty banter and teasing of other characters/"Oh … what trade was that, Mr. Curry?" shows how he copes with his mundane life **(2)** • The farcical nature of Hector's "makeover"/reference to Phil forcing Hector into the clothes/the balaclava … shows Phil's cruelty towards others **(2)** • The use of black humour in the descriptions of Phil's mother/"The old dear's impromptu dip" — euphemism describes his mother's suicidal tendencies **(2)** • The attempts to get Lucille to accompany Hector to the Staffie shows that, underneath, Phil is a compassionate character **(2)** • Uses humour to show off/appear to be 'top dog'/put people down … — eg "You can't even get the tin trunks off a chocolate soldier, Jack" **(2)** Many other answers are possible.

Text 2 — Drama — *The Cheviot, the Stag and the Black, Black Oil* by John McGrath

Question	Expected Answer(s)	Max Mark	Additional Guidance
5.	Candidates should analyse how language is used to create different tones in the Duke's speeches, by referring to at least two examples. For full marks candidates must make reference to at least two distinct tones, but not necessarily in equal measure. 2 marks are awarded for detailed/insightful comment plus quotation/reference. 1 mark for more basic comment plus quotation/reference. 0 marks for quotation/reference alone	4	Possible answers include: Lines 1—4 • persuasive, evoking national pride and loyalty through "the Queen"/use of precedent and tradition through "as always" • business-like/authoritarian in evoking "My Commissioner informs me …" Lines 8—10 • patronising in the assumption that they can be bought off for personal gain: "6 golden sovereigns" • arrogant/presumptuous: "step up in an orderly manner" Lines 12—18 • angry in the demands for "an explanation" and swearing "damn it" because of Highland defiance • frustration that his argument has failed: "Have you no pride …?" • scaremongering tone in the use of hyperbole/threats: "the cruel Tsar of Russia installed in Dunrobin Castle" • accusatory/hectoring tone in the series of questions

Question	Expected Answer(s)	Max Mark	Additional Guidance
6.	Candidates should analyse how both the stage directions and dialogue in lines 17–27 convey the local people's defiance of the Duke. For full marks candidates must cover both stage directions and dialogue, but not necessarily in equal measure 2 marks are awarded for detailed/insightful comment plus quotation/reference. 1 mark for more basic comment plus quotation/reference. 0 marks for quotation/reference alone.	4	Possible answers include: Stage Directions • *'Silence.'* Creates an unsettling atmosphere, showing the tension between the Highlanders and the Duke • *'Nobody moves.'* The inaction of the Highlanders shows a passive resistance • *'OLD MAN stands'* shows the shift from passive resistance to active resistance • *'in the audience'* makes the audience identify with the man as a representative of the people/puts the audience in the position of the tenants Dialogue • The old man's respectful, reasonable response adds weight to his argument: "I am sorry …"/"your Grace" • The old man takes the Duke's threat as the basis of his counter-argument: "we could not expect worse treatment" • Use of personal pronouns "We … you" emphasises the lack of identification that the Highlanders have with the Duke's cause • Climactically mocking the Duke by suggesting that the Duke conscripts the sheep • The humorous solidarity shown by the collective "Baa-aa"
7.	Candidates should explain how the MC's speech brings this section of the play to an ironic conclusion. 2 marks are awarded for detailed/insightful comment. 1 mark for more basic comment. 0 marks for quotation/reference alone.	2	Possible answers include: • Description of the fate of the one man who did enlist whose family was treated badly, in contrast to the promise of financial reward • Duke's expectations/efforts in contrast to the lack of response • The futility of the Highlanders' defiance: after they were cleared off the land they had to enlist anyway • Use of the phrase 'The old tradition of loyal soldiering' when it was based on desperation rather than duty
8.	Candidates should discuss how McGrath develops the theme of change/resistance to change in this and at least one other extract from the play. Candidates may choose to answer in bullet points in this final question, or write a number of linked statements.	10	Up to 2 marks can be achieved for identifying elements of commonality as identified in the question, ie the development of the theme of change/resistance to change in the play. A further 2 marks can be achieved for reference to the extract given. 6 additional marks can be awarded for discussion of similar references to at least one other part of the text. In practice this means: Identification of commonality (theme, characterisation, use of imagery, setting, or any other key element …) eg Cultural/economical and social changes that have affected Scotland (1 mark) Variety of responses from the population to these changes (1 mark) From the extract: 2 marks for detailed/insightful comment plus quotation/reference;

Question	Expected Answer(s)	Max Mark	Additional Guidance
8.	*(continued)*		1 mark for more basic comment plus quotation/reference;
			0 marks for quotation/reference alone.
			eg Change in the attitude of the common people to authority from unquestioning obedience to resistance (2 marks)
			From elsewhere in the play:
			2 marks for detailed/insightful comment plus quotation/reference;
			1 mark for more basic comment plus quotation/reference;
			0 marks for quotation/reference alone
			(Up to 6 marks).
			Possible answers include:
			Role of women as defenders of the community in resisting the introduction of Cheviot sheep to the Highlands for example, female members' direct appeal to the audience when recounting Patrick Sellar's evictions in their community **(2)**
			The erosion of Gaelic culture through the banning of language, music etc for example, the role of the MC in disseminating historical information **(2)**
			Forced emigration to the colonies to maximise profit at the behest of figures of authority for example, the Duke of Selkirk's movement of his Lowland tenants to Canada **(2)**
			The continued eviction of tenants to free up land for hunting for example, Lady Phosphate's preference for gaming estates at the expense of the tenants in the area **(2)**
			The continued exploitation of the Highlands by entrepreneurial outsiders for example, Andy McChuckemup plans to exploit the landscape through commercialisation **(2)**
			Many other answers are possible.

Text 3 – Drama – *Men Should Weep* by Ena Lamont Stewart

Question	Expected Answer(s)	Max Mark	Additional Guidance
9.	Candidates should explain two of Jenny's reasons for visiting the family home.	2	Possible answers: • Jenny wants to correct her mother's misunderstanding of Bertie's situation: the hospital will not let him come back to Maggie's very unhealthy slum tenement • Jenny wants to make sure her parents actively pursue the Corporation about getting a Council house, using Bertie's ill-health as a lever • When Jenny was considering suicide by drowning, she thought of her father and all the love and kindness he had shown her when she was a child • Jenny regrets her ill-treatment, partly influenced by Isa, of her parents; she has come back to admit her guilt and regret

Question	Expected Answer(s)	Max Mark	Additional Guidance
10.	Candidates should analyse how Lily and Jenny's differing attitudes are shown in lines 22–42. For full marks, both Lily and Jenny's attitudes must be covered, although equal coverage is not necessary. 2 marks awarded for detailed/insightful comment plus quotation/reference. 1 mark for more basic comment plus quotation/reference. 0 marks for quotation/reference alone.	4	Possible answers: Lily: • does not believe in couples living together unless they're married — "livin in sin" • is contemptuous, highly critical of the money or gifts Jenny has received; she implies that what Jenny is doing is little better than prostitution — "We've had an eye-fu o yer wages o sin"; "she'll hae earned it, Maggie. On her back." • suggests strongly that Jenny has damned herself in exchange for material possessions "The wages o sin's nae deith, it's fancy hairdos an a swanky coat an pur silk stockins" • assumes that a woman who lives with a man outwith marriage will inevitably be punished, disappointed, discarded — "till yer tired business man gets tired o you an ye're oot on yer ear" • is unswervingly conventional, is determined not to behave in a way society might find unacceptable — "I've kept ma self-respect" Jenny: • sees nothing wrong with couples living together outside marriage — "Aye, if ye want tae ca it sin! I don't." • is dismissive of conventional morality — "You seem tae ken yer Bible … I never pretended tae." • favours happiness over convention — "kind", "generous", "I'm happy, an I'm makin him happy" • sees no point in sacrificing all hope of happiness, love or companionship just to follow the norms of society — "Aye. An that's aboot a ye've got."
11.	Candidates should analyse the dramatic impact of at least two of the stage directions in lines 43–62. 2 marks awarded for detailed/insightful comment plus quotation/reference. 1 mark for more basic comment plus quotation/reference. 0 marks for quotation/reference alone.	4	Possible answers: (Her hands to her head): • conveys the depth of Maggie's distress and unhappiness. The argument between Lily and Jenny, which she has just brought to an end, has pushed her to her wits' end • creates a dramatic pause before Maggie goes on to reflect that the happiness she had felt on seeing Jenny return has gone • emphasises Maggie prefers to avoid confrontation and often ignores the reality of her problems (She draws a couple of chairs together … watching): • conveys Jenny's desire to discuss important matters with Maggie • Jenny only draws up two chairs, not three, clearly signaling she is excluding Lily from the discussion • Lily feels she is an important enough figure in the family and has the right to listen, so she withdraws but only a little (She doesn't even look at Lily): • conveys Jenny's determination to get somewhere with Maggie (Maggie nods): • shows the start of Maggie's acceptance that she must listen to Jenny and perhaps act on her advice. (She opens her handbag … She gasps) • given the Morrisons' poverty, producing the "roll of notes" has a powerful physical impact on Maggie (John comes in … lips tighten) • conveys his conflicting emotions about his daughter: initial pleasure at seeing her followed by his anger at her current situation

Question	Expected Answer(s)	Max Mark	Additional Guidance
12.	Candidates should discuss how Jenny's growing maturity is made clear and should refer to appropriate textual evidence to support their discussion. Candidates may choose to answer in bullet points in this final question, or write a number of linked statements.	10	Up to 2 marks can be achieved for identifying elements of commonality as identified in the question, ie how Jenny's growing maturity is made clear. A further 2 marks can be achieved for reference to the extract given. 6 additional marks can be awarded for discussion of similar references from at least one other part of the text. In practice this means: Identification of commonality eg: Jenny's concern for her family shows a sense of responsibility (1 mark) her earlier behaviour was self-centred and immature (1 mark) From the extract: 2 marks for detailed/insightful comment plus quotation/ reference; 1 mark for more basic comment plus quotation/reference; 0 marks for quotation/reference alone. eg Jenny's admission of her previous lack of respect towards her mother shows her willingness to accept responsibility for her actions (2 marks) OR "Listen, Mammy. We canna wait for a hoose … So while ye're waitin, ye're goin tae flit tae a rented hoose." shows that Jenny is now capable of taking control where her mother has been unable to do so (2 marks) From at least one other part of the play: 2 marks for detailed/insightful comment plus quotation/ reference; 1 mark for more basic comment plus quotation/reference; 0 marks for quotation/reference alone (Up to 6 marks). Possible answers include: Jenny shows little sympathy for her parents' financial plight "I'm chuckin the shop"/she does not want to be disgraced by bringing home the "chipped apples and bashed tomaties" to help eke out the family budget **(2)** Jenny's late arrival home from the "pickshers" and her impudent response to John's concern shows that she is selfish and often irresponsible **(2)** Jenny's desperate attempts to carve her own identity often result in cruel, unloving behaviour towards her parents — "Ye needna worry! When I leave this rotten pig-stye I'm no comin back. There's ither things in life … " **(2)** Jenny's guilt over abandoning her home and family becomes apparent through her attempts to reassure Maggie/"Ma, ye've got Dad and Alec and the weans. Ye'll no miss me oot of the hoose." **(2)** Mrs Bone and Mrs Harris' description of Jenny as "a right mess" reveals the difficult circumstances Jenny has managed to overcome before returning to the family home **(2)** Many other answers are possible.

SCOTTISH TEXT (PROSE)

Text 1 — Prose — *Mother and Son* by Iain Crichton Smith

Question	Expected Answer(s)	Max Mark	Additional Guidance
13.	Candidates should analyse the writer's use of language in lines 1–22 to reveal the nature of the relationship between mother and son. 2 marks awarded for detailed/insightful comment plus quotation/reference. 1 mark for more basic comment plus quotation/reference. 0 marks for quotation/reference alone.	4	Possible answers include: • pattern of relationship has been set/it had happened before/likely to happen again — "beginning again …" • Their conflict followed a regular pattern — "always …"/emphasis on repeated pattern of sentence structure — "You know well enough" • He is tired of the inevitable, repetitive conflicts — "spoke wearily" • She dominates him by hurtful comments — "same brutal pain stabbed him" • little chance of success in being understood/making his point — "retired defeated" • mother appears to give the son the chance to change/take responsibility but doesn't really mean it — "if you'll only say"
14.	Candidates should identify the tone of the mother's words in lines 27–28 and analyse how this tone is created. 1 mark awarded for identification of appropriate tone. Analysis: 2 marks awarded for detailed/insightful comment plus quotation/reference; 1 mark for more basic comment plus quotation/reference. 0 marks for quotation/reference alone.	3	Possible answers include: **Tone:** • cruel/vicious/dismissive/critical … • dismissive put-down — "Lessons aren't everything." • repetition of accusatory "you" — "You aren't a mechanic." • Repeated use of negatives — "aren't"/"can't" … • short, quick-fire list of complaints/criticisms — "You … Why don't you hurry up with that tea?" • accusatory question — "Why don't you hurry up with that tea?" • escalating list of her perception of his inadequacies — "You aren't a mechanic … Fat good you'd be at a job."
15.	Candidates should analyse how the language of lines 29–38 conveys the son's reaction to his mother's words. 2 marks awarded for detailed/insightful comment plus quotation/reference. 1 mark for more basic comment plus quotation/reference. 0 marks for quotation/reference alone.		Possible answers include: • defeated in the face of mother's constant criticism — "despairingly leaning"; "head on his hands" • acceptance of inadequacies — "wasn't a mechanic"; "never could understand" • deepening lack of self-esteem/self-doubt — "something had gone wrong" • unhappy/despairing — "sad look on his face"
16.	Candidates should discuss how Iain Crichton Smith uses contrasting characters to explore theme. Candidates may choose to answer in bullet points in this final question, or write a number of linked statements.	10	Up to 2 marks can be achieved for identifying elements of commonality as identified in the question, ie contrast used to explore character and/or theme. A further 2 marks can be achieved for reference to the extract given. 6 additional marks can be awarded for discussion of similar references from at least one other short story. <u>In practice this means:</u> Identification of commonality eg: Iain Crichton Smith will often create contrast between characters from different backgrounds (1 mark) with differing personalities (1 mark) **OR** the sense of an outsider in a closed community or alien environment (1 mark) such as restricted island setting or war-time situation (1 mark)

Question	Expected Answer(s)	Max Mark	Additional Guidance
16.	*(continued)*		From the extract:
			1 × relevant reference to technique/idea/feature
			1 × appropriate comment (2 marks)
			(maximum of 2 marks only for discussion of extract)
			eg The domineering mother contrasts with the submissive son — "her spiteful, bitter face"/"his head in his hands" (2 marks)
			The mother's directness contrasts with the son's tentative responses — "you'd be no good in a job"/"I'll take a job tomorrow … if you'll only say" (2 marks)
			From at least one other text:
			2 marks for detailed/insightful comment plus quotation/reference;
			1 mark for more basic comment plus quotation/reference;
			0 marks for quotation/reference alone
			(Up to 6 marks).
			Possible answers include:
			• *The Telegram* — the fat woman and thin woman contrast as the thin woman is an incomer whereas the fat woman has always lived in this village — highlights small-mindedness of village "she was an incomer from another village and had only been in this one for thirty years or so" **(2)**
			• *The Telegram* — contrasting attitudes towards education/aspiration — "thin woman was ambitious: she had sent her son to university …" whereas the fat woman has lived there all her life/is more conventional/her son was only an ordinary seaman but both are equally affected by the war **(2)**
			• *The Red Door*: Murdo contrasts with the rest of the islanders through his ultimate willingness to be different when he accepts the red door instead of re-painting it **(2)**
			• *The Painter*: painter sees the fight as an artistic opportunity whereas the other villagers are horrified by his apparent lack of concern for the violence — "… a gaze that had gone beyond the human and was as indifferent to the outcome as a hawk's might be." **(2)**
			• *The Crater*: contrast in attitude between Lt Robert Mackinnon and Sergeant Smith to the war. Mackinnon is sensitive/horrified by the brutality of war whereas Sergeant Smith is stolidly accepting — happy to be back **(2)**
			Many other answers are possible.

Text 2 — Prose — *The Wireless Set* by George Mackay Brown

Question	Expected Answer(s)	Max Mark	Additional Guidance
17.	For full marks, candidates should explain how Mackay Brown creates a sense of both community life and the role of the wireless set within it. 0 marks for reference/quotation alone.	2	Possible answers include: • "passed the shop and the manse and the schoolhouse" — postman's journey encapsulates the centres of community life • "the island postman" — suggests he is a central part of the community/small community requiring only one postman • "Joe Loss and his orchestra" — alien (from London) music intruding into island life via wireless set • Contrast traditional island life ("croft"/"track") with new, modern music (from outside/London)

Question		Expected Answer(s)	Max Mark	Additional Guidance
18.	(a)	Candidates should analyse how Mackay Brown reveals the postman's attitude to Betsy in lines 6–15. 2 marks may be awarded for detailed/insightful comment plus quotation/reference. 1 mark for more basic comment plus quotation/reference. 0 marks for reference/quotation alone.	2	Possible answers include: • Repetition/parallel expressions in "Is there anybody with you?" and "There should be somebody with you" — reveals his insistence that she have support before he gives her the bad news — sympathetic/concerned • "miser parting with a twenty pound note" — image reveals his extreme reluctance to tell her/telling her the news is compared with parting with a thing that is precious : protective towards her/relishing power the knowledge gives him • "disappearing on his bike round the corner"- already left (by the time she has read the telegram) suggests he doesn't know how to deal with her/his concern is not deep/he has now moved on and left her to someone else to care for her (the missionary)
	(b)	Candidates should analyse how Mackay Brown uses language to convey the differing reactions of the missionary and Betsy to the news in lines 16–22. 0 marks for reference/quotation alone.	2	Possible answers include: Missionary: • "He died for his country"/"He made the great sacrifice" — platitudes/conventional clichés suggest insincerity/no real sympathy Betsy: • "It's time the peats were carted" suggests that Betsy is taken up with the work on the land rather than facing her personal tragedy/a coping strategy • "That isn't it at all" suggests Betsy's simple dismissal of the missionary's cliché/reveals her honesty in the face of his platitudes • "Howie's sunk with torpedoes. That's all I know" — blunt statement of the fact shows that she is forced to face up to the brutal reality of what has happened
19.		Candidates should refer to both sides of the contrast: the couple's real feelings and the missionary's perception of their feelings. 2 marks awarded for detailed/insightful comment plus quotation/reference. 1 mark for more basic comment plus quotation/reference. 0 marks for quotation/reference alone.	4	Possible answers include: The couple: • "How many lobsters … I got two lobsters … I got six crabs" determined focus on practicalities/modest numbers which define their frugal life/getting on with normalities of life as coping mechanism • "The wireless stood, a tangled wreck, on the dresser" — utter destruction of the object which 'brought the war' shows Hugh's agony The missionary's view: • "I'll break the news to him" — slightly officious/patronising attempt to take charge of the situation — he does not realise that Hugh already knows • "awed by such callousness" — complete failure to understand their stoical way of dealing with extreme grief • "slowly shaking his head" — demonstrates that the missionary doesn't understand their coping strategy/thinks they don't care • "My poor man" — tries to impose what he thinks their reaction should be

Question	Expected Answer(s)	Max Mark	Additional Guidance
20.	Candidates should discuss how the writer deals with the relationship between the island community and the outside world. Candidates may choose to answer in bullet points in this final question, or write a number of linked statements.	10	Up to 2 marks can be achieved for identifying elements of commonality as identified in the question, ie the relationship between the island community and the outside world. A further 2 marks can be achieved for reference to the extract given. 6 additional marks can be awarded for discussion of similar references from at least one other short story. <u>In practice this means:</u> Identification of commonality eg George Mackay Brown often reveals the intrusion of the modern or violent outside world (1 mark) into the traditional/safe/secure world of an island community (1 mark). From the extract: 2 marks for detailed/insightful comment plus quotation/ reference; 1 mark for more basic comment plus quotation/reference; 0 marks for quotation/reference alone. eg The music belongs to another world outside the island – "The wireless was playing music inside, Joe Loss and his orchestra." (2 marks) **OR** The news of the Howie's death, arriving by telegram, shows the destructive intrusion of the war on the local community (2 marks) From at least one other text: 2 marks for detailed/insightful comment plus quotation/ reference; 1 mark for more basic comment plus quotation/reference; 0 marks for quotation/reference alone (Up to 6 marks). Possible answers include: *Tartan* – the Vikings' journey through the village – apparently aggressive/predatory but villagers' silent, brooding presence follows them to shore – they leave hastily/gaining little from the raid **(2)** *Tartan* – the Vikings are searching for anything valuable to plunder but, ironically, give a silver coin to a child because of his wit (the only money to change hands in the raid) **(2)** *Tartan* – Vikings threaten violence/pillaging/attacking dark-haired woman but the only death is Kol, murdered by the villagers while he lies drunk **(2)** *The Eye of the Hurricane* – the narrator, Barclay's, slightly patronising attempt to relate to the island people shown in his description of them: "I had come to live ... among simple, uncomplicated people" **(2)** *A Time to Keep* – the "missionary" (title suggests patronising attempt to bring enlightened religion to the community) offers comfort on death of Ingi but his words are hollow and meaningless and are rejected by Bill: "She's in the earth"/"The ground isn't a particularly happy place to be." **(2)** Many other answers are possible.

Text 3 – Prose – *The Trick is to Keep Breathing* by Janice Galloway

Question	Expected Answer(s)	Max Mark	Additional Guidance
21.	Candidates should analyse how Galloway makes the reader aware of Joy's efforts to cope. 2 marks may be awarded for detailed/insightful comment plus quotation/reference. 1 mark for more basic comment + quotation/reference. 0 marks for quotation/reference alone.	2	Possible answers include: • Repetition of "I" eg "I wanted"; "I made"; "I kept going" emphasises all the things she was trying to do/creates a listing effect • Comparison to Bunyan's Pilgrim and Dorothy emphasises her determination • Reference to "endurance test" demonstrates the effort needed just to keep going • "all I had to do was last out" emphasises that she is trying to convince herself that she can cope
22.	Candidates should analyse how the writer uses language to convey Joy's desperation for Michael's presence. 2 marks awarded for detailed/insightful comment plus quotation/reference. 1 mark for more basic comment plus quotation/reference. 0 marks for quotation/reference alone.	4	Possible answers include: • Repetitive sentence structure in lines 9–14 emphasises her obsession with Michael • Use of list in sentence beginning "I saw him in cars" emphasises the number and variety of places she imagines seeing him • Use of question "How could he be …?" emphasises that she wants to believe/is trying to convince herself that he is still alive • Use of the senses eg smell ("I started smelling …") and sight ("I saw him …") emphasises that she can imagine his presence/wants his presence • "roaring past"; "drifting by"; "hovering in a cloud" emphasises that he is always just out of reach • "sunk my face into his clothes" emphasises how she totally immerses herself; wants to feel his presence • "howled" emphasises how much despair she feels at his absence • "invisible presence" emphasises her emptiness; imagines he is there but cannot see him
23.	Candidates should analyse how the writer conveys Joy's feelings of despair. For full marks at least two different examples must be commented on. 2 marks awarded for detailed/insightful comment plus quotation/reference. 1 mark for more basic comment plus quotation/reference. 0 marks for quotation/reference alone.	4	Possible answers include: • Sentence structure "Please god …" – plea/prayer emphasises her desire to die • "mashed remains"; "marrowbone jelly oozing" – word choice creates vivid visual image of the aftermath of boulders crashing through the roof; emphasises her desire to be wiped out completely • Use of humour in the Health Visitor's words emphasises her sarcasm/bitterness towards the medical professionals who are supposed to be helping her • "shrinking" emphasises that she feels as if she is disappearing • "shiver" emphasises her coldness/fear • Use of contrast in the final paragraph helps us to understand her despair at her situation
24.	Candidates should discuss how the writer conveys Joy's fear/anxiety about relating to other people and should refer to appropriate textual evidence to support their discussion. Candidates may choose to answer in bullet points in this final question, or write a number of linked statements.	10	Up to 2 marks can be achieved for identifying elements of commonality as identified in the question, ie evidence of Joy's fear/anxiety about relating to other people. A further 2 marks can be achieved for reference to the extract given. 6 additional marks can be awarded for discussion of similar references from at least one other part of the text. <u>In practice this means:</u> Identification of commonality eg Fear/anxiety is ever-present in Joy's view of the world around her and how she relates to other people (1 mark) shown through a range of narrative techniques/descriptions of her experiences (1 mark).

Question	Expected Answer(s)	Max Mark	Additional Guidance
24.	(continued)		From the extract:
			2 marks for detailed/insightful comment plus quotation/reference;
			1 mark for more basic comment plus quotation/reference;
			0 marks for quotation/reference alone.
			eg Health Visitor's clichéd comments reveal (Joy's perception of) her lack of understanding of the depth of Joy's problems and show that they cannot relate to one another (2 marks)
			OR
			Joy's direct statement ("Needing people … wearing me out") reveals her inability to cope with forming relationships which she, nevertheless, recognises she needs (2 marks)
			From at least one other part of the text:
			2 marks for detailed/insightful comment plus quotation/reference;
			1 mark for more basic comment plus quotation/reference;
			0 marks for quotation/reference alone
			(Up to 6 marks).
			Possible references include:
			• Joy's attempts to distance herself from/avoid contact with her sister, Myra "Tell me where you live" **(2)**
			• Anxiety about visits from the Health Visitor — Joy refers to herself as a patient to distance herself from her illness and putting on a brave front by not being honest about how much she is struggling/how deep her depression is **(2)**
			• Anxiety about meeting doctors — eg referring to them by numbers, "Doctor 1, Doctor 2" which shows her refusal to engage with them on a personal level **(2)**
			• Fear of the phone — eg. after she self-harms she says "I can't face the phone tonight either" showing that, even when desperate, she cannot use the phone to seek help **(2)**
			• Fear/avoidance of communication — eg. despite having a landline, Joy prefers to use the phone box nearby because the landline represents people coming in/she can't control who is calling **(2)**
			Many other answers are possible.

Text 4 — Prose — *Sunset Song* by Lewis Grassic Gibbon

Question	Expected Answer(s)	Max Mark	Additional Guidance
25.	Candidates should explain how Chris is feeling in lines 1—8. 2 marks are awarded for detailed/insightful comment plus quotation/reference. 1 mark for more basic comment plus quotation/reference. 0 marks for quotation/reference alone.	2	Possible answers include: • Chris's desire to arrive at the Stones displays great mental strength like the strength of the metal iron; • the strength of Chris's will in her single-mindedness; • peace and restfulness of Chris lying down after her exertions; • sense of Chris's complete freedom from tension; Chris feels at peace with nature; • Physical symptoms indicative of exertion or distress
26.	Candidates should analyse how the writer conveys the impact her mother's death has had on Chris in lines 9—23. 2 marks are awarded for detailed/insightful comment plus quotation/reference. 1 mark for more basic comment plus quotation/reference. 0 marks for quotation/reference alone.	4	Possible answers include: • "as a dark cold pit" — the simile suggests Chris's misery and difficulty in escaping from so much sorrow; • "and the world went on … the world went on and you went with it" — repetition reinforces the fact that Chris has no choice but to carry on with her life, despite her personal tragedy; • "something died in your heart and went down with her to lie" — suggests that emotionally Chris has suffered a loss which will accompany her mother to her grave;

Question	Expected Answer(s)	Max Mark	Additional Guidance
26.	*(continued)*		• "the child in your heart died then" — shows Chris's acknowledgement of the abrupt end of childhood for her; • "hands ready to snatch you back … over-rough" — image conveys a past where Chris knew she would be rescued from harm; • "the Chris of the books and the dreams died with it" — all that might have been must be cast aside because reality has taken over from fantasy; • "the dark, quiet corpse that was your childhood" — stark image of death conveys the certainty of this childhood stage of Chris's life being over.
27.	Candidates should analyse how the writer conveys the horror of Chris's memory of her mother's death in lines 23–45. 2 marks are awarded for detailed/insightful comment plus quotation/reference. 1 mark for more basic comment plus quotation/reference. 0 marks for quotation/reference alone.	4	Possible answers include: • Description of Mistress Munro as a terrifying presence: "uncaring", "black-eyed futret", "snapping", "terrified" • Pathetic fallacy showing Chris's despair: "awful night", "rain-soaked parks" • Chris's initial feelings of shock/numbness: "dazed and dull-eyed" • Description of mother's body as beautiful heightening the horrific nature of Chris's loss: "sweet to look at" • Chris's movement from denial to the agony of grief: "hot tears wrung from your eyes like drops of blood" • Chris's thoughts conveyed directly to show her utter despair, including repetition: "Oh mother, mother, why did you do it?"
28.	Candidates should discuss how Grassic Gibbon presents Chris's growing to maturity in this and at least one other part of the novel. Candidates may choose to answer in bullet points in this final question, or write a number of linked statements.	10	Up to 2 marks can be achieved for identifying elements of commonality as identified in the question, ie Chris's growing to maturity. A further 2 marks can be achieved for reference to the extract given. 6 additional marks can be awarded for discussion of similar references to at least one other part of the text by the writer. <u>In practice this means:</u> Identification of commonality (theme, characterisation, use of imagery, setting, or any other key element …) Eg Her evolving identification with the land. (1 mark) This helps her to resolve her internal conflict and find her own identity at a time of personal and societal change. (1 mark) From the extract: 2 marks for detailed insightful comment plus quotation/reference; 1 mark for more basic comment plus quotation/reference; 0 marks for quotation/reference alone. eg During a time of change she finds comfort in the permanence of the Standing Stones (2 marks) **OR** Mistress Munro's role in reminding Chris of her familial responsibilities leads to her leaving behind her childhood and assuming the role of mother: "you'll find little time for dreaming and dirt when you're keeping house at Blawearie" (2 marks) From at least one other part of the text: 2 marks for detailed/insightful comment plus quotation/reference; 1 mark for more basic comment plus quotation/reference; 0 marks for quotation/reference alone (Up to 6 marks).

Question	Expected Answer(s)	Max Mark	Additional Guidance
28.	*(continued)*		Possible answers include: • Chris's loss of her father and decision to stay on the land which shows her increased sense of her identity being tied up with the land/taking responsibility for her own future **(2)** • Chris falling in love with and marrying Ewan further links her to the land as Ewan represents the agricultural way of life **(2)** • Her pregnancy and the birth of her son which shows her taking on responsibility and starting new life with her own family **(2)** • The return of Ewan as a soldier and the apparent destruction of their relationship when she displays resilience and determination to endure as an independent woman **(2)** • The death of Ewan which brings about redemption/reconciliation in her eyes as he "went into the heart that was his forever" **(2)** Many other answers are possible.

Text 5 – Prose – *The Cone-Gatherers* by Robin Jenkins

Question	Expected Answer(s)	Max Mark	Additional Guidance
29.	Candidates should analyse how language is used to create a positive picture of Lady Runcie-Campbell in lines 1–19. 2 marks are awarded for detailed/insightful comment plus quotation/reference. 1 mark for more basic comment plus quotation/reference. 0 marks for quotation/reference alone.	4	Possible answers include: • Her attractiveness: "clear courteous musical voice"/"charming" speaker/"loveliness"/"outstanding beauty of face" • Her sense of fairness and justice: "earnestness of spirit"/"almost mystical sense of responsibility"/"passion for justice, profound and intelligent"/"determination to see right done, even at the expense of rank or pride" • Her ability to bring out the best in people: "ability to exalt people out of their humdrum selves" • Her Christian beliefs/altruism/spirituality: "almost mystical sense of responsibility"/"associated religion ... with her perfume"/"her emulation of Christ"
30.	Candidates should analyse two instances of the use of language to convey the contrast between the two characters in lines 23–43. 2 marks are awarded for detailed/insightful comment plus quotation/reference. 1 mark for more basic comment plus quotation/reference. 0 marks for quotation/reference alone.	4	Possible answers include: **Openness and duplicity:** Duror 's desire to corrupt Lady Runcie-Campbell' – "it would implicate her in his chosen evil"; in contrast she "looked at him frankly and sympathetically", suggesting her honesty and compassion **Beauty/Purity and ugliness:** Setting in the room suggests beauty – "sunny scented room" which contrasts with the evil thoughts in Duror's mind – "black filth" **Contrast in physical appearance** She is beautiful and "vital"; in contrast he is unkempt and ill-looking – "hadn't shaved". **Light and dark** Setting of the room suggests light/"glittering rings" contrasts with "black filth" **Good and evil:** Reference to the goodness of nature in the birdsong – "everywhere birds sang"-which contrasts with Duror's evil thought which "crept up until it entered his mouth, covered his ears, blinded his eyes, and so annihilated him"

Question	Expected Answer(s)	Max Mark	Additional Guidance
31.	Candidates should explain why Lady Runcie-Campbell now feels more able to identify with Peggy's situation. 2 marks may be awarded for a detailed/insightful explanation. 1 mark for a more basic explanation.	2	Possible answers include: • The war (and the fact she is separated from her husband as a result) has demonstrated to Lady Runcie-Campbell what it is like to miss a loved one — she links this to Peggy Duror's illness as her 'war' and understands how she and Duror must feel • The war has stopped Lady Runcie-Campbell being able to appreciate aspects of everyday life: "flowers ... friends", something Peggy has been deprived of for years • Word-choice such as "dreadful separations"/"cut off" may also be commented on, showing the hurt/pain caused by being apart • Candidates may also notice that her sympathies lie with Peggy rather than Duror — she empathises with a wife who is missing her husband (and perhaps fails to acknowledge his lack of emotion)
32.	Candidates should discuss how Duror is presented not just as an evil character, but one who might be worthy of sympathy or understanding, and should refer to appropriate textual evidence to support their discussion. Candidates can answer in bullet points in this final question, or write a number of linked statements. For the full 6 marks on elsewhere in the text, both evil and sympathy must be covered, although coverage will not necessarily be balanced.	10	Up to 2 marks can be achieved for identifying elements of commonality as identified in the question, ie how Duror is presented not just as an evil character, but one who might be worthy of some sympathy. A further 2 marks can be achieved for reference to the extract given. 6 additional marks can be awarded for discussion of similar references from at least one other part of the text. <u>In practice this means:</u> Identification of commonality eg: Duror's evil character is primarily shown through his persecution of those whom he perceives as imperfect (1 mark) yet some sympathy can be felt because of personal circumstances (1 mark) From the extract: 2 marks for detailed/insightful comment plus quotation/reference; 1 mark for more basic comment plus quotation/reference; 0 marks for quotation/reference alone. eg His duplicitous behaviour towards Lady Runcie-Campbell, yet some sympathy could be evoked by awareness of his own immorality (2 marks). **OR** his intention in this extract is to damage the cone gatherers, but we have some sympathy for the burden he carries with his wife (2 marks). From at least one other part of the text: 2 marks for detailed/insightful comment plus quotation/reference; 1 mark for more basic comment plus quotation/reference; 0 marks for quotation/reference alone (Up to 6 marks). Possible answers include: Duror as evil: • Duror lurking in the wood, spying on the cone-gatherers/aiming his gun at them suggests that he sees them as animals/inferior beings to be hunted/suggests his devious nature **(2)** • His determination to drive them out of the wood shows selfish protection of his own territory in the face of their geuine need **(2)** • The lies he spreads about Calum (eg. with reference to the doll) shows his desire to crush his innocence and/or destroy others' views of him **(2)**

Question	Expected Answer(s)	Max Mark	Additional Guidance
32.	*(continued)*		Sympathy for Duror: • His nightmare about Peggy before the deer drive/his collapse at the end of the deer drive shows that he is mentally ill — reflected in many of his thoughts **(2)** • His mother-in-law accuses him of spending more time with his dogs than with his wife suggests his loneliness and isolation **(2)** Many other answers are possible.

SCOTTISH TEXT (POETRY)

Text 1 — Poetry — *To a Mouse, On turning her up in her Nest, with the Plough, November 1785* by Robert Burns

Question	Expected Answer(s)	Max Mark	Additional Guidance
33.	Candidates should analyse how at least two aspects of the speaker's personality are established. 2 marks awarded for detailed/insightful comment plus quotation/reference. 1 mark for more basic comment plus quotation/reference. 0 marks for quotation/reference alone.	4	Possible answers include: **Sympathetic** • shows awareness of mouse's vulnerability — "poor, earth — born companion,/An' fellow-mortal" • apologetic tone of "I'm truly sorry" • reflected in the language emphasising the mouse's vulnerability — "wee", "cowrin", "tim'rous", "poor", "panic" **Understanding** • of the mouse's need to live/the modest nature of its needs — "A daimen icker in a thrave" **Affectionate** • tone of diminutives — "beastie"/"breastie"; • reassurance in direct address: "Thou need na start …" **Forgiving** • the mouse's thieving put into the context of its need to "live" **Reflective** • his apologetic tone of "I'm truly sorry" suggests speaker's regret for man's destruction of the environment **Generous** • "'S a sma' request" suggests his willingness to share; "blessin" in allowing the mouse a living
34.	Candidates should analyse how the poet's language creates pity for the mouse and its predicament by dealing with at least two examples. These examples could be of the same, or of different technique(s). 2 marks awarded for detailed/insightful comment plus quotation/reference. 1 mark for more basic comment plus quotation/reference. 0 marks for quotation/reference alone.	4	**Possible answers include:** Word choice • "wee bit" or "wee bit heap" or "silly" underline the smallness and fragility of the mouse's nest • "housie" — as above; "house" (as opposed to nest) humanises the mouse • "strewin" — emphasises the power and harshness of the wind in the utter destruction of the nest; emphasises the fragility and flimsiness of the nest, so easily blown away • "bleak December's" — the harshness of the weather/season reinforces the desperation of the mouse's situation • "ensuing" — sense of inevitability, unavoidable harshness • "bare an' waste"; — emphasises/reinforces the devastation caused by winter and the hopelessness/harshness of the mouse's situation • "winds" or "snell" or "keen" or "blast" — (unrelenting) harshness of weather to emphasise vulnerability of mouse without its nest • "sleety dribble" — depicts the coldness and misery in store for the mouse without shelter

Question	Expected Answer(s)	Max Mark	Additional Guidance
34.	*(continued)*		• "cruel coulter" — harshness/malice of the plough; sense of a force set against the mouse • "thole" — underlines suffering in store for mouse Personification • "housie"/"house or hald" — compares the mouse's nest to a human habitation encouraging empathy from the reader • "Now thou's turn'd out" — suggests forced eviction, homelessness Alliteration • "weary Winter" — underlines the difficulty/hopelessness posed by the coming cold • "Beneath the blast" — emphasises the harshness of the elements and the shelter the mouse might have had • "crash! the cruel coulter" — harsh sounds mirror the harsh action • "But house or hald" — underlines the complete loss the mouse has suffered • "Cranreuch cauld" — underlines the harshness of the cold the mouse will have to endure Onomatopoeia • "crash!" — adds drama to the sudden destruction; relives the experience from the mouse's perspective to make us feel the disaster Contrast • "cozie here" with "blast" (and any of the other weather words) — reinforce pity for mouse; hope for warmth and safety replaced with coldness and vulnerability • "thought to dwell" with " now thou's turned out" — reversal of fortune creates pity Repetition • "An'" — used at the start of lines to emphasise sense of all the problems/difficulties piling up to add to the mouse's predicament • words to do with harshness of weather — reinforce the mouse's vulnerability in face of the remorseless elements • "December — winter — winter" — emphasises the inescapable nature of the elements and the vulnerable mouse Tone • emotional, empathetic tone underlined by frequent use of exclamation marks, underlining the pitiful nature of the mouse's situation • empathetic — in the speaker putting himself in mouse's • situation — "Til crash! the cruel coulter" — and relating what has happened as a disaster • sympathetic — towards the effort now destroyed without hope of mending — "has cost thee mony a weary nibble"
35.	Candidates should explain how the final two verses highlight the contrast between the speaker and the mouse. 2 marks awarded for detailed/insightful comment plus quotation reference. 1 mark for more basic comment plus quotation/reference. 0 marks for quotation/reference alone.	2	Possible answers include: • the mouse is fortunate only living in the present whereas mankind must suffer the anxiety and trouble which come from being conscious of the past and the future • the penultimate verse deals with the mouse and the speaker's shared experience(s) whereas the final verse contrasts the emotions/feelings of the speaker and the mouse • the final verse starts with a direct comparison "Still thou are blest, compared wi'me!"

Question	Expected Answer(s)	Max Mark	Additional Guidance
36.	Candidates should discuss how Burns uses a distinctive narrative voice to convey the central concerns of *To a Mouse* and at least one *of* his other poems. Candidates can answer in bullet points in this final question, or write a number of linked statements.	10	Up to 2 marks can be achieved for identifying elements of commonality as identified in the question, ie how Burns uses a distinctive narrative voice to convey the central concerns in *To a Mouse* and at least one of his other poems. A further 2 marks can be achieved for the reference to the extract given. 6 additional marks can be awarded for discussion of similar references in at least one other poem by Burns. <u>In practice this means:</u> Identification of commonality eg the creation of a persona/ speaker in a dramatic situation and/or communicating directly with reader (1 mark) allows Burns to explore a variety of themes — hypocrisy/social class/love religion/nature etc (1 mark) From the extract: 2 marks for detailed/insightful comment plus quotation/ reference; 1 mark for more basic comment plus quotation/reference; 0 marks for quotation/reference alone. eg The regretful tone adopted by the persona allows Burns to reflect on man's destruction of nature and the impermanence of existence. (2 marks) **OR** The persona's compassion for the mouse allows Burns to comment on how even the "best laid plans" can be destroyed by fate. (2 marks) From at least one other text: 2 marks for detailed/insightful comment plus quotation/ reference; 1 mark for more basic comment plus quotation/reference; 0 marks for quotation/reference alone (Up to 6 marks). Possible answers include: In comments on other poems by Burns, possible references include: • *A Poet's Welcome to his Love-Begotten Daughter* — the emotions of the defensive/combative speaker/persona are appropriate for the heartfelt challenge to contemporary religious and moral attitudes **(2)** • *Address to the Deil* — humorous, ironic speaker/persona is appropriate for poet's satirical critique of Calvinism **(2)** • *A Man's A Man For A' That* — a spokesman, champion of equality and fraternity speaking as the voice of a community/nation **(2)** • *Holy Willie* — creation of hypocritical character for dramatic monologue is an apt vehicle for poet's religious satire **(2)** • *Tam O'Shanter* — character of moralising, commentating narrator allows Burns to point out the vagaries of human nature/undermine the apparent moral 'message' of the poem **(2)** Many other answers are possible.

Text 3 — Poetry — *War Photographer* by Carol Ann Duffy

Question	Expected Answer(s)	Max Mark	Additional Guidance
37.	Candidates should analyse how imagery is used to create a serious atmosphere. A detailed/insightful comment on one example may be awarded 2 marks. More basic comments can be awarded 1 mark each. Identification of image alone = 0 marks	2	Possible answers include: • The metaphor "spools of suffering" links the content of the photographic images in the spools to the subjects of the photographs to highlight the awareness of the (on-going, cyclical) misery endured by the subjects. • The image "spools … ordered rows" compares the meticulous arrangement of the spools to the graves in a (war) cemetery to highlight the scale of deaths witnessed/ the violent nature of the deaths. • The image of the "dark room" with its red light as a "church" compares the interior lighting within the darkroom to that of a church to highlight the gloomy, funeral atmosphere of the darkroom. • Word choice of "red" suggests danger (of war zone/ pictures) or blood (represents the horror of the war zone) • The image of the photographer as "a priest … intone a Mass" suggests a similarity between the role of the photographer and the priest in terms of the seriousness of the processes they are involved in/the importance of their roles in spreading the word. • The image "All flesh is grass" compares human life to short lived "grass" to highlight the transient nature of human life (especially in times of conflict).
38.	Candidates should analyse how Duffy conveys the contrast between the photographer's perception of life in Britain and life in the war zones he covers. For full marks both sides of the contrast should be dealt with but not necessarily in equal measure. 2 marks awarded for detailed/insightful comment plus quotation/reference. 1 mark for more basic comment plus quotation/reference. 0 marks for quotation/reference alone.	4	Possible answers include: • The word choice of "Rural England" suggests the idealised view of England as predominantly countryside which is leafy, peaceful, natural, wholesome. • The juxtaposition of "ordinary pain" suggests how trivial and unimportant the problems faced in Britain are compared to those in war zones. • The word choice of "simple weather" and/or "dispel" suggests how shallow/easily addressed the problems faced in Britain are. • The word choice of "explode" suggests the unpredictability and danger of life in the war zone. • The word choice of "nightmare heat" suggests extreme climactic conditions endured (with suggestion of oppressive or threatening atmosphere). • An extended contrast could be drawn between the stereotypical feature of "rural England" — "fields" and "running children" and how this is contrasted with reality of life in the war zone — "exploded" and "nightmare heat". • The word choice of "hand, which did not tremble then"- emphasises contrast between his ability to cope with the job at the time and the impact on him now as he reflects on it
39.	Candidates should analyse how poetic technique is used to convey the distressing nature of the photographer's memories. 2 marks awarded for detailed/insightful comment plus quotation/reference; 1 mark for more basic comment plus quotation/reference. 0 marks for reference/quotation alone.	2	Possible answers include: • Word choice — "twist" suggests the subject's body distorted by pain/injury; writhing in agony. • Word choice — "half-formed ghost" suggests memories of death/being haunted by the memories. • Word choice of "cries" suggests the anguish of the man's wife. • Enjambment "cries/of this man's wife" suggests emotional turmoil, uncontained by ordinary line structure. • Word choice of "blood stained" suggests the scale of the violence remembered/the indelible nature of the memory. • use of sense words such as "blood stained" and "cries" suggests the vivacity of the memory. • Word choice of "foreign dust" suggests abandoned and forgotten.

Question	Expected Answer(s)	Max Mark	Additional Guidance
40.	Candidates should analyse how the poet's use of poetic technique conveys the indifference of the readership of the newspapers to the suffering shown in them. 2 marks awarded for detailed/insightful comment plus quotation/reference; 1 mark for more basic comment plus quotation/reference. 0 marks for reference/quotation alone.	2	Possible answers include: • Word choice – "A hundred agonies" suggests the emotional power/quantity of images that the public respond to in a limited way. • Word choice – "black and white" suggests the veracity of the images that the public respond to in a limited way. • The contrast in numbers, "hundred" with "five or six", illustrates the public's limited capacity for images of this horrific nature. • Word choice of "prick with tears" suggests the public's limited emotional response to the images • The juxtaposition/alliteration of "between the bath and the pre-lunch beers" suggests the brief impact of the suffering shown in the images. • The positioning/tone of "they do not care" reinforces sense of the British public's indifference to the suffering.
41.	Candidates should discuss the link between the past and present in this poem by Duffy and at least one other poem. Candidates may choose to answer in bullet points in this final question, or write a number of linked statements.	10	Up to 2 marks can be achieved for identifying elements of commonality as identified in the question, ie the way one's past influences one's present. A further 2 marks can be achieved for reference to the extract given. 6 additional marks can be awarded for discussion of similar references to at least one other poem by the poet. <u>In practice this means:</u> Identification of commonality eg Past exerts a powerful influence on the present (1 mark) this can be negative, haunting or add further complexity to life (1 mark). From the extract: 2 marks for detailed/insightful comment plus quotation/reference; 1 mark for more basic comment plus quotation/reference; 0 marks for quotation/reference alone. "half-formed ghost" suggests haunted by the memories of conflicts that he has witnessed (2 marks) From at least one other text: 2 marks for detailed/insightful comment plus quotation/reference; 1 mark for more basic comment plus quotation/reference; 0 marks for quotation/reference alone (Up to 6 marks). Possible answers include: • *Originally* – sense of childhood security lost in moving to unfamiliar environment still remembered vividly in adulthood shown in "big boys … shouting words you don't understand" • *Anne Hathaway* – happy memories of the past with her late husband influencing her thoughts in the present "we would dive for pearls" **(2)** • *Mrs. Midas* – intimacy of past relationship intensifies pain of absolute separateness in present memory of "his hands, his warm hands on my skin" **(2)** • *Havisham* – pain of betrayal in youth has become the defining bitterness of age "ropes on the backs of my hands I could strangle with" **(2)** • *Havisham* "the dress yellowing" – wedding dress losing its bright whiteness symbolises the tarnishing/loss of her youthful dreams/ideals **(2)** Many other answers are possible.

Text 3 – Poetry – *My Rival's House* by Liz Lochhead

Question	Expected Answer(s)	Max Mark	Additional Guidance
42.	Candidates should explain why the speaker feels uncomfortable in her rival's house. 2 marks may be awarded for detailed/insightful comment. 1 mark for more basic comment.	2	Possible answers may include: • the decorative materials look expensive but are cheap suggesting the rival's welcome is false/only superficial – "ormolu and gilt, slipper satin" • the furnishings seem luxurious at first glance but, in reality, are uncomfortable suggesting an unwelcoming atmosphere – "cushions so stiff … can't sink in" • disconcerting reflections in polished surfaces suggest deceptive nature of rival/too perfect to be true – "polished clear enough to see distortions in" • rival's almost aggressive pride in the perfection of the house – "ormolu and gilt, slipper satin"
43.	Candidates should analyse how the poet conveys a tense atmosphere by referring to at least two examples from these lines. 2 marks awarded for detailed/insightful comment plus quotation/reference. 1 mark for more basic comment plus quotation/reference. 0 marks for reference/quotation alone.	4	Possible answers may include: • "Silver sugar-tongs … salver" – suggests the rival is trying to intimidate the speaker with a display of wealth • "glosses over him and me" – gives the impression the rival thinks the speaker's relationship with the son is unimportant • "I am all edges … shell – suggests the speaker's sense of her own fragility/anxiety • "squirms beneath her surface" – suggests the speaker is aware that she will never be able to get to grips with her rival's hidden nature • "tooth … nail … fight" suggests the animalistic/visceral nature of the rivalry • "Will fight, fight foul …" – repetition of 'fight' emphasises the ongoing/intense nature of the rivalry • "Deferential, daughterly …" – irony as she is well aware of her rival's true feelings and is also putting up a façade
44.	Candidates should discuss how the speaker's resentment of her rival is made clear in at least two examples. 2 marks awarded for detailed/insightful comment plus quotation/reference. 1 mark for more basic comment plus quotation/reference. 0 marks for reference/quotation alone.	4	Possible answers may include: • "first blood to her" – grudging acknowledgement of mother's blood relationship/boxing imagery suggests speaker views this as a bitter match • "never, never can escape scot free" – repetition of "never" emphasises speaker's reluctant admission that she will never truly have her partner to herself • "sour potluck of family" suggests the speaker's bitter feelings about family ties • "And oh how close …" – mocking tone to suggest speaker's resentment • minor sentences "Lady of the house. Queen Bee." – suggest speaker's derogatory dismissal/summation of her rival's position • repetition of "far more" suggests the speaker's fearful view of the threat posed by her rival • "I was always my own worst enemy … taken even this from me" – speaker's sardonic comment reveals her awareness of her rival's power/destructive qualities • brevity of final two lines encapsulates the idea that the rivalry will never end
45.	Candidates should discuss how Lochhead uses descriptive and/or symbolic detail to explore personality in this and in at least one other poem. Candidates can answer in bullet points in this final question or write a number of detailed linked statements.	10	Up to 2 marks can be achieved for identifying elements of commonality as identified in the question, ie how Lochhead uses descriptive and/or detail to explore personality A further 2 marks can be achieved for the reference to the extract given. 6 additional marks can be awarded for discussion of similar references in at least one other poem by Lochhead. In practice this means: Identification of commonality eg details of description and/or symbolism of objects or activities (1 mark) can help to focus on key personality elements developed in the poem (1 mark).

Question	Expected Answer(s)	Max Mark	Additional Guidance
45.	(continued)		From the extract:
			2 marks for detailed/insightful comment plus quotation/reference;
			1 mark for more basic comment plus quotation/reference;
			0 marks for quotation/reference alone.
			eg Process of the rival's making tea for the speaker in such a superficially proper way is both patronising and, she senses, a precursor for more open hostility (2 marks)
			From at least one other text:
			2 marks for detailed/insightful comment plus quotation/reference;
			1 mark for more basic comment plus quotation/reference;
			0 marks for quotation/reference alone
			(Up to 6 marks). Possible answers include:
			• *Last Supper* — "So here she is, tearing foliage," reveals savagery of revenge underlying 'civilised' making of meal **(2)** • *Last Supper* — "cackling round the cauldron" in their desire to criticise the faithless boyfriend, the friends have become consumed by malice themselves **(2)** • *For my Grandmother Knitting* — "the needles still move/their rhythms" even though woman is old and frail, the need to provide for her family still defines her **(2)** • *For my Grandmother Knitting* — "deft and swift/you slit the still-ticking quick silver fish." evokes the dexterity and skill as a young woman **(2)** • *View of Scotland/Love Poem* "Down on her hands and knees … on Hogmanay" conveys mother's commitment to ritual, but not the spirit, of celebration **(2)**
			Many other answers are possible.

Text 4 — Poetry — *Visiting Hour* by Norman MacCaig

Question	Expected Answer(s)	Max Mark	Additional Guidance
46.	Candidates should analyse how the poet's use of language establishes his response to the surroundings. 2 marks awarded for detailed/insightful comment plus quotation/reference. 1 mark for more basic comment plus quotation/reference. 0 marks for quotation/reference alone.	2	Possible answers include: • Opening line of the poem "The hospital smell" is blunt and matter-of-fact defining the odour universal to all hospitals. • Unusual imagery of "combs my nostrils" combines the senses of touch and smell to convey the pungent nature of the odour. It is so strong it is almost palpable. • Quirky word choice of "bobbing" is designed to disguise his discomfort/shut out the unpleasant reality he is facing/The disembodied nature of "nostrils/bobbing" indicates how dislocated he feels at this point as he struggles to remain detached. • Reference to unpleasant colours "green/yellow" connote sickness and echo his inner turmoil as he prepares to face the reality of his situation. • Word choice of "corpse" hints at the seriousness of the patient's position/his preoccupation with death. The impersonal terminology creates a darker tone, thus foreshadowing the inevitable.

Question	Expected Answer(s)	Max Mark	Additional Guidance
46.	*(continued)*		• "Vanishes" has connotations of magic/make-believe/disappearing forever suggesting that there is no afterlife and that, for him, death is final. • Religious imagery of "vanishes heavenward" introduces the hoped for final destination for those, unlike him, who believe in an afterlife. Ironic imitation of the "soul's" final journey is an observation conveying his view that this visiting hour will not be about recovery.
47.	Candidates should analyse how the poet's use of language conveys his sense of his own inadequacy. 2 marks awarded for detailed/insightful comment plus quotation/reference. 1 mark for more basic comment plus quotation/reference. 0 marks for quotation/reference alone.	4	Possible answers include: • Repetition in stanza 3 "I will not feel" emphasises the sharp contrast between the acuteness of his senses in his previous observations and his endeavours to keep his emotions entirely contained • "I" repeated three times illustrates the intensely personal difficulty he is experiencing in keeping his anguish in check. • Climax of "until I have to" shows his acknowledgement of his own avoidance. • Adverbs "lightly, swiftly" create a sense of immediacy and a change to a lighter tone. They suggest the tactful/sensitive/deliberate way in which the nurses work. This contrasts with his feelings of inadequacy. • Inversion of "here … there" echoes the busy and varied nature of the nurses' demanding jobs yet they remain focused. • Word choice of "slender waists" conveys their slight physical frames and sets up the contrast with the following expression — "miraculously … burden" — to highlight the poet's admiration for their dignified demeanour whilst working in this difficult environment whereas he is struggling to cope. • Word choice of "miraculously" has connotations of wonder and awe, suggesting he finds it inconceivable that the nurses could withstand so much emotional suffering. • Word choice of "burden/pain" echoes the emotional and physical responsibilities of their job highlighting its exacting nature. • Repetition of "so much/so many" illustrates his observations that a large proportion of a nurse's job is dealing with death and the dying ie it is a regular occurrence. • Word choice of "clear" shows their ability to remain professional and not form deep emotional attachments to their dying patients.

Question	Expected Answer(s)	Max Mark	Additional Guidance
48.	Candidates should analyse how the poet's use of language emphasises the painful nature of the situation for both patient and visitor. For full marks, both patient and visitor must be dealt with for full marks, although not necessarily in equal measure. 2 marks awarded for detailed/insightful comment plus quotation/reference. 1 mark for more basic comment plus quotation/reference. 0 marks for quotation/reference alone.	4	Possible answers include: Patient • Metaphor "white cave of forgetfulness" suggests that her reduced mental capacity offers her some protection/refuge from the horrors of her situation OR diminishes her insight into her own situations/lessens her ability to communicate • Imagery of a flower/plant "withered hand … stalk" suggests her weakness and helplessness. The image is ironic as flowers are traditional tokens of recovery for hospital patients. • The unconventional inverted vampire image "glass fang/guzzling/giving" emphasises the reality that the patient is being kept alive medically as her body is decaying and death is imminent. Candidates may choose to deal with this as word choice/alliteration/onomatopoeia. All are acceptable approaches and should be rewarded appropriately. • Imagery of "black figure/white cave" suggests the patient is dimly aware of her surroundings but the "black figure" who has now entered her environment symbolises her approaching death. • Word choice of "smiles a little" indicates that the patient has, perhaps, accepted the reality of her situation/does have a sense of the caring nature of the visit Visitor • Personal pronouns "her/me/she/I" indicate that both are suffering albeit in different ways. The patient suffers the physical agony of dying but the visitor has to face the emotional anguish of her loss. • Repetition of "distance" highlights that on a literal level he has arrived at her bedside but there is still a gulf between them as he cannot help her. • Word choice "neither … cross" conveys he is no longer an observer but a helpless participant who now feels acute emotional misery. • Word choice of "clumsily" highlights his feelings of inadequacy and ineptitude in the situation in which he finds himself. Either/both: • Symbolic reference to "books that … read" creates a tone of futility/despair as the pleasure to be gained from reading will never be experienced again. • Oxymoron/pun "fruitless fruits" effectively conveys the hopelessness of the situation for both patient and visitor. Just as fruits are traditional gifts brought to hospital to aid recuperation, "fruitless" ironically reveals that this patient will never recover so there is no hope. The agony of her loss is, therefore, laid bare.

Question	Expected Answer(s)	Max Mark	Additional Guidance
49.	Candidates should discuss the significance of loss in this poem and in at least one other by MacCaig and should refer to appropriate textual evidence to support their discussion. 0 marks for reference/quotation alone. Candidates can answer in bullet points in this final question, or write a number of linked statements.	10	Up to 2 marks can be achieved for identifying elements of commonality as identified in the question, ie MacCaig's presentation of the theme of loss. A further 2 marks can be achieved for reference to the extract given. 6 additional marks can be awarded for discussion of similar references to at least one other poem by the poet. <u>In practice this means:</u> Identification of commonality loss is a universal human experience(1 mark) Which can have a profound and long-lasting effect on the individual (1 mark) From the extract: 2 marks for detailed/insightful comment plus quotation/reference; 1 mark for more basic comment plus quotation/reference; 0 marks for quotation/reference alone. eg Fear of loss of the loved one influences the speaker's perception of everything in the hospital eg 'what seemed a corpse' (2 marks) OR Sense of despair at end of visit due loss of communication with the loved on- nothing has been achieved 'fruitless fruits; (2 marks) From at least one other text: 2 marks for detailed/insightful comment plus quotation/reference; 1 mark for more basic comment plus quotation/reference; 0 marks for quotation/reference alone (Up to 6 marks). Possible answers include: • *Sounds of the Day* — profound impact of loss when a relationship ends shown through contrast between sounds — meaning life — and the 'silence' after parting **(2)** • *Sounds of the Day* use of 'numb' as final word emphasizes finality and intensity of negative feelings associated with the relationship ending **(2)** • *Memorial* — all consuming, all pervading nature of loss in the death of a loved one shown in 'Everywhere she dies' **(2)** • *Memorial* — despite passage of time, his life is now a 'memorial' devoted to her memory 'I am her sad music' **(2)** • *Aunt Julia* loss of opportunity to communicate with his aunt shown in 'absolute silence' of her death/grave, by the time he could have spoken Gaelic to her **(2)** Many other answers are possible.

Text 5 — Poetry — *An Autumn Day* by Sorely Maclean

Question	Expected Answer(s)	Max Mark	Additional Guidance
50.	Candidates should analyse how the poet's use of language emphasises the impact of this experience. 2 marks awarded for detailed/insightful comment plus quotation/reference. 1 mark for more basic comment plus quotation/reference. 0 marks for quotation/reference alone.	4	Possible answers include: • Reference to "that slope" suggests that the specific place is imprinted on the mind of the persona • "soughing" is surprising, suggesting the deadly shells make a gentle noise • "six dead men at my shoulder" — a matter-of-fact tone, suggesting that the persona has become accustomed to the extraordinary and the traumatic. • "waiting … message" suggests a communication with a higher power, as if the dead soldiers are in a state of limbo • "screech" conveys the disturbing nature of the noise from shells • "throbbing" suggests pain and discomfort • "leaped … climbed … surged" makes clear the rapid spread of deadly fire • "blinding … splitting" shows how the shell robs the persona of his senses.
51.	Candidates should analyse how the poet uses at least two examples of language to emphasise the meaninglessness of the men's deaths. 2 marks awarded for detailed/insightful comment plus quotation/reference. 1 mark for more basic comment plus quotation/reference. 0 marks for quotation/reference alone.	4	Possible answers include: • "the whole day" suggests that their deaths have been ignored • "morning … midday … evening" emphasising the time continues as normal/is never-ending • "sun … so indifferent" — the sun, rather than being a primary life-force, is portrayed as being cold and lacking in nurturing qualities • juxtaposition of "painful" and "comfortable/kindly" highlights the ironic nature of the landscape ignoring the men's deaths • "In the sun … under the stars" highlight the starkness of death in the midst of the continuous nature of time/life's cycle • contrast of "six men dead" and "stars of Africa/jewelled and beautiful" emphasises the triviality of the men's deaths beside the greatness/majesty of nature
52.	Candidates should explain what the speaker finds puzzling when he reflects on the men's deaths. 2 marks may be awarded for detailed/insightful comment. 1 mark for more basic comment	2	Possible answers include: • he is puzzled by the random/indiscriminate nature of death —"took them and did not take me" • he is puzzled as these deaths seem to contradict the beliefs/religious teaching of his background — the notion of the Elect

Question	Expected Answer(s)	Max Mark	Additional Guidance
53.	Candidates should discuss how MacLean uses nature to convey the central concern(s) of this and at least one other poem. Candidates may choose to answer in bullet points in this final question, or write a number of linked statements.	10	Up to 2 marks can be achieved for identifying elements of commonality as identified in the question, ie how MacLean uses nature to convey the central concerns of his poetry A further 2 marks can be achieved for the reference to the extract given. 6 additional marks can be awarded for discussion of similar references from at least one other poem by MacLean. <u>In practice this means:</u> Identification of commonality eg vivid images from nature (1 mark) allow MacLean to explore a variety of themes — war/heritage and tradition/love/relationships etc (1 mark) From the extract: 2 marks for detailed/insightful comment plus quotation/reference; 1 mark for more basic comment plus quotation/reference; 0 marks for quotation/reference alone. eg The grandeur contained in the imagery of the "stars of Africa, jewelled and beautiful" highlights humanity's insignificance. (2 marks) **OR** Autumn is used to suggest the transience of life/inevitability of death in the continuous cycle of nature. (2 marks) From at least one other text: 2 marks for detailed/insightful comment plus quotation/reference; 1 mark for more basic comment plus quotation/reference; 0 marks for quotation/reference alone (Up to 6 marks). Possible answers include: • *Hallaig*: the native trees of Raasay are used to symbolise the traditional ways of life/inhabitants who have been removed as a consequence of The Clearances **(2)** • *Screapadal*: the beauty of the natural setting allows the persona to reflect on his connection with the Hebrides **(2)** • *Screapadal*: the peaceful nature of the seal and basking shark is contrasted with the submarine/threat of destruction from humans **(2)** • *Shores*: the sea coming into "Talisker bay forever" depicts the fulfilling qualities of love **(2)** • *I gave you Immortality*: **the permanence of nature symbolises his undying love for Eimhir (2)** Many other answers are possible.

Text 6 — Poetry — *Two Trees* by Don Paterson

Question	Expected Answer(s)	Max Mark	Additional Guidance
54.	Candidates should analyse how the poet's use of poetic technique in lines 1–12 emphasises the importance of the story of the trees. 2 marks are awarded for detailed/insightful comment plus quotation/reference. 1 mark for more basic comment plus quotation/reference. 0 marks for quotation/reference alone.	4	Possible answers include: • Temporal sequence of 'One morning … Over the years …' suggests the ever-present/universal nature of the story • Interest in character of Don Miguel as obsessive: 'one idea rooted' • Allegorical representation/characterisation/symbolism of trees: 'the magic tree' suggest powerful nature of the story • Impact of the tree on the villagers: 'not one kid in the village didn't know'
55.	Candidates should analyse how language is used to create an impression of 'the man'. 2 marks will be awarded for 1 detailed/insightful comment plus reference. 1 mark for more basic comment plus reference. 0 marks for reference/quotation alone.	4	Possible answers include: • "The man" is unnamed, remains faceless/anonymous • "had no dream" suggests lack of imagination or empathy • "dark" suggests sense of foreboding • "malicious" suggests evil intent • "whim" suggests casual, thoughtless act • "who can say" suggests his actions were inexplicable/unaccountable • "axe"/"split the bole" suggests a violence/brutality in his actions
56.	Candidates should explain the irony of the final two lines. 2 marks awarded for one detailed/insightful comment. 1 mark for more basic comment.	2	Possible answers: • Idea of trees having no human qualities despite earlier allusions • Trees are essentially prosaic with no magical qualities • The definitive statement that the poem is only about trees when it is clearly not
57.	Candidates should discuss how Paterson develops the theme of relationships. Candidates may choose to answer in bullet points in this final question, or write a number of linked statements.	10	Up to 2 marks can be achieved for identifying elements of commonality as identified in the question, ie the theme of relationships. A further 2 marks can be achieved for reference to the extract given. 6 additional marks can be awarded for discussion of similar references to at least one other short story by the writer. In practice this means: Identification of commonality eg the profound and complex nature of intimate relationships on the individual (1 mark) and the potential fragility of human relationships (1 mark). From the extract: 2 marks for detailed/insightful comment plus quotation/reference; 1 mark for more basic comment plus quotation/reference; 0 marks for quotation/reference alone. eg "so tangled up" suggests complex mutual dependency which can be either damaging or productive (2 marks)

Question	Expected Answer(s)	Max Mark	Additional Guidance
57.	*(continued)*		**OR**
			"nor did their unhealed flanks weep every spring" suggests the resilience of the human spirit/the pain of separation/longing for intimacy (2 marks)
			From at least one other text:
			2 marks for detailed/insightful comment plus quotation/reference;
			1 mark for more basic comment plus quotation/reference;
			0 marks for quotation/reference alone
			(Up to 6 marks).
			Possible answers include:
			• *Waking with Russell* — father/son bond explored through transformative power of love showing it is unconditional — "pledged myself forever" **(2)**
			• *Waking with Russell* — "lit it as you ran" suggests love providing mutual benefit, enriching lives **(2)**
			• *The Ferryman's Arms* — relationship with self when he plays pool alone, suggesting the conflict between different aspects of the self **(2)**
			• *The Thread* — development of the thread image shows fragility of family relationship/resilience gained through trauma **(2)**
			• *The Thread* — "the great twin-engined wingspan of us" suggests the uplifting exhilaration of sharing experiences with loved ones **(2)**
			Many other answers are possible.

SECTION 2 — Critical Essay

Please see the assessment criteria for the Critical Essay on page 172.

HIGHER ENGLISH
2016

PAPER 1 — READING FOR UNDERSTANDING, ANALYSIS AND EVALUATION

Marking Instructions for each question

Question		Expected Answer(s)	Max Mark	Additional Guidance
1.		For full marks there should be comments on at least two examples. Possible answers are shown in the "Additional Guidance" column.	2	Possible answers: • emphatic/categorical nature of opening sentence conveys the topic in an unequivocal manner • "hugely important" conveys the gravity of the topic • use of question/repeated use of questions invites the reader to think about the topic • humorous tone created, e.g. mockery of their lack of basic political awareness • use of stereotypical teenage concerns leads the reader to agree or disagree with the writer • climactic nature of final sentence
2.	(a)	Candidates must attempt to use their own words. No marks for straight lifts from the passage. 2 marks may be awarded for detailed/insightful comment. 1 mark for more basic comment. Possible answers are shown in the "Additional Guidance" column.	2	Possible answers: Writer's viewpoint: • assumption that today's teenagers will be just like her generation ("my younger self") • no idea how to make important decisions/lack of awareness or knowledge ("clueless") • preoccupied with relationships with contemporaries ("increased obsession with their peer group") • distracted/influenced by technology ("unpatrolled access to social media", "constant barrage of entertainment") Scientific research: • the teenage brain is not fully formed ("undeveloped teenage brain") • (inadequate frontal lobes means) higher order thinking/judgements are challenging for teenagers ("think in the abstract...impulses") • teenagers' inability to make personal choices precludes them from influencing issues affecting other people ("life-changing decisions for themselves")
	(b)	For full marks there should be comments on at least two examples. 2 marks may be awarded for detailed/insightful comment plus quotation/reference. 1 mark for more basic comment plus quotation/reference. 0 marks for quotation/reference alone. Possible answers are shown in the "Additional Guidance" column.	4	Possible answers: • the delaying of the final clause of the first sentence ("when I would have agreed …. status quo") suggests the plausibility of the case against lowering the voting age • "clueless" suggests an inability to make responsible decisions • "(increased) obsession" suggests an irrational fixation with social standing • "unpatrolled" suggests the potential damage of unlimited access/malign influence of social media on young people • "constant" suggests the unremitting distraction of media products • "barrage", an intense military bombardment, suggests the destructive influence of the media • the list "social media… entertainment" suggests range of lifestyle features on which they place greater importance

Question		Expected Answer(s)	Max Mark	Additional Guidance
2.	(b)	*(continued)*		• "disengagement" suggests an apathetic attitude towards politics • "smartphone-fixated" suggests the supposedly trivial/self-absorbed nature of the teenagers' concerns • "undeveloped" suggests that the brain is not fully functioning/is not capable of fully undertaking a task • the list "enables us to think in the abstract … control our impulses" suggests the seeming amount/variety of mental processes teenagers can't properly engage in
3.		2 marks may be awarded for detailed/insightful comment. 1 mark for more basic comment. Possible answers are shown in the "Additional Guidance" column.	2	Possible answers: The example of Malala's achievements at such a young age is used to show that young people should be allowed to vote/challenge the view that young people are too irrational or immature Someone with Malala's qualities could not vote in the UK elections merely because of age shows how ridiculous the age restriction is/adults with ridiculous views can vote, yet someone like Malala would not be allowed to. Candidates could approach this question in a number of ways (e.g. Malala reference acts as a link between negative views of young people and more positive views).
4.		For full marks, candidates must deal with both word choice and sentence structure, but not necessarily in equal measure. 2 marks may be awarded for detailed/insightful comment plus quotation/reference. 1 mark for more basic comment plus quotation/reference. 0 marks for quotation/reference alone. Possible answers are shown in the "Additional Guidance" column.	4	Possible answers: Word choice: • "scarcely (exempt)" suggests a scathing condemnation of adult failings • "limited brain power/inadequately brained" suggests adults' lack of intelligence • "incivility" suggests the rude behaviour exhibited by adults • "tantrums" suggests immature outbursts of temper • "profanity" suggests the offensive nature of the language used by adults • "prejudice" suggests the intolerance displayed by adults • "time-wasting" suggests a lack of commitment/desire to shirk work • "unedifying" suggests setting a poor example • "illiterate" suggests lack of sophistication in opinion • "non-taxpaying" suggests devious, unwilling to accept civic responsibilities • "ignorant" suggests ill-mannered/lack of awareness Sentence structure: • parenthesis "as politicians must hope" emphasises/isolates the writer's point about political hypocrisy • list "incivility, tantrums, …. tabloid websites" emphasises the variety/scale of the unacceptable behaviour exhibited by adults (a comment on the anti-climactic nature of the list, introducing a mocking tone is also possible) • parallel sentence structure of the lists "sport, music, creating computer software" and "incivility, tantrums, … tabloid websites" to emphasise the negative behaviour of adults in comparison to teenagers

Question	Expected Answer(s)	Max Mark	Additional Guidance
4.	*(continued)*		• parallel sentence structure of the lists "incivility, tantrums, … tabloid websites" and "inadequately brained, illiterate, non-taxpaying or ignorant" to reinforce the negative behaviour exhibited by adults • climactic nature of final sentence culminating in condemnatory use of "chilling"
5.	2 marks may be awarded for detailed/ insightful comment. 1 mark for more basic comment. Possible answers are shown in the "Additional Guidance" column.	3	Possible answers: • from their earliest years they have been exposed to technological advances • they have the capacity to absorb a variety of sources to establish their own outlook on important issues • they have enough knowledge of how the media works not to be taken in by those who try to deceive them
6.	For full marks there should be comments on at least two examples. 2 marks may be awarded for detailed/ insightful comment plus quotation/reference. 1 mark for more basic comment plus quotation/reference. 0 marks for quotation/reference alone. Possible answers are shown in the "Additional Guidance" column.		Possible answers: • sequence "No … Yes … But" builds to climactic turnaround emphasising the positive qualities of teenagers • positioning of "But" in the paragraph/sentence to indicate change to positive view of teenagers • parenthesis of "idealism … open-mindedness" to identify/clarify the "more loveable teenage qualities" • list of "loveable teenage qualities" to emphasise the scale/variety of qualities • "idealism" suggests lack of cynicism/belief in making the world a better place • "energy" suggests passion and commitment to making a difference • "sense of injustice" suggests their desire to right wrongs in the world • "open-mindedness" suggests their tolerance and lack of prejudice • "starved" suggests that at the moment politics is in dire need of/sorely lacks/is deprived of the positive qualities young people exhibit • "inject some life" suggests the rejuvenating effect of young people on political debate OR the sudden force/strength/impact of their introduction into political debate
7.	For full marks candidates must deal with both tone and contrast, but not necessarily in equal measure. 2 marks may be awarded for detailed/ insightful comment plus quotation/reference. 1 mark for more basic comment plus quotation/reference. 0 marks for quotation/reference alone. Possible answers are shown in the "Additional Guidance" column.	4	Possible answers: Tone: • conversational tone of "Naturally" suggests shared understanding between writer and reader about validity of teenage concerns • tongue-in-cheek tone. "If voting has to be rationed …" Writer uses humour to approach the topic in a subversive manner • ironic tone of "only have a year to wait" builds on previous examples of irony e.g. the reference to "epistocracy"/the irony of the powers of old and teenage voters, to mock the opposing viewpoint • blunt, matter-of-fact tone of "We could compromise" suggests the initial plausibility of this solution • incredulous tone created by listing the responsibilities currently conferred ("after they have already married … fight for their country") highlights the absurdity/inconsistencies of current policy • scathing tone of "believe they know so much better" underlines the arrogance of adults

Question	Expected Answer(s)	Max Mark	Additional Guidance
7.	(continued)		• sarcasm/mockery of the final sentence ("doing our young people a great big favour") to suggest the absurdity of not recognising a teenager's right to vote
			Contrast:
			• development of old vs young argument — old allowed to vote but not around to live with the consequences, young not allowed to vote but have to live with the consequences
			• list of fairly trivial things ("fireworks") contrasted with life-changing decisions ("donated an organ") — stresses random/illogical nature of what people are and are not allowed to do
			• final sentence emphasises the contrast between adults who consider themselves superior set against the young people whose rights are being denied
8.	Candidates can use bullet points in this final question, or write a number of linked statements. Key areas of disagreement are shown in the grid. Possible answers are shown in the "Additional Guidance" column.	5	The following guidelines should be used: 5 marks — identification of three key areas of disagreement with detailed/insightful use of supporting evidence 4 marks — identification of three key areas of disagreement with appropriate use of supporting evidence 3 marks — identification of three key areas of disagreement 2 marks — identification of two key areas of disagreement 1 mark — identification of one key area of disagreement 0 marks — failure to identify any key areas of disagreement and/or misunderstanding of the task **NB** A candidate who identifies only two key areas of disagreement may be awarded up to a maximum of 4 marks, as follows: • 2 marks for identification of two key areas of disagreement **plus**: **either** • a further mark for appropriate use of supporting evidence to a total of 3 marks **or** • a further 2 marks for detailed/insightful use of supporting evidence to a total of 4 marks A candidate who identifies only one key area of disagreement may be awarded up to a maximum of 2 marks, as follows: • 1 mark for identification of one key area of disagreement • a further mark for use of supporting evidence to a total of 2 marks

	Areas of Disagreement	Passage 1	Passage 2
1.	Intellectual ability	Teenagers are capable of intellectual maturity, for example reference to Malala	Young people may have political knowledge but not the intellectual development of an adult, for example the writer refers to her daughter
2.	Areas of political debate	Teenagers would focus on issues of relevance to them like student debt, minimum wage	Debate will continue to focus on traditional areas of concern like the economy and the NHS
3.	Independence of thought	As part of iGeneration, they have developed an independent political stance	Influenced by parents to turn out to vote
4.	Response to manipulation	Too media aware to be taken in by politicians/spin doctors	Susceptible to media manipulation by cynical politicians
5.	Commitment	Potential to sustain long term commitment to political issues, for example the environment	Give up on voting very quickly
6.	Responsibilities/rights	Teenagers already have a large number of rights/responsibilities and therefore should be allowed to vote	Teenagers have a limited number of rights/responsibilities and therefore should not be allowed to vote
7.	Impact of teenage voters	Teenager voters would invigorate/ energise political life	Teenage voters would be detrimental/would make no difference to the political process

PAPER 2 – CRITCAL READING

SECTION 1 – Scottish Text

For all Scottish Texts, marking of the final question, for 10 marks, should be guided by the following generic instruction in conjunction with the specific advice given for the question on each Scottish Text:

Candidates can answer in bullet points in this final question, or write a number of linked statements.

0 marks for reference/quotation alone.

Up to 2 marks can be achieved for identifying elements of commonality as identified in the question.
A further 2 marks can be achieved for reference to the extract given.
6 additional marks can be awarded for discussion of similar references to at least one other part of the text (or other story or poem) by the writer.

In practice this means:

Identification of commonality (2) (e.g.: theme, characterisation, use of imagery, settng, or any other key element ...)

from the extract:

1 × relevant reference to technique/idea/feature (1)
1 × appropriate comment (1)
(maximum of 2 marks only for discussion of extract)

from at least one other text/part of the text:

2 marks for detailed/insightful comment plus quotation/reference

1 mark for more basic comment plus quotation/reference

0 marks for quotation/reference alone

(Up to 6 marks).

Detailed Marking Instructions for each question

SECTION 1 — Scottish Text

SCOTTISH TEXT (DRAMA)

Text 1 — *Drama — The Slab Boys* by John Byrne

Question	Expected Answer(s)	Max Mark	Additional Guidance
1.	2 marks may be awarded for detailed/ insightful comment plus quotation/reference. 1 mark for more basic comment plus quotation/reference. 0 marks for quotation/reference alone.	2	Possible answers include: • Challenging/obstructive: "What're you wanting him for?" • Assertive: repetition of "I'll take it." • Taking control away from Jack: "That's all right. I'll take it." • Defiant: "I'll take it, I said."/"I'm authorised!" • No respect for Jack/ignoring him shown by *(Exits.)* to take the call when Jack has said not to
2.	2 marks may be awarded for detailed/ insightful comment plus quotation/reference. 1 mark for more basic comment plus quotation/reference. 0 marks for quotation/reference alone.	4	Possible answers include: • Sadie's incongruous casting of herself as a martyr: "Too bloody soft, that's my trouble..." • Incongruity of reference to casters instead of feet. • Lucille's shocked overreaction to finding Sadie in the slab room: "Waaaahh! God!" • Play on word "shy": Sadie means "fifteen bob shy" whereas Lucille thinks she means lacking in confidence (opposite of what Spanky is) • Ludicrousness of description of Sadie's husband's antics at last year's dance — "leapfrogging over ... beehive hairdo" • Juxtaposition of Lucille's question about leg injury sustained during this behaviour
3.	For full marks both Sadie and Lucille should be covered but not necessarily in equal measure. 2 marks may be awarded for detailed/ insightful comment plus quotation/reference. 1 mark for more basic comment plus quotation/reference. 0 marks for quotation/reference alone.	4	Possible answers include: Sadie: • Critical of men/contemptuous/thinks they are useless: reference to negative connotations of "real rubbish" and "dross" • Impossibility of finding a decent man: anti-climactic effect of "sift through the dross ... real rubbish" • Blames her choice of husband for her disappointment with life: dismissive tone of "all you've got to show's bad feet and a display cabinet" Lucille: • She is confident in her own chance of finding a better man than Sadie's: powerful rebuttal of Sadie's viewpoint of men "They're not all like that, for God's sake" • Determined not to define herself by choice of man: confident assertion of "Not this cookie, Lucille Bentley ... Woman of the World"
4.	Candidates can answer in bullet points in this final question, or write a number of linked statements.	10	Up to 2 marks can be achieved for identifying elements of commonality as identified in the question, i.e. the role of women. A further 2 marks can be achieved for reference to the extract given. 6 additional marks can be awarded for discussion of similar references to at least one other part of the text by the writer. In practice this means: Identification of commonality (2) E.g. play is mainly about men/the male experience of work/thwarted ambition (1) but women important in terms of what they represent/the relationships they offer to the men (1)

Question	Expected Answer(s)	Max Mark	Additional Guidance
4.	(continued)		From the extract: 2 marks for detailed/insightful comment plus quotation/reference 1 mark for more basic comment plus quotation/reference 0 marks for quotation/reference alone Maximum of 2 marks only for discussion of extract. E.g. Lucille represents the confident young woman who sees herself as independent/equal to any man and does not need to validate herself through a relationship **(2)** From at least one other part of the text: as above for up to 6 marks Possible references include: • Lucille "every slab boy's dream" — she is seen as a traditional representation of femininity/objectified in terms of her desirability **(2)** • Phil's mother — source of worry for Phil/reverse of the nurturing role of mother, e.g. his story about her breakdown and its impact on him **(2)** • Lucille provides the motivation/cause of the extreme mockery of Hector: he is dressed up ridiculously to impress her **(2)** • Sadie's role as "surrogate mother" providing food (tea trolley cakes) and nagging the slab boys to behave properly **(2)** • Sadie is represented as a clichéd/stock female character in a male-dominated world, providing humour in the play on the receiving end of Phil and Spanky's banter/scene where she hits Phil on the head **(2)**

Text 2 — Drama — The Cheviot, the Stag and the Black, Black Oil by John McGrath

Question	Expected Answer(s)	Max Mark	Additional Guidance
5.		2	Possible answers include: Tone: • Astonishment • Incredulity • Outrage Analysis: • Dismissive nature of "Re" contrasts with the serious nature of the accusation • Repeated use of questions suggests inability to believe they could think this of him • "Can you believe" emphasises the unlikely nature of the accusation • Repetition of "no" emphasises the obvious lack of motivation
6.	2 marks are awarded for detailed/insightful comment plus quotation/reference. 1 mark for more basic comment plus quotation/reference. 0 marks for quotation/ref alone.	4	Possible answers include: Language: • use of "Therefore" implies unquestioning acceptance of Sellar's defence • understatement of the crimes with language such as "ignored a custom" • directing the jury with phrases such as "I would ask them ..." • using language which suggests the crime — damaged property ("barns" and "the burning of the house of Chisholm") — whilst ignoring the deaths of the tenants

Question	Expected Answer(s)	Max Mark	Additional Guidance
6.	*(continued)*		• "contradictory nature" contrasts with "real evidence" suggesting that the judge gives greater credence to evidence which defends Sellar • use of "And … And …" suggests an accumulation of evidence for Sellar's defence • he directs the jury to ignore contradictory evidence and focus on character assessment with references to the accused "humanity" and being "in all cases … most humane" • the inappropriately friendly greeting, "hello, Archie" suggests he is complicit in Sellar's defence
7.	2 marks are awarded for detailed/insightful comment plus quotation/reference. 1 mark for more basic comment plus quotation/reference. 0 marks for quotation/ref alone.	4	Possible answers include: • "Every reformer of mankind" suggests he/those he works for are bringing about grand-scale improvement as many others have before • "errors, frauds and quackery" suggests that he dismisses the opposition as duplicitous and mistaken: • "at bottom" suggests the fundamental truth/ rightness of what the reformers are doing • "patience" suggests resilience and commitment in the face of adversity • his references to "zeal and enthusiasm" present the reformers as being motivated, committed and dynamic • "generous" suggests reformers are selflessly working for the good of mankind • "exertions" suggests the tireless efforts to make improvements • "public yet unostentatious" suggests generosity combined with modesty • "distresses of the widow, the sick and the traveller" list of clichéd examples of needy people to emphasise Sutherland's wide-ranging philanthropic role
8.	Candidates may choose to answer in bullet points in this final question, or write a number of linked statements.	10	Up to 2 marks can be achieved for identifying elements of commonality as identified in the question, i.e. McGrath's presentation of authority A further 2 marks can be achieved for reference to the extract given. 6 additional marks can be awarded for discussion of similar references to at least one other part of the text by the writer. <u>In practice this means:</u> Identification of commonality **(2)** E.g. the self-seeking nature of authority in a variety of guises **(1)** Their cruel treatment of the people over whom they should exercise stewardship **(1)** From the extract: 2 marks for detailed/insightful comment plus quotation/reference; 1 mark for more basic comment plus quotation/ reference; 0 marks for quotation/reference alone. Maximum of 2 marks only for discussion of extract. E.g. The judge's involvement with the defence illustrates collusion within the establishment **(2)** Sellar's speech shows hypocrisy by presenting the inhumane actions of Lord and Lady Stafford in a positive light **(2)**

Question	Expected Answer(s)	Max Mark	Additional Guidance
8.	*(continued)*		From elsewhere in the text: as above for up to 6 marks Possible answers include: • List of Sutherland's estates, properties and sources of wealth, e.g. "huge estate in Yorkshire", "a large slice of the Liverpool-Manchester Railway" suggests his self- serving, selfish and materialistic view of his privileges as a lord **(2)** • Hypocrisy of Sellar and Loch in lamenting the problems of the lifestyle of the crofters as an excuse to remove them and exploit the land they live on **(2)** • Cruelty and violence towards vulnerable crofters shown in example of old woman and her grandchildren forced to live in an exposed sheep-cot when their home was seized **(2)** • Sinister behaviour of Lord Crask and Lady Phosphate turning guns on audience to show threat their kind pose "We'll show you we're the ruling class" **(2)** • Sutherland's attempts to manipulate the people into enlisting suggests that they are seen as a resource to be exploited, not people to be respected **(2)**

Text 3 — *Drama — Men Should Weep* by Ena Lamont Stewart

Question	Expected Answer(s)	Max Mark	Additional Guidance
9.	For full marks, both relationships should be covered but not necessarily in equal measure. 2 marks awarded for detailed/insightful comment plus quotation/reference. 1 mark for a more basic comment plus quotation/reference. 0 marks for quotation/reference alone.	4	Possible answers include: Relationship with Maggie: • "…gives Maggie a pat" — gesture suggests an easy intimacy between them • "they exchange warm smiles" — suggests their affection is mutual, natural, spontaneous • "Ye dry, John? I'll pit the kettle on." — suggests Maggie anticipates his needs and wants to care for him • "He didna mean onythin." — Maggie's assertion is an attempt to justify his behaviour, to keep the peace with Lily Relationship with Lily: • "turning to Lily" — lack of respect shown by the fact John only acknowledges Lily after being in the room some time • "with as much of a smile as he can muster" — suggests being polite to Lily requires considerable effort on his part, is not natural or easy • "An how's Lil?" — suggests deliberate provocation by using a form of her name he knows she dislikes • "Don't you two stert up!" — Maggie's remark shows an awareness of repeated confrontations between John and Lily/highlights childish nature of John's behaviour towards Lily • "Goad help us!" — John finds Lily's constant criticism and undermining of him tiresome/irritating/exasperating

Question	Expected Answer(s)	Max Mark	Additional Guidance
10.	For full marks both Lily and Maggie should be covered, though not necessarily in equal measure. 2 marks awarded for detailed/insightful comment plus quotation/reference. 1 mark for a more basic comment plus quotation/reference. 0 marks for quotation/reference alone.	4	Possible answers: Lily: • ridicules him by presenting an idealised vision of the domestic world he believes men would create. "if you was a wumman"/"everythin just perfect"/"the weans a washed and pit tae bed at six"/"everythin' spick an span"/"naethin tae dae till bedtime but twiddle yer thumbs" • points out the impracticalities of his ideas in the face of the reality of the demands placed on Maggie every day "hoose-fu o weans"/"and a done aul granny tae look after." • Emphatic nature of "And ony wumman'll tell ye" undermines his status as a man Maggie: • mocks his ability to do anything useful around the house despite his claims that he could organise things more efficiently. "Ye should see him tryin tae mak the breakfast on a Sunday; ye'd get yer kill." • highlights his inability to multi-task when he actually tries to do household chores. "If he's fryin bacon, he's fryin bacon, see? ... intae the pan a at the same time." Lily and Maggie • mock John, showing how silly they think his ideas are by throwing his words back at him in unison. "He'd hae a system!"
11.		2	Possible answers include: • Lily is annoyed by John's insinuation that she is expecting the Morrisons to feed her • She feels a lack of appreciation for the fact that she often provides the family with food/has brought the tin of beans • She is annoyed by John's suggestion that she would chase after a man if she had the opportunity • She is annoyed at their ingratitude in the light of the fact that (their son) Alec still owes her money
12.	Candidates may choose to answer in bullet points in this final question, or write a number of linked statements.	10	Up to 2 marks can be achieved for identifying elements of commonality as identified in the question, i.e. John's role within the family. A further 2 marks can be achieved for reference to the extract given. 6 additional marks can be awarded for discussion of similar references to at least one other part of the text by the writer. <u>In practice this means:</u> Identification of commonality (2) E.g. John conforms to assumptions about the male role within the family (1) however he often does not fulfil this traditional role and feels frustrated/despondent as a result (1) From the extract: 2 marks for detailed/insightful comment plus quotation/reference; 1 mark for more basic comment plus quotation/reference; 0 marks for quotation alone. Maximum of 2 marks only for discussion of extract

Question	Expected Answer(s)	Max Mark	Additional Guidance
12.	*(continued)*		E.g. John's obvious consideration for Maggie does not stop him from accepting her assumption that she should make him tea when he comes in, although she is exhausted **(2)** From elsewhere in the text: as above for up to 6 marks Possible answers include: • John's willingness to share in Maggie's household duties is very limited/he sees domestic work as very much the preserve of women Maggie: "Ye couldna even wash up a dish for me!" • John sees his role as father of Jenny is to protect her and be respected shown by his anger when she is out in the close with a man • He feels ashamed of his inability to provide for the family "Ye end up a bent back and a heid hanging wi shame for whit ye canna help." • He responds to Isa's flirtation/criticism of Maggie even though this is a betrayal of his wife for feelings which are much more superficial • He is proud and happy when he is able to provide for the family, in the traditional male role for example the Christmas present of the red hat for Maggie in Act 3 - a reminder of their "courting" days

SCOTTISH TEXT (PROSE)

Text 4 — *Prose — The Crater* by Iain Crichton Smith

Question	Expected Answer(s)	Max Mark	Additional Guidance
13.	2 marks awarded for detailed/insightful comment plus quotation/reference. 1 mark for more basic comment plus quotation/reference. 0 marks for quotation/reference alone.	2	Possible answers include: • Repetition of questions suggests his nervousness/confusion/frustration at a situation he cannot control • "We're like a bunch of actors" — comparison suggests a sense of unreality • Emphatic statement/repetition of "I'm" "I'm leading these men, I'm an officer" suggests self-doubt as he is trying to convince/reassure himself • "a huge mind breeding thought after thought" — suggests that he believes that something/someone beyond earthly beings must be controlling their actions
14.	2 marks awarded for detailed/insightful comment plus quotation/reference. 1 mark for more basic comment plus quotation/reference. 0 marks for quotation/reference alone.	4	Possible answers include: • "I am frightened." — simple statement/child-like language suggests the sudden realisation of the danger that he is in • Repetition of "fear" reinforces the pervasive nature of the feeling • "It was an older fear"/"the fear of being buried"/"the fear of wandering" use of repetition/word choice to emphasise the deep-rooted atavistic nature of the fear • "grey figures like weasels" symbolises the unknown/unnatural/indeterminate nature of the threat • reference to "web"/"spiders" — primitive fears/idea of being trapped

Question	Expected Answer(s)	Max Mark	Additional Guidance
15.	2 marks awarded for detailed/insightful comment plus quotation/reference. 1 mark for more basic comment plus quotation/reference. 0 marks for quotation/reference alone.	4	Possible answers include: • sequence of "thrustings", "hackings", "scurryings", "flowing" suggests unrelenting nature of the action • "thrustings and flashes" — dramatic language emphasises sudden combat/forceful violence • "scurryings and breathings as of rats" — evokes primitive fears • "Back. They must get back." — urgency of short sentences/repetition emphasises panic • "Mills bombs, hackings ..." — listing of horrors emphasises the range of danger they are in • "Over the parapet. They were over the parapet. Crouched they had run and scrambled" — staccato nature of sentence structure creates a sense of relief that they were safe for the moment • "Wright ... one arm seemed to have been shot off" use of ellipsis emphasises his sudden realisation of the horror of combat • "all those dead moons" description of desolate landscape evocative of death/emptiness is ever present
16.	Candidates can answer in bullet points in this final question, or write a number of linked statements.	10	Up to 2 marks can be achieved for identifying elements of commonality as identified in the question — i.e. the impact of extreme situations on characters A further 2 marks can be achieved for reference to the extract given. 6 additional marks can be awarded for discussion of similar references to at least one other part of the text. In practice this means: Identification of commonality **(2)** E.g. extremity of situation can bring out positive qualities in a character **(1)** and/or bring about their destruction **(1)** From the extract: 2 marks for detailed/insightful comment plus quotation/reference; 1 mark for more basic comment plus quotation/reference; 0 marks for quotation/reference alone. E.g. Sergeant Smith's practical, phlegmatic response to war is underlined by his matter of fact comment to the soldier who has lost his arm, focusing on the positive benefits **(2)** From at least one other text/part of the text: as above for up to 6 marks Possible answers include: • *In Church* when Colin MacLeod is faced with the threat of death from the 'priest' during his sermon we see his growing sense of unease and stoicism • *The Telegram* the thin woman's quiet heroism, coping with (apparent) reality of the bad news of her son's death as the elder seems to be approaching her house — she is able to comfort the fat woman at that moment • *The Painter* William Murray's detached attitude of the artist is developed as he coolly observes the fight and the emotional reactions of the villagers — isolates him further

Question	Expected Answer(s)	Max Mark	Additional Guidance
16.	*(continued)*		• *Mother and Son* the mother's unrelenting criticism of her adult son creates tension in the household resulting in his feelings of hopelessness and despair • *The Red Door* the mysterious painting of Murdo's door prompts him to consider the difficulty — and attractiveness - of breaking away from the conformity of his community.

Text 5 — *Prose — The Whaler's Return* by George Mackay Brown

Question	Expected Answer(s)	Max Mark	Additional Guidance
17.	Up to 2 marks awarded for detailed/insightful comment plus quotation/reference. 1 mark for more basic comment plus quotation/reference. 0 marks for quotation/reference alone.	4	Possible answers include: • "standing at a mirror … drove a pin through it" her actions reveal her vanity, determined focus on her appearance • "yellow hair … fine burnished knot" — build-up of 'golden' images suggests attractive, almost magical/captivating quality • "At last she got a fine …" suggests the length of time she spends on her hair and the length of time he watches her • Use of the list with repeated use of "and" emphasises her snobbish attitude towards the working men • "Out of her pretty mouth she spat on the stone floor" — contrast between daintiness of "pretty mouth" and coarseness of "spat" emphasises her unpleasant action which contrasts with her lovely appearance
18.	Up to 2 marks awarded for detailed/insightful comment plus quotation/reference. 1 mark for more basic comment plus quotation/reference. 0 marks for quotation/reference alone.	4	Possible answers include: • "wearing his decent suit" suggests he is pleased he is looking his best in order to impress her • "smiled at him sweetly" suggests the special nature of the moment because of the perceived approval/acceptance by 'unattainable' barmaid • "touched rims" suggests intimacy/gentle coming together • "whisky trembled" suggests nervous, tremulous excitement • "transported" — shows intensity of experience for Flaws taken beyond normality • "glittered at him with eyes, teeth, hair, rings" word choice/listing suggests the all-encompassing nature of her allure
19.		2	Possible answers include: • "shame" because he was being dishonest about what he is in order to be accepted • "resentment" because he has been unfairly rejected/humiliated/missed his opportunity

Question	Expected Answer(s)	Max Mark	Additional Guidance
20.	Candidates can answer in bullet points in this final question, or write a number of linked statements.	10	Up to 2 marks can be achieved for identifying elements of commonality as identified in the question, i.e. the importance of journeys, both literal and metaphorical.
			A further 2 marks can be achieved for reference to the extract given.
			6 additional marks can be awarded for discussion of similar references from at least one other short story.
			In practice this means: Identification of commonality **(2)** E.g.: journeys can be physical challenges for survival **(1)** and these are mirrored by metaphorical journeys as a rite of passage **(1)**
			From the extract: 2 marks for detailed/insightful comment plus quotation/reference; 1 mark for more basic comment plus quotation/reference; 0 marks for quotation alone. E.g. The episode in the bar, when Flaw's deception is rewarded with humiliation, is a learning moment on his journey to fulfilment **(2)**
			From at least one other text: as above for up to 6 marks
			Possible answers include:
			• *The Eye of the Hurricane* – Cpt. Stevens' speech on the 'voyage' of life is a quiet moment in the final storm of his life • *A Time to Keep* – journey through the year in time and life involving marriage, birth, death and rebirth • *Tartan* – the Vikings' journey across the island seeking treasure: allegorical journey meeting the human condition in the form of death, fear, betrayal... • *The Bright Spade* – the men set off on a physical/metaphorical journey into the snow to save the community which leads to their heroic, but pointless, deaths • *The Bright Spade* – the community's journey through winter reflects the harsh nature of life and the ever-present threat of death faced by the community

Text 6 – Prose – *The Trick Is To Keep Breathing* by Janice Galloway

Question	Expected Answer(s)	Max Mark	Additional Guidance
21.	2 marks may be awarded for detailed/insightful comment plus quotation/reference. 1 mark for more basic comment plus quotation/reference. 0 marks for quotation/reference alone.	3	Possible answers include: • Word-choice shows attempt to think positively, e.g. "cheap"/"opened up"/"fresh" • "it also meant travel"/"it made me feel free" suggests the idea of freedom as the bus stop is outside the door • Repetition – "my own place, my home" emphasises she is pleased/proud to possess the cottage/be independent • Sentence structure – lists the number and variety of domestic chores she undertook to try to be positive about her new home "I papered ... the place fresh" • Use of short sentences makes it sound matter-of-fact/keeping her emotions in check – "The parting wasn't bitter. We wanted to be civilised and polite" • "I figured they were good signs. Everybody needs to cry now and then" – she turns a negative into a positive

Question	Expected Answer(s)	Max Mark	Additional Guidance
22.	Up to 2 marks awarded for detailed, insightful comment plus quotation/reference. 1 mark for more basic comment plus quotation/reference. 0 marks for quotation/reference alone.	3	Possible answers include: • Word-choice "uneasy" suggests her feelings of concern as she is worried/uncomfortable • Word-choice "tried" suggests she did not succeed in forgetting/continues to be concerned • Personification of the mushroom — "where it had settled"/"left a little pink trail like anaemic blood"/"baby mushrooms"/"just to let them alone in case"/"dangerous"/emphasises that she sees them as almost human/actions are deliberately menacing • "LOOK" in bold and/or capitals emphasises her panic • Minor sentence "In case" suggests they are a real threat
23.	Candidates should deal with both sides of the contrast but not necessarily in equal measure. Up to 2 marks awarded for detailed, insightful comment plus quotation/reference. 1 mark for more basic comment plus quotation/reference. 0 marks for quotation/reference alone.	4	Possible answers include: Cottage: • "Dry rot." abrupt statement/repetition/positioning at the start of both paragraphs emphasises the scale and the extent of the problem • "Sinister" emphasises that Joy sees the dry rot as something evil/deliberately menacing • Metaphor "eaten from the inside by this thing" emphasises that she sees her cottage as a victim of something alien/evil/monstrous • "multiply ... as we slept" emphasises the sense of menace as the rot creeps up on them while they are vulnerable • Word choice "silent spores" also increases the feeling of an invisible evil presence • Word choice "creeping red clouds" emphasises the silent predatory nature of the rot/like it is alive House: • Word choice "cheerful"/"bright" emphasises the attractiveness of and happiness within the house • "full of windows" gives the impression of openness and light • Emphasis on colour — "yellow walls and white woodwork" is bright/cheerful symbolising a new start
24.	Candidates may choose to answer in bullet points in this final question, or write a number of linked statements.	10	Up to 2 marks can be achieved for identifying elements of commonality as identified in the question, i.e. the impact of Joy's relationship with Michael A further 2 marks can be achieved for reference to the extract given. 6 additional marks can be awarded for discussion of similar references from at least one other part of the text. In practice this means: Identification of commonality **(2)** E.g. Michael brings a short period of happiness to Joy **(1)** and, therefore, his sudden, tragic death is all the more shocking for her **(1)**. From the extract: 2 marks for detailed/insightful comment plus quotation/reference; 1 mark for more basic comment plus quotation/reference; 0 marks for quotation alone.

Question	Expected Answer(s)	Max Mark	Additional Guidance
24.	*(continued)*		E.g. throughout the extract Joy repeats "We" to suggest a sense of unity/belonging as she feels protected and complete when she is with Michael **(2)** From at least one other part of the text: as above for up to 6 marks Possible answers include: • The effect of Michael's death and its contribution to Joy's depression — reference to the flashbacks of Michael's drowning convey the still-present horror of that experience • The effect on her ability to cope with day to day life, e.g. work — the Head Teacher doesn't want her to make a fuss when Michael's wife is invited to the Memorial Service • Her casual relationships with men following Michael's death reveal her difficulties in coping with his loss • Her unwillingness to accept Michael's death shows the power of the relationship, still, in her life, e.g. deliberately spilling his aftershave to create a sense of his presence • Her anorexia develops after Michael's death and this allows her some control — she realises she has gone past her time for eating/she bakes but doesn't eat any of it

Text 7 — *Prose — Sunset Song* by Lewis Grassic Gibbon

Question	Expected Answer(s)	Max Mark	Additional Guidance
25.	2 marks awarded for detailed/insightful comment plus quotation/reference. 1 mark for more basic comment plus quotation/reference. 0 marks for quotation/reference alone.	4	Possible answers include: • "a cold and louring day" — sense of gloom is heightened by the combination of the two adjectives • "under the greyness" — dullness which seems all-encompassing • "squelched" — onomatopoeic word which catches the gurgling and sucking sound when walking in wet mud emphasising the sodden conditions she's walking through • "oozing" — again suggests the unpleasantness of the gradual flow of a smell of decay from the wet earth • "sodden" — suggests a thorough soaking which adds to the disagreeable impression of the conditions • "sheltered" is contrasted with "drenched" to highlight the extent of the rain damage to the crops • The very long sentence from "The wet fields" to "*endures*" gives a sense of the much wider world beyond, which is emphasised by the constant movement south to several places beyond Chris's immediate world • "ancient tower that the Pictish folk had reared" suggests Chris's awareness of the achievements of settlers long ago • "below the hands of the crofter folk" shows Chris's awareness of previous generations of farmers working this land • "Standing Stones" their presence provides a link with ancient times emphasising her sense of connection to the many generations before (and their worship) • General awareness that people are transient — "they lasted but as a breath" — but the landscape remains constant

Question	Expected Answer(s)	Max Mark	Additional Guidance
26.	2 marks awarded for detailed/insightful comment plus quotation/reference. 1 mark for more basic comment plus quotation/reference. 0 marks for quotation/reference alone.	4	Possible answers include: • "weeping"/"stricken and frightened" suggests Chris has now realised that her plans to leave the land were foolish and she recognises that the land is part of who she is • "she could never leave it" sums up what Chris has realised/accepted about her relationship with the land • "this life … acrid" — repeated use of "and" shows a build up of all the challenging aspects of the constant physical effort which Chris (ironically) does not want to leave behind • "bound and held as though they had prisoned her here" suggests no possibility of escape • "fine bit plannings" suggests Chris's plans had been childish and vague, without a basis in reality • "the dreamings of a child" suggests that Chris's plans were unrealistic, fantasy, immature • "over toys it lacked" suggests a peevish desire for a passing childish phase • "toys that would never content it when it heard the smore of a storm …" suggests that Chris's previous plans were part of a childish world of playthings which cannot compare to the more lasting pleasures of nature and farming the land • "She could no more teach a school than fly" suggests how unrealistic her dreams were by comparing them to the fantasy idea of flying • "for all the fine clothes and gear she might get and hold" suggests that her desire to pursue her education was at least in part a desire for superficial possessions • "hated and loved" explains the dilemma that Chris has with the land
27.	2 marks awarded for detailed/insightful comment plus quotation/reference. 1 mark for more basic comment plus quotation/reference. 0 marks for quotation/reference alone.	2	Possible answers include: • *"Mighty be here, Chris, where are you going?"* — Auntie's words suggest she feels she should have power over Chris/treats her as though she were a child who needs to ask permission • *"I'm away to Stonehaven to see Mr Semple, can I bring you anything?"* — Chris' determination to make her own decisions and establish her independence • *"Away to Stonehive? What are you jaunting there for? I'll transact any business you have"* — Uncle Tam reacts as though Chris is wasting time on an outing, when he, as the man, should deal with business/legal matters
28.	Candidates can answer in bullet points in this final question, or write a number of linked statements.	10	Up to 2 marks can be achieved for identifying elements of communality as identified in the question, i.e. the idea that "nothing endures". A further 2 marks can be achieved for reference to the extract given. 6 additional marks can be awarded for discussion of similar references to at least one other part of the text by the writer. In practice this means: Identification of commonality **(2)** E.g. Chris's life undergoes constant change as a result of family deaths and changes in her circumstances. **(1)** just as the farming community changes as a result of the devastating effects of the war **(1)**

Question	Expected Answer(s)	Max Mark	Additional Guidance
28.	*(continued)*		From the extract: 2 marks for detailed/insightful comment plus quotation/reference; 1 mark for more basic comment plus quotation/reference; 0 marks for quotation alone. E.g. Chris's growing independence reflects her transition from child to woman when she makes a mature decision to stay on the land and stands up to her Aunt and Uncle who try to dictate what she should do **(2)**. From at least one other part of the text: as above for up to 6 marks Possible answers include: • The death of Jean Guthrie forces Chris to relinquish her childhood dreams and educational aspirations and adopt the role of the woman of the house • The impact of the war on the landscape with the felling of the trees leads to soil erosion making the land harder to farm • Post-war economic exploitation of the land leads to the loss of small farms and the crofters' way of life • The mechanisation of farming, e.g. at the harvest demonstrates agricultural change and progress and the emergence of a new technological world • The end of an era as indicated in the "Morning Star" eulogy suggesting the end of a way of life, culture and a community

Text 8 — *Prose — The Cone-Gatherers* by Robin Jenkins

Question	Expected Answer(s)	Max Mark	Additional Guidance
29.	2 marks awarded for detailed/insightful comment plus quotation/reference. 1 mark for more basic comment plus quotation/reference. 0 marks for quotation/reference alone.	4	Possible answers include: • "yew trees" suggests evil/death as they are often found in graveyards • "dark caverns" suggests underground places (possibly idea of Hades?) where Roderick cannot see/place which is creepy/frightening/dangerous … • "evil presences" extremity of word choice suggests someone/something undefined there to do wrong/cause hurt/create danger • "lurker" suggests someone watching and waiting with harmful intent • "No sunshine" negative term suggests darkness/cold and, therefore, connotations of evil/danger • Reference to Roderick's feelings suggests sinister atmosphere as he is uneasy, e.g. "cold"/"frightened"/"sick at heart". These suggest he is clearly upset/rattled/scared by the presence in the wood
30.	2 marks awarded for detailed/insightful comment plus quotation/reference. 1 mark for more basic comment plus quotation/reference. 0 marks for quotation/reference alone.	4	Possible answers include: • Roderick begins to work out what is going on in Duror's mind, e.g. he realises Duror is spying on the cone-gatherers to collect evidence of their "wrong-doing" (although he does not realise how sinister Duror's thoughts actually are, yet he is closer to the truth than any of the other characters) • He recognises some of the hypocrisy/irony in Duror's thinking — "Duror himself shot deer on Sundays", yet he might use working on a Sunday as an example of the cone-gatherers' "wrong-doing"

Question	Expected Answer(s)	Max Mark	Additional Guidance
30.	*(continued)*		• He is insightful enough to recognise that Duror dislikes the cone-gatherers and wants them removed from the wood: "Why then did he hate the cone-gatherers and wish to drive them away?" • Roderick has an understanding of the "struggle between good and evil" — and recognises the cone-gatherers as good and Duror as evil • He understands that "Good did not always win" based on his reading (references to Christian from *The Pilgrim's Progress* and Sir Galahad's struggles) • He recognises there is something wrong with Duror — "Had Duror gone mad" — and links this to the "change" his mother and Mrs. Morton had been discussing • He makes the link between Duror and the "perils in the wood" which Mrs. Morton had warned him about: without understanding fully, intuitively, he is the closest to understanding what is going on with Duror
31.	2 marks may be awarded for a detailed/insightful comment plus reference. 1 mark should be awarded for a more basic comment plus reference. 0 marks for reference/quotation alone.	2	Possible answers include: • Duror's presence is responsible for Roderick hiding rather than going to the cone-gatherers' hut as intended • Duror is responsible for Roderick's feelings of fear • Roderick's thoughts and fears involve Duror — his imaginings and his attempt to work out why Duror thinks and acts as he does • Duror motivates Roderick to think about the battle between good and evil
32.	Candidates may answer in bullet points in this final question, or write a number of linked statements.	10	Up to 2 marks can be achieved for identifying elements of commonality as identified in the question, i.e. the conflict between good and evil. A further 2 marks can be achieved for reference to the extract given. 6 additional marks can be awarded for discussion of similar references to at least one other part of the text by the writer. In practice this means: Identification of commonality **(2)** E.g. Conflict between good and evil is symbolised through Duror's irrational hatred of the innocent Calum **(1)** Calum has an affinity with nature whereas Duror destroys it **(1)** From the extract: 2 marks for detailed/insightful comment plus quotation/reference; 1 mark for more basic comment plus quotation/reference; 0 marks for quotation alone. E.g. Roderick works out that the cone-gatherers represent goodness and Duror evil shown by his perceptive reaction to Duror's presence outside the hut and is beginning to understand that the struggle between good and evil never ends (2) From at least one other text/part of the text: as above for up to 6 marks

Question	Expected Answer(s)	Max Mark	Additional Guidance
32.	(continued)		Possible answers include: • References to the war as an influence of evil, destroying the landscape/many men/families contrasts with the gentleness of Calum/nature as a life force • Calum is presented as a Christ-like figure of goodness, sacrificed in a Biblical way at the end of the novel whereas Duror is presented as evil in his thoughts and deeds, e.g. lurking at the start of the novel • Roderick is presented as the future of hope/goodness, having inherited a sense of fairness and justice from his grandfather and mother — his desire to be like the cone gatherers identifies him with Calum's innocence • Lady Runcie-Campbell's faith is presented as goodness as this encourages her to visit Peggy Duror/be lenient towards the cone-gatherers following the deer drive/weeps at the end of the novel, yet she sends the cone-gatherers into the storm rather than allowing them to stay in the beach-hut — corrupted by Duror • Mr. Tulloch's continued support of the cone-gatherers is seen as good; he demonstrates fairness and justice following the deer drive and their expulsion from the beach-hut and at the end when Lady Runcie-Campbell insists they rescue Roderick from the tree — this contrasts with influence of Duror

SCOTTISH TEXT (POETRY)

Text 9 — Poetry — A Poet's Welcome to His Love-Begotten Daughter; The First Instance that entitled him to the Venerable Appellation of Father by Robert Burns

Question	Expected Answer(s)	Max Mark	Additional Guidance
33.	2 marks awarded for detailed/insightful comment plus quotation/reference. 1 mark for more basic comment plus quotation/reference.	2	Possible answers include: • "Thou's welcome, wean" suggests warm/congratulatory/proud tone in defiance of convention • "My sweet wee" acknowledges ownerships/suggests intimacy and protectiveness • "My (sweet wee) lady!" — deliberately gives the child status despite the circumstances of her birth • "Daddy" — familiar/informal title underlines the closeness of the bond he acknowledges between them • "mishanter fa' me" — determination not to feel shame/embarrassment
34.	2 marks awarded for detailed/insightful comment plus quotation/reference. 1 mark for more basic comment plus quotation/reference.	4	Possible answers include: • "fornicator" — blunt statement of their accusation showing his refusal to be intimidated/troubled by it • "kintry clatter" — reduces the accusations to trivial gossip/alliteration emphasises the noisy meaninglessness of it • "the mair they talk, I'm kent the better" — balance in the comparatives suggests relishing his notoriety • "clash!" makes all the gossip seems like discordant noise/climactic nature of positioning at end of the short line

Question	Expected Answer(s)	Max Mark	Additional Guidance
34.	*(continued)*		• "auld wife's tongue's" belittling connotations — people who think like this are old-fashioned/out of touch/not worth listening to • "I hae fought for"/"Baith kirk and queir" defiant tone emphasises his determination to take them on/individual taking on authority and institution
35.	2 marks awarded for detailed/insightful comment plus quotation/reference. 1 mark for more basic comment plus quotation/reference. 0 marks for quotation/reference only.	4	Possible answers include: • "Tho' I should be the waur bestead...bienly clad" juxtaposition/contrast of "I" and "thou" to emphasise his commitment to support her, whatever the cost to himself • word choice of "brat" and "wedlock's bed" emphasises his defiant attitude in the face of social convention • "fatherly I kiss and daut thee" use of terms of physical tenderness as an expression of his love for her/the attention he lavishes on her • "Thy mither's person, grace an' merit" list of conventional female virtues emphasises his loyalty and commitment to the baby's mother despite the circumstances • "An' thy poor, worthless daddy's spirit" word choice creates self-deprecating humour showing that he doesn't take himself too seriously
36.	Candidates can answer in bullet points in this final question, or write a number of linked statements.	10	Up to 2 marks can be achieved for identifying elements of commonality as identified in the question, i.e. Burns' treatment of the religious and/or moral concerns of his time A further 2 marks can be achieved for the reference to the extract given. 6 additional marks can be awarded for discussion of similar references in at least one other poem by Burns. Jn practice this means: Identification of commonality **(2)** E.g. Burns challenges/criticises the rigid/intrusive/hypocritical aspects of moral/religious beliefs of his time **(1)** while presenting a warmer, more human alternative **(1)** From the extract: 2 marks for detailed/insightful comment plus quotation/reference; 1 mark for more basic comment plus quotation/reference; 0 marks for quotation/reference alone. E.g. "But be a loving father to thee, And brag the name o' 't." demonstrates his love for and commitment to her, as well as his pride, despite the criticism he will face from those representing conventional religion and morality **(2)** From at least one other text: as above for up to 6 marks Possible references include: • *Address to the Deil* — humorous, ironic speaker/persona is appropriate for poet's satirical critique of Calvinism • *A Man's A Man For A' That* — a spokesman, champion of equality and fraternity speaking as the voice of a community/nation as he criticises the hierarchical nature of society • *Holy Willie* — creation of self-righteous character who justifies his own sins as an apt vehicle for his critique of the perceived religious hypocrisy of the time

Question	Expected Answer(s)	Max Mark	Additional Guidance
36.	*(continued)*		• *Tam O'Shanter* — character of moralising, commentating narrator allows Burns to point out the vagaries of human nature/undermine the apparent moral 'message' of the poem • *To a Mouse* uses the symbol of the homeless mouse to make a comment about the suffering of the tenant farmers of his day.

Text 10 — *Poetry* — *Mrs Midas* by Carol Ann Duffy

Question	Expected Answer(s)	Max Mark	Additional Guidance
37.	Both sides of the contrast must be dealt with for full marks but not necessarily in equal measure. 2 marks awarded for detailed/insightful comment plus quotation/reference. 1 mark for more basic comment plus quotation/reference. 0 marks for quotation/reference alone.	4	Possible answers include: Stanza 1 — the atmosphere of ordinariness/security suggested by: • "poured a glass of wine/started to unwind/relaxed" all suggest the routine process of starting to enjoy the free time at the end of the day • "kitchen filled … itself" conveys the domesticated/homely environment • "blanching the windows/opened one/wiped the other" suggest the mundane activities involved in the preparation of the meal Stanza 2 — the atmosphere of extraordinariness/threat/disbelief suggested by: • "visibility poor/dark" signals a change in mood from previous stanza to one of mystery • "twig in his hand … gold" suggests a supernatural occurrence • "pear … like a lightbulb" suggests the unnatural appearance of her husband • "fairy lights" the incongruity of putting these up in September/connotations of something magical
38.	2 marks awarded for detailed/insightful comment plus quotation/reference. 1 mark for more basic comment plus quotation/reference. 0 marks for quotation/reference alone.	2	Possible answers include: • "He drew the blinds" the furtive action suggests a concealment/attempt to isolate them from the outside world • "strange, wild, vain" conveys her confusion/concern at the change in his demeanour • "spitting out the teeth … rich" suggests the negative effects of his greed/inappropriateness of his behaviour at the table • "shaking hand" demonstrates the anxiety she feels over his actions • "glass, goblet, golden chalice" suggests the stages of the unnatural transformation of the glass before her eyes
39.	2 marks awarded for detailed/insightful comment plus quotation/reference. 1 mark for more basic comment plus quotation/reference. 0 marks for quotation/reference alone.	4	Possible answers include: • "I finished the wine/I made him sit" highlights her practical nature/ability to regain her composure • Sequencing of "I made/I locked/I moved" suggests she quickly takes control of the situation demonstrating her strength of character/domineering nature • "The toilet I didn't mind" shows her pride in material possessions/keeping up appearances • Use of statement/(rhetorical) questions "I couldn't believe my ears"/"But who has …/about gold?" suggests her no-nonsense approach to life's problems • "keep his hands to himself … lock the cat in the cellar … At least … smoking for good" all suggest a humorous side to her character in being able to make light of such a serious situation

Question	Expected Answer(s)	Max Mark	Additional Guidance
40.	Candidates can answer in bullet points in this final question, or write a number of linked statements.	10	Up to 2 marks can be achieved by identifying elements of commonality as identified in the question, i.e. attempts of characters to cope with life-changing situations. A further 2 marks can be achieved for reference to the text given. 6 additional marks can be awarded for discussion of similar references to at least one other poem by the poet. <u>In practice this means:</u> Identification of commonality **(2)** E.g. Duffy presents characters who develop various coping "strategies" either consciously or unconsciously **(1)** some more successful in allowing them to accept or move on, whilst others are still struggling **(1)** From this extract: 2 marks for detailed/insightful comment plus quotation/reference; 1 mark for more basic comment plus quotation/reference; 0 marks for quotation/reference alone. E.g. she attempts to cope by using humour to make light of the horrifying implications of the situation **(2)** From at least one other text: as above for up to 6 marks Possible comments include: • *Anne Hathaway* she focuses on happy memories of when her husband was alive and the depth of their passionate love for one another to cope with the pain of her loss • *Havisham* the speaker imagines violent acts against her one time lover in order to cope with the rejection she feels but is still stuck in the past • *War Photographer* the inability of the photographer to rid himself of his experiences in warzones despite his attempts to adopt a professional distance • *Originally* the speaker attempts to adapt her language in order to fit in to her new environment but feels a sense of loss as a result of this • *Valentine* the speaker attempts to cope with the loss of her illusions about love by rejecting the clichés of love in favour of a more cynical view

Text 11 — *Poetry — The Bargain* by Liz Lochhead

Question	Expected Answer(s)	Max Mark	Additional Guidance
41.	At least two examples should be included for full marks. 2 marks awarded for detailed/insightful comment plus quotation/reference. 1 mark for more basic comment plus quotation/reference. 0 marks for quotation/reference alone.	4	Possible answers include: • "river fast and high" suggests the relationship isn't going smoothly/could run into trouble • "You and I" Individual personal pronouns separated by "and" suggests that even though they seem physically together, they are drifting apart • "twitch and fret" — connotations of unsettled, jumpy. Refers not only to the police horses but the speaker's awareness of her failing relationship • "rubbing the wrong way" — beginnings of disagreement/discomfort of being in the crowd echoes their feelings towards each other

Question	Expected Answer(s)	Max Mark	Additional Guidance
41.	*(continued)*		• "ready to let fly" — the impending violence of the fans suggests conflict/her fear that her lover is preparing to leave her • "looking back, looking forward" — repetition to highlight the uncertainty in the relationship/don't know whether to look to the past or the future
42.	2 marks awarded for detailed/insightful comment. 1 mark for more basic comment. 0 marks for quotation/reference alone.	2	Possible answers include: • Alliteration of "b" in "but the boy...beautiful Bakelite/Bush" suggests energy/upbeat attitude of boy to activity • Positive connotations of "beautiful/Bakelite" suggests bright, upbeat mood • Fast pace/internal rhyme of "buttonpopping stationhopping" suggests enthusiastic enjoyment of music • List of three positive aspects of boy's experience in "doesn't miss a beat", "sings along", "it's easy" suggests the boy's happiness
43.	At least two examples should be included for full marks. 2 marks awarded for detailed/insightful comment plus quotation/reference. 1 mark for more basic comment plus quotation/reference. 0 marks for quotation/reference alone.	4	Possible answers include: • "splintering city" — suggests city is broken or divided, just as the relationship is fractured • "wintry bridges" — cold and uninviting, which suggests the distance/lack of connection in the relationship • "black" — suggests neglect and poverty in this area, which reflects the deteriorating nature of the relationship • "every other tenement ... on its gable end" — pun suggests the open and frank nature of the people which contrasts with lack of openness in the relationship now • "I know it's cold" — pathetic fallacy suggests lack of harmony/closeness in their relationship • "wet dog reek ... damp clothes" — emphasises the unpleasant smell which permeates the area, symbolic of the state of their relationship
44.	Candidates can answer in bullet points in this final question, or write a number of linked statements.	10	Up to 2 marks can be achieved for identifying elements of commonality as identified in the question, i.e. Lochhead's exploration of the theme of difficult relationships. A further 2 marks can be achieved for reference to the extract given. 6 additional marks can be awarded for discussion of similar references to at least one other poem. In practice this means: Identification of commonality **(2)** E.g. Lochhead explores the various problems in relationships **(1)** and in doing this gives us new insights/increases our understanding of universal human problems **(1)** From the poem: 2 marks for detailed/insightful comment plus quotation/reference; 1 mark for more basic comment plus quotation/reference; 0 marks for quotation/reference alone. E.g. the projection of the disintegrating relationship onto the surroundings "splintering city ... wintry bridges" **(2)**

Question	Expected Answer(s)	Max Mark	Additional Guidance
44.	*(continued)*		OR The portrayal of the tension/uncertainty within the relationship "looking back … which way" **(2)** From at least one other text: as above for up to 6 marks Possible answers include: • *My Rival's House* the difficult relationship of the speaker and her prospective mother-in-law due to her overprotectiveness of her son "this son she bore … never can escape" • *My Rival's House* the awkwardness and insecurity of the speaker in the face of the unwelcoming attitude of the rival "I am all edges, a surface, a shell" • *Last Supper* the bitterness and resentment as a result of the disintegration of a relationship "betrayal with a kiss" • *Last Supper* the predatory nature of the spurned as they seek new relationships "get hungry and go hunting again" • *For my Grandmother Knitting* repetition of "there is no need" emphasises the grandmother's diminishing importance within the family

Text 12 — *Poetry — Memorial* by Norman MacCaig

Question	Expected Answer(s)	Max Mark	Additional Guidance
45.	2 marks awarded for detailed/insightful comment plus quotation/reference. 1 mark for more basic comment plus quotation/reference.	3	Possible answers include: • Blunt/matter-of-fact opening statements convey the simple truth that her death surrounds him • Repetition of "everywhere" and/or "dies" reinforces the fact that he cannot escape from this • Present tense shows it is still vivid in his mind • Patterned list of phrases "no sunrise … mountain" emphasises the inescapable nature of her death as these are places not usually associated with death. Placement of "but" after the list highlights the pleasure he previously took has become tainted by her death • Paradox "silence of her dying sounds" conveys the devastating impact of her death as its intensity blocks out everything else. It, in itself, is his only focus • Imagery of "carousel of language" is intricate and candidates may consider it in different ways. Sensible interpretations should be rewarded which link/contrast it to the ideas suggested by "the silence of her dying". E.g. the frivolous, noisy, joyous nature of a fairground; the endless, circular movement which has no purpose other than to entertain; the connotations of childhood freedom and innocence • Imagery of "web" connotes: a deadly trap possibly suggesting his grief is so powerful it eliminates all other emotions/interconnectedness or interwoven human emotions — no escape from absolute quiet • Word choice/imagery of "stitches" further illustrates that his despair is so firmly secured in his psyche that all future happiness will be overpowered/vanquished

Question	Expected Answer(s)	Max Mark	Additional Guidance
45.	*(continued)*		• Candidates may also make a case for "web/ stitches" having more positive connotations, e.g. of his memories of happier times being secured/ fastened/locked away. As before, sensible interpretations, which are justified with evidence, should be considered • Rhetorical question "How can …" creates a pessimistic tone highlighting that his grief is so prevalent he can see no escape • Word choice of "clasp" suggests a tight grip showing the close bond and the strength of his feelings towards his loved one. Thus, this conveys the impact her death has had on him • Imagery of "thick death" portrays death as something impenetrable which he can never break through or recover from emotionally • Word choice of "intolerable distance" conveys his feelings on the inevitable, unbearable barrier between the living and the dead. Highlights his wider beliefs about the finality of death being a gap which can never be bridged
46.	2 marks awarded for detailed/insightful comment plus quotation/reference. 1 mark for more basic comment plus quotation/reference.	4	Possible answers include: • Repetition/echoing in opening line "she grieves … grief" informs of her sympathy/comfort for him in his sorrow, thus reinforcing their love • Present tense of "dying" and "she tells me" conveys his vivid recollection that at the end of her life she was still concerned about the impact, on him, of her death • References to nature "bird … fish" are contradictions of the normal order of things. He sees death as a reversal of existence and so their relationship has been permanently altered./Equally death is being presented as part of the natural cycle of things symbolised by the bird and the fish • Imagery of "crocus is carved ….shapes my mind" offers a brief respite in mood as he appreciates her invocation of nature to highlight that death is part of the circle of life. As such, her death inspires him to be more creative in his work/be precise in the words he uses • The dash/"But" introduces a contrast/change of mood to one of melancholy about his loved one being forever lost to him • Word choice of "black words" continues this mood and hints at his despair about the finality of death forever separating them • Oxymoron "sound of soundlessness" echoes his anguish in stanza 1 about the intense nature of his all-consuming grief • Word choice of "that name" is vague and unspecific highlighting his view of the implausibility of reunion after death • Imagery of "nowhere …. continuously going into" is ambiguous in nature conveying his bleak outlook that her death is a never-ending journey with no certainty or hopeful conclusion

Question	Expected Answer(s)	Max Mark	Additional Guidance
47.	2 marks awarded for detailed/insightful comment plus quotation/reference. 1 mark for more basic comment plus quotation/reference.	3	Possible answers include: • "she can't stop dying" shows how her death is constantly on his mind. The present (continuous) tense illustrates its vividness and clarity which threatens to overwhelm him • "she makes me" conveys their bond and the strength of his love for her, which will prevail through time • "elegy" shows he has become a living testament to the profound nature of grief as an elegy would usually be written as a tribute to her. Instead he subverts the notion to show how profound his melancholy is • "masterpiece" normally relates to an outstanding piece of work/impressive creation. This satirically conveys his belief that his grief is so penetrating it has transformed him into a work of art/treasure/monument • "true fiction" — oxymoron suggests that unlike a story, his anguish is real and links to the "ugliness of death" to convey his horror and anger regarding his fundamental belief in the reality of the situation • "sad music" sums up the central idea about the pervasive nature of grief and despair. The pessimistic ending highlights the all-consuming nature of grief and how it remains forever with him
48.	Candidates may choose to answer in bullet points in this final question, or write a number of linked statements.	10	Up to 2 marks can be achieved for identifying elements of commonality as identified in the question, i.e. reaction to suffering A further 2 marks can be achieved for reference to the extract given. 6 additional marks can be awarded for discussion of similar references to at least one other poem. <u>In practice this means:</u> Identification of commonality **(2)** E.g. reaction to suffering is part of the human condition **(1)** can be experienced as life-affirming or life-denying **(1)** From the poem: 2 marks for detailed/insightful comment plus quotation/reference; 1 marks for more basic comment plus quotation/reference; 0 marks for quotation alone. E.g. the all-consuming and enduring impact of his grief "Everywhere I go she dies" **(2)** From at least one other text: as above for 6 marks Possible answers include: • *Visiting Hour* the speaker's denial/numbness in reaction to severity of the patient's condition and his refusal to accept the inevitable • *Aunt Julia* the speaker's mental pain and regret over the loss of his Aunt and all that she represents in terms of Scotland's heritage • *Assisi* the beggar's reaction to physical suffering: acceptance and gratitude for the little he has in the face of neglect and hypocrisy

Question	Expected Answer(s)	Max Mark	Additional Guidance
48.	*(continued)*		• *Sounds of the Day* the speaker underestimates the depth and enduring nature of his suffering when the relationship ends • *Visiting Hour* the all-consuming despair felt by the speaker at the futility of his efforts to communicate with or to alleviate the suffering of his loved one

Text 13 — *Poetry — Shores* by Sorley MacLean

Question	Expected Answer(s)	Max Mark	Additional Guidance
49.	2 marks awarded for detailed/insightful comment plus quotation/reference. 1 mark for more basic comment plus quotation/reference. 0 marks for quotation/reference alone.	4	Possible answers include: • Sense of immense scale of the landscape conveyed by place names, word choice of "ocean", reference to "between Scotland and Tiree" • Use of Gaelic place names in English translation emphasises speaker's appreciation of the depth of history/his sense of heritage • The enormity of the physical landscape suggested by personification/comparison with a giant of "great white mouth"/"two hard jaws" • "while the ocean was filling ... forever" suggests speaker is appreciative of the never ending power of nature • "Prishal bowed his stallion head" comparison to intimidating, wild, elemental force • Use of hyperbole: of "between the world and eternity" emphasises his sense of wonder at the vast timeless quality of nature
50.	2 marks awarded for detailed/insightful comment plus quotation/reference. 1 mark for more basic comment plus quotation/reference. 0 marks for quotation/reference alone.	4	Possible answers include: • "till doom"/"measuring sand, grain: by grain"/"for the sea draining drop by drop" geological timescale to highlight depth of speaker's commitment, devotion and patience • "And if ... Mull"/"And if ... Moidart" — parallel structure and references to places that he wishes they could be together in, suggests that his strong love for these places is mirrored in his love for the person/wishes to share them with his lover • "that wide solitude ... wait there forever" extreme nature of the vocabulary emphasises that even in this vast, empty setting he is willing to wait for his lover • "a synthesis of love" suggests the link between his love for sea and land and love for his woman • Reference to "ocean and sand" emphasises the never ending nature of his love by comparison with never-ending natural phenomena/gives a sense of his love as elemental, like the force of nature itself
51.	Candidates may choose to comment on either language or ideas or both. 2 marks awarded for detailed/insightful comment plus quotation/reference. 1 mark for more basic comment plus quotation/reference. 0 marks for quotation/reference alone.	2	Possible answers include: Language: • Personification of "unhappy" contrasting the sea with his own contented state as conveyed in the rest of the poem • Nature is shown as powerful/threatening "surging sea"/"dragged the boulders"/"threw them over us" as it was earlier • Promise of "I would build the rampart wall" reaffirms his desire to preserve his love from threats and make sure that it will endure • Threat is described as "an alien eternity" linking back to the idea of infinite time and its sublime power

Question	Expected Answer(s)	Max Mark	Additional Guidance
51.	*(continued)*		Ideas: • Desire to protect his love emphasises the strong feelings that he has conveyed in the rest of the poem for his lover • Nature as a powerful, frightening force is emphasised here, and in the rest of the poem • Eternity of his love is compared to the eternity of natural, elemental forces
52.	Candidates can answer in bullet points in this final question, or write a number of linked statements.	10	Up to 2 marks can be achieved for identifying elements of commonality as identified in the question, i.e. discuss how MacLean explores the impact of time on human experience. A further 2 marks can be achieved for reference to the extract given. 6 additional marks can be awarded for discussion of similar references to at least one other poem by the poet. In practice this means: Identification of commonality **(2)** E.g.: human experience is essentially transitory **(1)** but aspects of life, e.g. love, appreciation of nature have greater permanence **(1)** From the extract: 2 marks for detailed/insightful comment plus quotation/reference; 1 mark for more basic comment plus quotation/reference; 0 marks for quotation/reference alone. E.g. declaration of love which will never end – the constant quality of his love emphasised by comparisons with measuring the sea "drop by drop" and the sand, "grain by grain" **(2)** From at least one other text: as above for up to 6 marks Possible answers include: • *Screapadal* the elemental beauty of the place has outlived its human occupation, which is essentially ephemeral • *An Autumn Day* death in war can be sudden and without warning or time and opportunity to prepare • *I Gave You Immortality* the immortality bestowed by the celebration of love in the poem contrasts with actual human response of the woman • *Heroes* youth, inexperience of the soldier who is killed emphasises the lack of heroism/common vulnerability of humanity and transience of human life • *An Autumn Day* the indifference of nature to the suffering of humanity shown in the passing of a whole day as the men's bodies lie in the sunshine

Text 14 — *Poetry — The Thread* by Don Paterson

Question	Expected Answer(s)	Max Mark	Additional Guidance
53.	2 marks awarded for detailed/insightful comment plus quotation/reference. 1 mark for more basic comment plus quotation/reference.	4	Possible answers include: • "Made his landing … so hard … ploughed" echoes a crash landing suggesting his arrival on earth was potentially life-threatening • positioning of "so hard" emphasises the intensity of the danger • "ploughed straight back into the earth" alludes to the burial of the dead suggesting the fragility of life • "They caught him" conveys the medical team's active role/intervention in saving his life • "by the thread" suggests how precarious his survival was • "pulled him up" suggests last minute intervention to save his life
54.	2 marks awarded for detailed/insightful comment plus quotation/reference. 1 mark for more basic comment plus quotation/reference.	2	Possible answers include: • "I thank what higher will" suggests his continuing gratitude for the intervention of a benign force guiding their destiny/looking after them • structure of "to you and me and Russ" suggests a unified, cohesive group • "great twin-engined … us" suggests the stability and resilience of the family grouping • "roaring" suggests life and vitality of the family • "somehow" suggests the miraculous nature of his survival • "out-revving … universe" suggests immense energy and power of the family unit and their activities
55.	2 marks awarded for detailed/insightful comment plus quotation/reference. 1 mark for more basic comment plus quotation/reference.	4	Possible answers include: • "All that trouble … dead" reprises the trauma of the boy's birth • "all I thought … week" contrasts with the present happiness • "thread holding all of us" returns to fragility of life/ suggests bond which holds family together • "look at our tiny house" concludes flight metaphor suggesting take-off/elation/joy • "tiny house" symbolic of vulnerability/closeness of small family unit • "white dot … mother waving" suggests the traditional, supportive role of the mother within the family unit

Question	Expected Answer(s)	Max Mark	Additional Guidance
56.	Candidates may choose to answer in bullet points in this final question, or write a number of linked statements.	10	Up to 2 marks can be achieved for identifying elements of commonality as identified in the question, i.e. the fragility of human life.
			A further 2 marks can be achieved for reference to the extract given.
			6 additional marks can be awarded for discussion of similar references to at least one other poem by the poet.
			<u>In practice this means:</u> Identification of commonality **(2)** E.g. the threat of death is ever-present in our sense of ourselves as human beings **(1)** anticipation/survival of this threat can be a powerful force at all stages of life **(1)**
			From the extract: 2 marks for detailed/insightful comment plus quotation/reference; 1 mark for more basic comment plus quotation/reference; 0 marks for quotation/reference alone. E.g. image of the 'thread' fastening Jamie to life reinforces the sense of the fragile and precarious nature of life as death is always a possibility **(2)**
			From at least one other text: as above for up to 6 marks
			Possible answers include:
			• *Nil Nil* reference to gall stone — all that's left of pilot — kicked into gutter emphasises how casually life can be disposed of and a human being can be reduced to an object • *The Ferryman's* Arms speaker waiting for the ferryman — reference to Greek mythology — ferry journey to afterlife suggests sense that we as living human beings are waiting for death/passing the time until the inevitability of death happens • *Nil Nil* decline of football team from (modest) glory days to no one coming to see their match creates a nihilistic picture of the inevitable decline of humanity towards death • *11.00: Baldovan* the boys' return to world where they no longer feel part of things/world seems to have changed suggests sense that life moves on without us and individuals are forgotten and dispensable • *Waking with Russell* the speaker, faced with the vulnerability of his new born child, commits himself to nurture and protect him from danger.

SECTION 2 — Critical Essay
Please see the assessment criteria for the Critical Essay on page 172.

Acknowledgements

Permission has been sought from all relevant copyright holders and Hodder Gibson is grateful for the use of the following:

The article 'Cutting down a tree is worse than fox hunting' by Janice Turner © The Times/News Syndication, 12 January 2013 (SQP Reading for Understanding, Analysis and Evaluation pages 2 & 3);
Article is adapted from 'Trees, me, and all of us' by Colin Tudge. Reproduced by kind permission of Colin Tudge. (SQP Reading for Understanding, Analysis and Evaluation page 5);
An extract from 'The Slab Boys' © 1982 John Byrne. 'The Slab Boys' was first performed at the Traverse Theatre, Edinburgh, on 6 April 1978. All right whatsoever in this play are strictly reserved and application for performance etc. should be made to the Author's agent: Casarotto Ramsay & Associates Limited, Waverley House, 7–12 Noel Street, London W1F 8G (rights@casarotto.co.uk). No performance may be given unless a licence has been obtained (SQP Critical Reading pages 2 to 4);
An extract from 'The Cheviot, the Stag and the Black, Black Oil,' by John McGrath. © John McGrath, 1981. Published by Bloomsbury Methuen Drama, an imprint of Bloomsbury Publishing Plc. (SQP Critical Reading pages 5 & 6);
An extract from 'Men Should Weep' © Ena Lamont Stewart, 1947. Reproduced by permission of Alan Brodie Representation Ltd (www.alanbrodie.com) (SQP Critical Reading pages 7 & 8);
An extract from 'In Church' by Iain Crichton Smith, taken from 'The Red Door: The Complete English Stories 1949–76', published by Birlinn. Reproduced by permission of Birlinn Ltd. www.birlinn.co.uk (SQP Critical Reading pages 10 & 11);
An extract from 'A Time to Keep' by George Mackay Brown, published by Polygon. Reproduced by permission of Birlinn Ltd. www.birlinn.co.uk (SQP Critical Reading page 12);
An extract from 'The Trick is to Keep Breathing' by Janice Galloway, published by Vintage, reprinted by permission of The Random House Group Limited (SQP Critical Reading pages 14 & 15);
An extract from 'Sunset Song' by Lewis Grassic Gibbon, published by Jarrold Publishing, 1932. Public domain (SQP Critical Reading page 16);
An extract from 'The Cone-Gatherers' by Robin Jenkins, published by Canongate Books Ltd. (SQP Critical Reading pages 18 & 19);
An extract from 'Holy Willie's Prayer' by Robert Burns. Public domain (SQP Critical Reading pages 20 & 21);
The poem 'Originally' by Carol Ann Duffy, taken from 'The Other Country' (Anvil, 1990). Reproduced by permission of the author c/o Rogers, Coleridge & White Ltd., 20 Powis Mews, London W11 1JN (SQP Critical Reading page 22);
An extract from the poem 'For My Grandmother Knitting' by Liz Lochhead, taken from 'A Choosing: Selected Poems', published by Polygon. Reproduced by permission of Birlinn Ltd. www.birlinn.co.uk (SQP Critical Reading pages 24 & 25);
The poem 'Sounds of the Day' by Norman MacCaig, taken from 'The Poems of Norman MacCaig', published by Polygon. Reproduced by permission of Birlinn Ltd. www.birlinn.co.uk (SQP Critical Reading page 26);
The poem 'Heroes' by Sorley Maclean, taken from 'Sorley Maclean Selected Poems' (edited by Whyte and Dymock), published by Polygon. Reproduced by permission of Birlinn Ltd. www.birlinn.co.uk (SQP Critical Reading pages 28 & 29);
An extract from 'The Ferryman's Arms' from 'Nil, Nil' by Don Paterson. Published by Faber & Faber, 2004. Reproduced by permission of the author c/o Rogers, Coleridge & White Ltd., 20 Powis Mews, London W11 1JN (SQP Critical Reading page 30);
An extract adapted from the article 'Goodbye birds. Goodbye butterflies. Hello… farmageddon' by Isabel Oakeshott © The Times/News Syndication, 19 January 2014 (2015 Reading for Understanding, Analysis and Evaluation pages 2 & 3);
The article 'Pasture to the Plate' by Audrey Ayton, taken from The Observer Supplement, 10 July 1994. Copyright Guardian News & Media Ltd 2016 (2015 Reading for Understanding, Analysis and Evaluation pages 3 & 4);
An extract taken from 'The Slab Boys' © 1982 John Byrne. 'The Slab Boys' was first performed at the Traverse Theatre, Edinburgh, on 6 April 1978. All right whatsoever in this play are strictly reserved and application for performance etc. should be made to the Author's agent: Casarotto Ramsay & Associates Limited, Waverley House, 7–12 Noel Street, London W1F 8G (rights@casarotto.co.uk). No performance may be given unless a licence has been obtained (2015 Critical Essay pages 2 & 3);
An extract from 'The Cheviot, the Stag and the Black, Black Oil,' by John McGrath. © John McGrath, 1981. Published by Bloomsbury Methuen Drama, an imprint of Bloomsbury Publishing Plc. (2015 Critical Essay page 6);
An extract from 'Men Should Weep' © Ena Lamont Stewart, 1947. Reproduced by permission of Alan Brodie Representation Ltd (www.alanbrodie.com) (2015 Critical Essay pages 8 & 9);
An extract from 'Mother and Son' by Iain Crichton Smith, taken from 'The Red Door: The Complete English Stories 1949–76', published by Birlinn. Reproduced by permission of Birlinn Ltd. www.birlinn.co.uk (2015 Critical Essay pages 12 & 13);
An extract from 'The Wireless Set' by George Mackay Brown, taken from the book 'A Time To Keep', published by Polygon. Reproduced by permission of Birlinn Ltd. www.birlinn.co.uk (2015 Critical Essay pages 14 & 15);
An extract from 'The Trick is to Keep Breathing' by Janice Galloway, published by Vintage, reprinted by permission of The Random House Group Limited (2015 Critical Essay page 16);
An extract from 'Sunset Song' by Lewis Grassic Gibbon, published by Jarrold Publishing, 1932. Public domain (2015 Critical Essay pages 18 & 19);
An extract from 'The Cone-Gatherers' by Robin Jenkins, published by Canongate Books Ltd. (2015 Critical Essay pages 20 & 21);
The poem 'To a Mouse' by Robert Burns. Public domain (2015 Critical Essay pages 22 & 23);
The poem 'War Photographer' by Carol Ann Duffy, taken from 'New Selected Poems 1984–2004' (Picador, 2004). Reproduced by permission of the author c/o Rogers, Coleridge & White Ltd., 20 Powis Mews, London W11 1JN (2015 Critical Essay page 24);